# The Time Inheritors

SUNY series, Education in Global Perspectives

Published in cooperation with the

**CIES** COMPARATIVE &
INTERNATIONAL
EDUCATION
SOCIETY

Series Editors:
Laura C. Engel, Claire Maxwell, and Miri Yemini (2022–2024)
Lesley Bartlett, Jun Li, M. Najeeb Shafiq,
and Frances Vavrus (2018–2022)

# The Time Inheritors

## How Time Inequalities Shape
## Higher Education Mobility in China

CORA LINGLING XU 许玲玲

**SUNY**
**PRESS**

**EU GPSR Authorised Representative:**
**Logos Europe,** 9 rue Nicolas Poussin, 17000, La Rochelle, France
contact@logoseurope.eu

For information, contact State University of New York Press, Albany, NY
www.sunypress.edu

**Library of Congress Cataloging-in-Publication Data**

Name: Xu, Cora Lingling, [date] – author.
Title: The time inheritors : how time inequalities shape higher
    education mobility in China / Cora Lingling Xu.
Description: Albany, New York : State University of New York Press, [2025] |
    Series: SUNY series, education in global perspectives | Includes bibliographical
    references and index.
Identifiers: LCCN 2024042825 | ISBN 9798855801903 (hardcover : alk. paper) |
    ISBN 9798855801927 (ebook) | ISBN 9798855801910 (pbk. : alk. paper)
Subjects: LCSH: Educational equalization—China. | Elite (Social sciences)—
    Education—China. | Universities and colleges—China—Admission. | Universities
    and colleges—China—Moral and ethical aspects. | Discrimination in higher
    education—China.
Classification: LCC LC213.3.C6 X82 2025 | DDC 378.51—dc23/eng/20241129
LC record available at https://lccn.loc.gov/2024042825

# Contents

## Part I: Theorization of Time Inheritance and Education Mobility

## Part II: How Time Inheritance Reproduces Inequalities

## Part III: How Time Inheritance Transforms Inequalities

# Illustrations

# Acknowledgments

This book would have been impossible without the support, guidance, and encouragements of the following people and organizations.

First and foremost, I thank the more than 100 research participants who generously gave their time to share their most intimate experiences of time and education mobility with me over the course of ten years. To this day I remain in touch with a great number of them, and I feel extremely honored by their trust in me.

I am indebted to my husband and best friend, Andreas Kotsakis, who went through the agony and joy of every single page of this book and its two previous iterations. Andreas supported me through the most difficult period of my academic life, during which significant portions of this book were written. My numerous conversations with Andreas gave me inspirations for the title of this book, *The Time Inheritors*—I am grateful for this significant contribution.

The four research projects on which this book is based are supported by a range of funding. I am thankful for the generous financial support of the Cambridge International Trust, Queens' College and the Faculty of Education at the University of Cambridge, the Sociological Review Foundation Seminar Series, and Keele and Durham Universities' various research funds.

The making of this book took a decade. At Cambridge University, I owe debt to Diane Reay, my PhD supervisor, and Yongcan Liu, my PhD advisor, for their invaluable guidance on my PhD project, the data of which contributed to this book. Diane's integrity and passion as a conscientious sociologist have been a major source of inspiration for this book.

Andy Gao facilitated the fieldwork of two of the projects. I am thankful for his continuous support over the years. Rachel Murphy, Chris Glass, and Arathi Sriprakash provided valuable feedback on and support of my research that went into the shaping of this book.

At Keele University, Lydia Martens, my research mentor, instilled in me the seed of writing a book. I benefited from the support of Farzana Shain, Lisa Dikomitis, Marie-Andrée Jacob, Mark Featherstone, and Reza Gholami for research projects that constitute parts of this book.

The publication journey of this book garnered the support of a global "village," too. I thank Derron Wallace for generously discussing ideas of this book, sharing his own experience, and making suggestions for the notion of "banked time," which eventually became part of this book's theoretical framework. Yi-lin Chiang shared her own publication experience with me and made informative suggestions during the early days of this book's publication journey; Wayne Furlong and Iris Ka Man Tang read the entire manuscript meticulously and provided insightful feedback; Matthew DeCoursey and Mona Jebril read and commented emphatically on chapters of this book; Sherzod Muminov, Anders Sybrandt Hansen, and Vikki Boliver read and made thoughtful suggestions for various iterations of my book proposals; Oakleigh Welply, Prue Holmes, Julie Rattray, Rille Raaper, Anna Llewellyn, and James Underwood provided emotional support during a difficult period of writing; Nicole Janz facilitated accountability peer support during the early days of writing this book—I thank them all for their invaluable friendship and contributions.

The writing of this book took place in the Durham University writing group that Helen Roche organized as well as the online writing group with Jack Xuebing Cao and Jade Zhiyu Lian. Thank you for making the space of writing so enjoyable.

I also benefited tremendously from the committed professional guidance of Rebecca Colesworthy, my editor at SUNY Press, and her team. I am grateful to Clare Maxwell, the SUNY Press–CIES series editor of Education in Global Perspectives, for her enthusiastic belief in the merit and importance of this book. I also wish to thank the three anonymous reviewers of my manuscript for recognizing the book's significance and making useful suggestions that helped strengthen it.

Laura Portwood-Stacer's Book Proposal Accelerator program gave me instrumental insights into book publication. Liz DeWolf, my developmental editor, aptly steered me toward the most suitable direction after reading two chapters from a previous iteration of the manuscript. Thank you both for your help.

I owe gratitude to Ying Du for his inspirations and suggestions for the book cover design. I also wish to acknowledge that two sections in chapter 6 and one section in chapter 8 were adapted from materials in my article "Time, Class and Privilege in Career Imagination: Exploring Study-to-Work Transition of Chinese International Students in UK Universities Through a Bourdieusian Lens" (2021, *Time & Society*, *30*[1], https://doi.org/10.1177/0961463x20951333). Some empirical materials of this book have previously been published in a number of other articles in peer-reviewed journals, including *The Sociological Review* ("Transborder Habitus in a Within-Country Mobility Context," 2018, https://doi.org/10.1177/0038026117732669), *International Studies in Sociology of Education* ("Political Habitus in Cross-Border Student Migration," 2018, https://doi.org/10.1080/09620214.2017.1415768; " 'Diaspora at Home,' " 2019, https://doi.org/10.1080/09620214.2019.1700821), *Policy Reviews in Higher Education* ("Tackling Rural-Urban Inequalities Through Educational Mobilities," 2020, https://doi.org/10.1080/23322969.2020.1783697), and *Journal of Current Chinese Affairs* ("When the Hong Kong Dream Meets the Anti-Mainlandisation Discourse," 2015, https://doi.org/10.1177/18681 0261504400302).

Last but not least, I would like to express my immense indebtedness to my family from rural China, my mother, my father, my brother, and his family. Without their support and nourishment, I would not have been where I am today. My aunt has been the most significant source of inspiration: A rural woman who has never been to school for one day, whose incredible tenacity and strength have defied but also manifested many constraints of inherited time inequalities. I dedicate this book to her and to other deprived, rural-origin women who sacrifice their own education for their families!

# Introduction

## The Significance of Inherited Time

Can one inherit time? The "legacy students" at Cornell can.

> Born in a small village in China, I never thought any of these [opportunities] would ever be possible during my childhood. Until now, many of my primary school classmates are still living in my village—some have become migrant workers in cities, and they usually leave their children in the village for education. At institutions like Cornell, however, I typically find myself surrounded by colleagues whose parents at least hold a bachelor's degree. For some of them, it's also possible that their parents, grandparents, and even great-grandparents were Cornell graduates—so-called legacy students. (Cao, 2021, p. 332)

This account is by Xiangkun Elvis Cao, an Impact Fellow at the prestigious MIT Climate and Sustainability Consortium who received his Ivy League PhD degree from Cornell University. The "legacy" of Cao's Cornell colleagues, some of whose parents, grandparents, and even great-grandparents were all Cornell graduates, captures what I call in this book "intergenerational time wealth inheritance"—these legacy students are examples of "time inheritors."

BBC News suggests that Ivy League institutions like Cornell and Harvard help the elite "skip the queue" and likens such legacy admission privilege to "a rocketship into the stratosphere of America's elite" (Levinson King, 2023, para. 15). The legacy students' higher education and career journeys can be substantially sped up thanks to their family's generationally accumulated prestige. They spend less time fidgeting about what decisions to make, about which university to choose, and save up valuable time to plan for the future.

In contrast, Cao has come a long way, being from a rural and impoverished family in China with parents and grandparents who did not have primary-level education. Instead of being guided to make informed decisions, Cao felt vulnerable about which major or university to choose, worrying about how to secure funds to sit the expensive TOEFL and GRE tests.[1] The time cost of navigating his rural-to-urban and transnational higher education journey was considerably higher than those of his legacy student colleagues. He wrote that his decision to pursue graduate studies meant "the opportunity cost of spending 5 years of my 20s. This opportunity cost is even higher for minorities since *we tend to have fewer opportunities in life*" (Cao, 2021, p. 334, my emphasis). Instead of inheriting generations of time wealth, Cao inherits what I call in this book "time debt." Cao and his primary school classmates belong to a different type of time inheritors whose opportunities in life are constrained by their time debt.

Time inheritance is unequal. Cao's struggles and dilemmas with time and opportunities in life are typical among the individuals researched in this book. Consider these snapshots:

Jiao had just sat Gaokao (the Nationwide Unified Examination for Admissions to General Universities and Colleges), one of the world's most competitive college-entrance examinations, and was exhilarated to learn that his marks could enable him to enter China's top two universities. However, he chose to enroll in a second-tier university in Wuhan, in China's southern Hubei Province.

Stephanie had just finished her education degree at a prestigious university in Beijing and was pumped to seek a professional job as a teacher back in her home city of Hong Kong. To her shock, she was told by the academic accreditation body that she needed three years' further training in Hong Kong before she could be hired as a teacher.

Bing was about to finish her family-sponsored degree course in the UK and was keen to try her hand at luxury goods sales. Yet her parents had just sent her an ultimatum about returning to her home city of Chongqing, where they had arranged a stable job with decent benefits for her.

These three snapshots are real scenarios encountered by participants in this book. What brought Jiao, a student from rural China with illiterate parents, to make this seemingly shortsighted decision at the juncture of university choice making? Why was Stephanie, a student from a low-income family in Hong Kong, not informed about this extra training required for pursuing a professional teacher's job? Why did Bing's parents, both highly educated and occupying jobs in China's state-owned enterprises, hurry her back home after her study abroad? These baffling questions all concern *time*. They reflect the complex and unequal scene of China's education mobility, which is underpinned by the key factor of intergenerational time inequalities. This is what I call in this book "time inheritance."

This book is centrally concerned with how intergenerational transfer of privilege or deprivation (McNamee & Miller, 1989) manifests in and through time among students of diverse social origins in China as they navigate the multifarious forms of education mobility. *Education mobility* refers to educationally motivated spatial movements of students from their home country or region to another. In China, education mobility encompasses rural-to-urban mobility, cross-border mobility (e.g., Hong Kong–mainland China), and transnational mobility (Xu & Montgomery, 2019). Using rich empirical data, I interrogate how time inequalities inherited across generations shape the life chances and trajectories of students from rural and deprived families like Jiao and Cao; to students from urban, low-income families like Stephanie; through to students from urban, affluent families like Bing. I ask, What is time inheritance, and how does it manifest in China's scene of education mobility? To what extent is social inequality reproduced or transformed by time inheritance? This book explores these and related questions, offering a critical account of the affecting influence of intergenerational time inequalities in the lives of educationally mobile Chinese youth today.

## Inheritance and Time

What is inheritance? Sociologists Stephen J. McNamee and Robert K. Miller Jr. (1989) maintain that the process of inheritance is the intergenerational transfer of "accumulated surplus." Such transfers of privilege manifest in two ways: "indirectly through the social and cultural advantages of initial placement at birth and directly through the bulk transfer of estates to designated heirs" (McNamee & Miller, 1989, p. 20). Existing literature on inheritance, whether on the sociology (Szydlik, 2004), the anthropology (Goody, 1962), or the economics (Piketty, 2014) of inheritance, has focused exclusively on the latter process—"the bulk transfer of estates to designated heirs." In contrast, the indirect transfer of "social and cultural advantages of initial placement at birth" is mostly dealt with by sociologists of education (Bernstein, 2003; Bourdieu, 1984; Bourdieu & Passeron, 1979; Lamont & Lareau, 1988; Lareau, 2003).

With regard to research on the inheritance of financial capital or real estate, it is clear within this literature that generational accumulation of financial and real estate wealth initially takes the form of active accumulation, such as in the building of enterprises and active trading of assets and products (Mumford, 2007; Szydlik, 2004). However, as Piketty (2014) points out, once such initial accumulation of financial capital is established, the passive income generated can surpass the income through active labor: "The inequality $r > g$ [$r$ represents the rate of return on capital, while $g$ represents the rate of economic growth] in one sense implies that the past tends to devour the future: wealth originating in the past automatically grows more rapidly, even without labor, than wealth stemming from work, which can be saved" (p. 378). This thus allows the owners and their heirs a great deal of time freedom—not only do they not have to partake in daily toils and laboring to generate a wage, but their passive income can bequeath them plenty of unoccupied time to engage in activities of their own choosing. This fits Bourdieu's (2000) depiction of time freedom, "time used freely for freely chosen, gratuitous ends" (p. 224).

As such, the inheritance of substantial economic wealth takes on two temporal facets. The first facet pertains to the fact that the accumulation and generation of financial assets and real estate takes (laboring) time, and thus inheriting such financial bequests is accepting the transfer of accumulated labor-time wealth. The second facet is related to the idea that once a person inherits such economic wealth, they become equipped with the capacity to free themselves from time that would otherwise be dedicated to wage labor, thus being able to enjoy temporal freedom and pursue whatever cause in life they prefer. This is "freed-up time."

In this literature on the inheritance of financial capital and real estate, a commonly discussed variable is "inheritance age." For instance, Piketty (2014) notes, "The difference between the average age of death and the average age of inheritance has always been around thirty years, for the simple reason that the average age of child-birth (often referred to as 'generational duration') has been relatively stable at around thirty over the long run (although there has been a slight increase in the early twenty-first century)" (p. 388). The fact that this inheritance age has slightly increased may mean that heirs tend to have to choose a profession to earn a living before they can inherit. People still, as Piketty notes, die eventually. Heirs, therefore, still inherit in the end. Intriguingly, the inheritance of "social and cultural privileges" is not bound by an inheritance age. Instead, such more indirect forms of inheritance begin as soon as the child is born. Sociologist Esping-Andersen (2005) argues, "I am sceptical about the standard assumption that generational inheritance is driven primarily by unequal investments in education. Instead, the decisive mechanisms probably concentrate in conditions prior to children's first encounter with the classroom. It is in early childhood that parental transmission is key. Poverty and economic insecurity are very problematic but the 'cultural capital' of families is arguably decisive" (p. 14).

Indeed, economists have confirmed that parental time investment in childcare strongly and positively correlates with the parents' own education and income levels and constitutes a "critical channel leading to the intergenerational transmission of education" (Du et al., 2023, p. 123; Guryan et al., 2008). Numerous sociological studies across different national contexts have repeatedly shown that the acquisition of valued cultural understanding and social skills begins at home (Maxwell & Aggleton, 2014; Maxwell & Yemini, 2019); the familial inculcation and primary socialization pass on invaluable cultural and social resources to the heirs who benefit from them but without "noticing" it. These social and cultural privileges are captured in concepts by sociologists including Bourdieu's (1986) "cultural and social capital," Basil Bernstein's (1962a, 1962b) "elaborated code," and Annette Lareau's (2003) "concerted cultivation."

All these concepts point to one shared characteristic: the "passive" time during which the heirs immerse themselves in an environment where they "effortlessly" become inculcated and educated. As such, they possess a sense of ease and even entitlement warranted by their tacit understanding of the social "codes" (after Bernstein), or "game rules" (after Bourdieu), of what the schooling or work setting will deem appropriate and legitimate (Forbes & Lingard, 2013; S. Friedman & Laurison, 2019; Maxwell & Aggleton, 2013). In this way, the indirect inheritance of cultural and social privileges is ultimately the inheritance of time that is spent in effortless inculcation of desirable cultural traits.

To summarize, in *The Time Inheritors*, I argue that in the two main forms of inheritance—the direct passing on of financial wealth and real estate and the indirect handing down of social and cultural privileges—time remains an important common root cause of inequalities. The inheritance of intergenerational privileges thus can be argued to be the inheritance of unequal time or temporal wealth. Importantly, while the existing literature on inheritance focuses on the familial realm, I argue that inheritance of temporal inequalities takes place also at the national and global levels.

When it comes to inherited time inequalities, there is a "time privilege continuum" (see figure 1.1). On one end of this continuum are the disadvantaged time inheritors, who live on "borrowed time"; on the other end of this continuum are the advantaged time inheritors, who live on "banked time." In chapter 1, I will detail the conceptual and empirical parameters of this time privilege continuum. I will point out how borrowed time and banked time are manifested in three different ways related to both quantitative and qualitative inheritance of time and across the familial, national, and international levels. The remainder of the book is then devoted to unpacking this central theoretical innovation and applying it to the Chinese context. As we will see, time inheritance both reproduces some (see part 2) and transforms other (see part 3) inequalities in China's higher education mobility arena.

## Education Mobility and Time Inequalities

Contemporary research on China's education inequality and mobility is championed by two distinct focuses: one on China's domestic education inequalities manifest through the rural–urban divides (Howlett, 2021; Kipnis, 2011; H. Li et al., 2015) and the ethnic hierarchies (Grose, 2010; J. Wu, 2016; M. Yang, 2017), and the other on Chinese students' cross-border (X. Gao, 2014; M. Gu & Tong, 2012; C. L. Xu, 2018b, 2019) and transnational educational moves (Chiang, 2022; V. L. Fong, 2011; Y. Ma, 2020; Martin, 2022; Xiang & Shen, 2009).

While the former literature accentuates the inequalities experienced by the rural-origin and ethnic minority students due to policy biases and social stigmas (E. Friedman, 2022; Murphy, 2020, 2022; J. Wu, 2016), the latter zooms in on the urban-origin middle-class students as they are privileged and resourceful enough to be within the top 2 percent of students with access to cross-border and transnational education mobility (Q. Gu & Schweisfurth, 2015a). Few empirical attempts, if any, have been carried out to portray a comprehensive picture of how inequalities play out across these divergent groups of students as they navigate through different forms of internal and external education mobility. Even less is known about how inequalities of time manifest across diverse student groups in education mobility.

## Time in Migration and Education Studies Research

Meanwhile, research on transnational migration (Collins & Shubin, 2015; Robertson, 2022; B. Wang & Collins, 2020) and research on education studies (Duncheon & Tierney, 2013; Lingard & Thompson, 2017) have separately but simultaneously demonstrated the crucial roles that time plays in shaping social inequality. Studies on transnational migration repeatedly show how middle-class migrants' agency interplays with institutional opportunities and constraints, especially the various national governments' migration regimes and policies. This literature generates nuanced and rich empirical insights about how these migrants live through their "everyday times," "individual times" (B. Wang, 2019; B. Wang & Collins, 2020), or indeed "migrant times" (Collins & Shubin, 2015) as they respond to and adjust their individual daily schedules and long-term plans as shaped by the institutional forces. In this process, sociologists such as Shanthi Robertson (2022) and Ken Sun (2021) accentuate how migrants' study, work, intimate, and retirement lives are notably affected by temporalities of migration policies and social environments of both home (e.g., Asia or Taiwan) and host societies (e.g., Australia and the United States).

In parallel, the literature on "time research in education," as Duncheon and Tierney (2013, p. 238) call it, focuses on education inequalities with regard to how the past, present, and future are framed in discourse (e.g., policy; Bennett & Burke, 2018; Clegg, 2010) and evidences how time allocation and expectations in schools or universities can further exacerbate social inequality among learners of different socioeconomic backgrounds. This focus on time notwithstanding, both bodies of literature pay insufficient attention to the mechanism that facilitates the intergenerational transfer of privilege, and they do not engage with the cross-national inequalities or opportunities presented to individuals of diverse social backgrounds from a temporal perspective.

Building on this outstanding scholarship, *The Time Inheritors* extends its empirical scope beyond the middle class and examines the "vertical" inequalities of time experienced by social agents of diverse sociopolitical backgrounds, ranging from the rural-origin and deprived to the urban working class, middle class, and upper middle class. As such, *The Time Inheritors* enriches our understanding of the sending country's (i.e., China's) social fabrics and pinpoints the complexity of migration and mobility. Moreover, *The Time Inheritors* draws our critical attention to intergenerational and inherited time inequalities that this body of literature does not address.

## Data Sets

To furnish an exposition of this central conceptual contribution, *The Time Inheritors* draws on nearly a decade of field research, including participant observation, focus groups, semistructured interviews with over 100 educationally mobile students, administrators, and parents.

### DATA SET 1

From 2013 to 2022, I conducted research on the experiences of 31 urban, middle-class mainland Chinese students who crossed the internal border to study in Hong Kong. This research explored their identity constructions amid increasingly tense mainland China–Hong Kong political relations as well as their longer-term life and career developments and political socialization. This research also involved the voices of another 12 local Hong Kong students in focus groups, which served as important contextual and triangulating sources of information.

### DATA SET 2

Between 2016 and 2022, I conducted multiple rounds of interviews with 23 Hong Kong students (mostly from low-income families) who pursued undergraduate studies in mainland China. While the initial focus was their political socialization, I followed them through to their postgraduation career-making stages, where I explored more nuanced insights about their career-development dilemmas and challenges.

### DATA SET 3

In 2017–2019, I researched 26 rural-origin academics' career and education trajectories. I conducted online and face-to-face interviews in Guangzhou and Hong Kong, China, and in the United Kingdom.

## Data Set 4

Between 2018 and 2020, I investigated Chinese international students who have received higher education in British universities, especially focusing on their study-to-work transition—including a survey to 400 respondents and in-depth interviews with 21 participants. I also conducted in-person field observations in Oxford, Keele, London, and Manchester as well as online observations via WeChat (refer to the appendix for the participants' profiles).

As shown clearly here, this focus on time inequalities arose organically from the four data sets: they all had different research focuses, which were not on time. As I engaged deeper with these data sets over the course of a decade, I found that the issue of time use and different understandings and lived experiences in relation to time were qualitatively different and significant across these participants of differentiated social origins. This empirical observation enabled me to understand the decision making and education mobility trajectories of my participants in a deeper and more nuanced way. Some of the difficulties that I previously encountered in interpreting the accounts of these participants became nonissues. I started to observe patterns of time use or "misuse" by different participants, which led me further to uncover the more systematic issues (e.g., inherited time wealth and debt) that have not been coherently discussed in existing scholarship. I ought to foreground the temporal inequalities embedded in these differing education-mobility trajectories.

This book is by no means denying the critical importance of inequalities pertaining to space and place in education mobility. Recognizing the substantial scholarship (including my own) that has been dedicated to space and place (Brooks & Waters, 2018; Y. W. Chan & Koh, 2017; Leung & Waters, 2017; Lipura & Collins, 2020; Waters & Brooks, 2021; Xiang & Shen, 2009; C. L. Xu, 2018b), I consider it my mission to accentuate the critical importance of time inequalities, especially inherited time inequalities, which is what I call "time inheritance."

*The Time Inheritors* brings these different research projects and data sets together conceptually and thematically. The multisited, online and offline ethnographic approach will facilitate an assemblage of a comprehensive picture of how time inheritance works in and through education mobility, embodied by the most disadvantaged through to the most privileged youth in China. The longitudinal nature of these data will furnish an expansion on existing scholarship's focus on Chinese youth's education mobility up to the undergraduate level and extend our investigative gaze to the subsequent post-first-degree career and life outlooks of the individuals concerned (Y. Ma, 2020; Xie & Reay, 2020; Xu, 2018b).

These researched students' markedly differentiated socioeconomic and geopolitical backgrounds and their divergence and convergence of education mobility experiences facilitate a systematic exposition of how multifarious inequalities (such as the rural–urban divide, class and political inequalities) within contemporary China intersect with globalization forces (such as global dominance of Western scholarship and higher education institutions), generating multiple unintended and little-documented consequences that are accentuated and crystalized through a focus on inherited time inequalities.

## Class in China and Differentiated Social Origins

### Class in Mainland China

Although class was deemed as less relevant in Maoist China (T. Lin & X. Wu, 2009), scholars have arrived at a consensus that class needs to be brought back to help understand social inequalities in post-reform-era China[2] (Breitung, 2009; M. K. Chan, 2003; Goodman, 2008, 2014). There have been different ways to approach class divisions in contemporary China. Scholars have demonstrated that the Erikson–Goldthorpe–Portocarero class scheme (EGP), which classifies all occupations using only six categories,[3] is inadequate for explaining China's rural–urban divides as reinforced by the *hukou* system (X. Wu, 2019, p. 371).

Instead, scholars such as Xueyi Lu [陆] (2002) proposed focusing on occupational, organizational, economic, and cultural differentiations and divided the Chinese population into ten social strata.[4] T. Lin and X. Wu (2009, p. 84) developed a "neo-Marxian class schema . . . taking into account three unique Chinese institutions": "the household registration system (*hukou* 户口), the work unit (*danwei* 单位), and the cadre-worker distinction," delineating a total of ten classes[5] in transitional China—in other words, after socialist China and since the opening up and reforming era. Given the vastness and complexity of China's rural society alone, scholars such as C. Wang [王] et al. (2018) argue for a pyramid-style social strata, encompassing rural cadres, rural enterprise owners, the rural self-employed (*getihu* 个体户), workers, part-time peasants, peasants, and the jobless.

In the urban sphere, Jin (2024, p. 68) observes that in the post-reform-era China over the past four decades,

> there arises an elite group who have the economic, social, cultural, and political capital to seize burgeoning business and social mobility opportunities with the development of reforms . . . on the other hand, new socially disadvantaged groups appear in cities, such as the millions of laid-off workers from state-owned businesses . . . rural-to-urban migrants . . . and low-income higher education graduates, who have been dubbed "蚁族" ("*yizu*," ant tribe, see Lian, 2009). The changes in the occupational structure owing to the development of new and modernised industries introduce the so-called new middle classes in China, such as white-collar officers, managers, and professionals. Together with the old middle classes, such as cadres and large enterprise leaders, they form middle-class strata in China and develop strategies and patterns of living and consumption that consolidate their economic and social advantages and produce class distinctions.

In contrast to these middle-class strata, Jin (2024, p. 69) understands the urban working class as "those who are in lower status occupations and who are struggling with structural inequalities and with senses of inferiority and inadequacy in comparison with others."

In view of this existing literature, in this book I use information including family's *hukou* origins, family monthly income, parental education levels and occupations, and self-identification to determine and depict the social positions of participants from mainland China. For the participants from urban China, I additionally point out the tier of cities they are originally from (for a detailed discussion of the inequalities due to city tiers, refer to chapter 10).

## CLASS IN HONG KONG

In Hong Kong, a capitalist society, the social structure is typically discussed along the Western Weberian class scheme that distinguishes the middle class from the working class, or the grass roots (*jiceng* 基层). T.-L. Lui (2003, p. 161) refers to its middle class as "those professional, administrative, and managerial salaried employees working in various sectors of the Hong Kong economy, whose market situations and working situations keep them distinct from other employees (such as routine non-manual workers, technicians, and supervisors)." This discussion has been framed in the context of Hong Kong's class structure since its "industrial takeoff" in the late 1960s and early 1970s. Scholars argue that prior to this, Hong Kong was primarily a colonial trading port that consisted of three classes: the colonials, the compradors, and the laborers. Since Hong Kong's industrialization, the society underwent a period of rapid economic development, which saw the emergence of its middle class. Some other research has noted four unequal social strata in Hong Kong society during the late 1990s and early 2000s:

> 1) the "well off" whose social positions and development status are largely immune from swings in the local economy; 2) the "socially secure" who occupy important positions of influence and who have been able to more or less insulate themselves against all but the most extreme development shifts occurring in Hong Kong; 3) the "socially insecure" who are employed and are "making it" . . . but with difficulty; and 4) a growing "underclass" of more or less permanently impoverished persons who possess limited means of extricating themselves from poverty. (Hong Kong Council of Social Service, 2000, pp. 6–7, cited in Chua et al., 2010, pp. 537–538)

If applied using T.-L. Lui's (2003) analysis, the "well off" could be referred to as the upper middle class, while the "socially secure" could be the middle class. In their analysis of social development in Hong Kong, Chua et al. (2010) refer to those situated lower than the "middle class" as the "lower-middle class," the "grassroots," and "low-income families" (Chua et al., 2010, pp. 543–545).

In general, social scientists tend to adopt a Marxist class structure (e.g., capitalist versus working class; B. C. Fong, 2014) or a Weberian class scheme to understand the social stratification in Hong Kong (T.-L. Lui, 2009). Despite the various terms and categorizations used, there is a consensus that Hong Kong's society is made up of an affluent, well-off class that owns substantial resources and political power (Chua et al., 2010, pp. 543–545)—this sometimes encompasses the "capitalist class" (B. C. Fong, 2014) and the "upper service class" (T.-L. Lui, 2009, p. 145). Immediately below this group is the broad "intermediate," or middle class (T.-L. Lui, 2009, p. 145), who assume professional, managerial, and administrative salaried positions (T.-L. Lui, 2003, p. 161) and are more "socially secure" than their "socially insecure," "under class," "working-class," "grassroots," and "low-income" counterparts (Chua et al., 2010, pp. 543–545).

In this study, I synthesize information including the participants' family monthly income (as compared with Hong Kong's median household income figures), parental education levels, parental occupations, and students' self-classification to deduce their class positions.

## DIFFERENTIATED SOCIAL ORIGINS

### *Places of Origin and Familial Socioeconomic Backgrounds*

There is a clear hierarchy among the four groups of participants whose accounts are featured in this book. At the bottom lie the rural-origin participants (*n* = 26), who are mostly from rural villages located in geographically remote areas. They are all from economically deprived families, having parents who were either full-time farmers or a combination of part-time peasants and migrant workers. Only three had parents who worked in factories (at managerial level) or state-owned collectives. However, it should be borne in mind that even for these three, their parents went out of work because of either the closing down of the factories or privatization of state-owned collectives (Jin, 2024). These socioeconomic conditions have led to these families' persistent struggles in supporting their children's education, which can be seen from their great difficulties in paying tuition fees from primary to university levels, as depicted in chapter 2. These families can be considered the bottom strata of the Chinese rural society (S. Lan, 2021; C. Wang [王] et al., 2018; C. L. Xu, 2020).

The second group of students come from the international metropolis of Hong Kong. While 9 of 23 among them are from typical middle-class families, the remaining 14 are from typical working-class or "grassroots" families, with both or either parent making no income (e.g., unemployed, retired, or having passed away) or occupying low-income jobs such as security guards, waitstaff, or cleaners (Chua et al., 2010). These students' self-reported family monthly incomes were also much lower than the median household income in Hong Kong. Such a "grassroots" status of the majority of these students meant that their families were situated at the bottom strata of Hong Kong's highly unequal society (O'Sullivan & Tsang, 2015; Piketty & Yang, 2022; C. L. Xu, 2019).

However, compared with their counterparts in the rural-origin group, their families struggled much less with paying their children's study expenses at the pre-university stages, partly because of Hong Kong's free education provision. At university level, these families were unable to sponsor their children to study abroad and chose the "cheaper" option of mainland China's universities to circumvent the study cost. Despite the much lower costs, however, some students, like Vivienne and Shane, had to work part-time jobs to pay for their own university-studies expenditures and even contribute financially to their families. The accounts of the Hong Kong students in this book are primarily from the 14 participants in this group, who are from low-income families whose parents had typical working-class jobs or had passed away.

The accounts of the urban students from mainland China were drawn from two data sets. The first data set is from a group of 31 students who came to Hong Kong to pursue their undergraduate studies, having given up offers from elite universities in mainland China. I began researching this group in 2013 and have remained in touch with 24 of them up to 2023. Among these 24, nine came from the first-tier cities of Beijing, Shanghai, and Guangzhou, and the remaining 15 were from lower-tier cities, including provincial capital cities but also smaller cities. All were from middle-class backgrounds, with parents having professional or civil service jobs or working in small or medium enterprises. These families had no difficulty affording their children's study expenses in Hong Kong but mostly could not afford to send them to study in the traditional Western study destinations such as the US, the UK, or Australia. While there are some variations—some came from more affluent backgrounds, such as Nianci and Guoxiang, and some from less prosperous backgrounds, such as Fei and Miusi—these families all belong to the middle-class brackets of contemporary urban China (Goodman, 2014; Jin, 2024).

The second group of urban students comprises 21 students whose families sent them to study in the UK for parts of their high school and/or their higher education degrees. I researched this group between 2018 and 2020. This group is the most privileged among all participants in this book. While 9 of 21 were from first-tier cities, the remaining 12 were from lower-tier cities such as Chengdu, Fuzhou, Mianyang, and Jingdezhen. They are of typically middle-class or upper-middle-class origins. Half were from families with business backgrounds, one third had parents working in the civil service or at management levels of state-owned enterprises, and the rest had parents with professional backgrounds, such as journalists and university professors. Most families were able to sponsor their children to study at least three to four years in the UK, and quite a few also had to pay for their children's international and private schooling in China or boarding schooling in the UK. These families are the most economically wealthy among these four groups and can be considered as representing the upper strata of China's contemporary urban families (Goodman, 2014; X. Wu, 2019).

## Parents' Education Levels and Familial Social Networks

Consistent with their socioeconomic backgrounds, the rural-origin participants' parents generally had low levels of education. None of this group's parents had been to a university or vocational college, and only five students had parents who had been to senior high school, the highest level of education attained by these parents. Sixteen students had parents who had achieved junior high school or primary education levels, while five had one or both parents who were illiterate. These low education levels aligned with their social networks, which were mostly confined to the rural environment, with little or no social networks or connections extended beyond their immediate village, township, or county seats. However, some participants had parents or elder siblings working as migrant workers in big cities such as Shenzhen or Hangzhou, although these connections did not provide them with educational support, such as advice in their university choice making.

Most participants in this group mentioned that they had never been to the county seats before senior high school and had never traveled to a city before their university stage. Xun (born in the 1980s in Hunan Province), for example, felt unable to travel alone to register at his university as he had never ridden a train before. Xun eventually asked his elder sister, who was working at a factory in Shenzhen, to accompany him to his university. This example illustrates the kind of social connections that these rural-origin participants could draw on when engaging in education-mobility endeavors. All participants suggested that their parents were unable to provide any educational support to them, such as advising in their educational choice making, but were mostly supportive of their educational pursuits, with the exception of Ku, whose father and stepmother did not support him beyond junior high school. Given their low socioeconomic status, these parents mostly expected their children who "made it" in the big cities to repay their monetary debts and moral debts in the forms of social favors (*renqing* 人情; see chapter 2 for more details).

The Hong Kong students' parents' education levels were relatively low. The 14 students from low-income, "grassroots" families all had parents with a secondary to primary level education. Their families' social networks were mostly within the lower strata of Hong Kong. These students generally reported few social connections that could advise them on their higher education options other than their secondary schools, with the exception of Charles, who has a university-educated aunt who pointed out to him that he could study in the mainland. In general, their parents were uninformed about the higher education options they had, and some had negative views about their children studying in the mainland; for example, Norman's parents thought he was out of his mind when they learned about his decision to study in Beijing.

For the first group of urban participants from mainland China who pursed undergraduate studies in Hong Kong, all of their parents were at least university graduates, with a few possessing PhD degrees. For example, both of Yu's parents were university professors with PhD degrees, and Nianci's father held a PhD degree, too. In terms of familial social networks, there is a range. On the top are those who have abundant resources and connections within the system (i.e., in the government's establishment)—such as Guoxiang, Zilong, and Miusi, who all had parents working as civil servants—or in the business world—such as Nianci and Longnv, who had parents who ran their own businesses. In the middle are those with plenty of professional connections, such as Yu, whose parents are university professors; Wen and Yingying, whose parents are doctors; and Keqin, whose parents are registered accountants. At the bottom are those who have fewer resources and connections, such as Fei, whose parents are a secondary school teacher and a retired real estate agent, and Lingshan, whose father is a sound-equipment shop owner and whose mother is a homemaker. In all cases, however, these parents were very supportive of their children's education pursuits, and many had very progressive educational philosophies (e.g., Yu's, Nianci's, Yingying's, and Lingshan's parents; see chapter 2 for further details).

For the second group of urban students from mainland China who pursued higher education studies (and, for some, high school) in the UK, all of their parents had at least university-level degrees, and one parent had a PhD degree (Yi's mother). In terms of familial social networks, all families had abundant social connections in their home cities, regardless of tiers. This explains why some parents were keen to urge their children to return home to inherit their social and political resources before they retired (see chapter 9). More importantly, many families had connections that went beyond their respective cities; for example, Dao's parents previously worked in Spain before returning to Shanghai, while other families like Man's had multiple family members or relatives who had migrated abroad. An even greater number had family friends who sent their children to study abroad, which brought them useful information and connections. This group's social networks are the most extensive across the four groups of participants. All parents were very supportive of their children's education. In fact, most were strategic about their children's educational options—for example, circumventing the students' poor Gaokao results or less-than-desirable academic aptitude (e.g., "not study material") by sending them to study abroad (see chapter 3). These parents were also supportive of their children's lifestyle and career pursuits; some parents not only paid for their children's overseas education expenditures but also invested in their business ventures and bought properties abroad for them, such as Man's and Li's parents (see chapter 8).

In view of these four groups' places of origin, socioeconomic backgrounds, parents' education levels, and familial social networks, a steep hierarchy can be seen in terms of these participants' access to not only economic but also cultural and social resources. These differentiated social origins have significant implications for the participants' respective time inheritances, which concomitantly shape their educational experiences and life options.

## Structure of the Book

In *The Time Inheritors*, I explore how intergenerational transfer of privilege or deprivation manifests in and through time in the scene of education mobility in China. In part 1, I lay the theoretical and conceptual foundations for the entire book, explicating the Bourdieusian origin, lineage, and application of the central concept of time inheritance as well as supporting concepts such as banked time and borrowed time. This is achieved through evoking and contrasting empirical evidence of education mobility from participants who are of vastly different socioeconomic backgrounds in China.

Part 1 encompasses three chapters. Chapter 1 outlines the overarching theoretical framework of the book—namely, the time inheritance framework as informed by Bourdieu (1986, 1988, 2000) and Serafin (2016). Chapter 2 proposes that differentiated time inheritance of families across social origins shapes how education is constructed in a temporal sense, straddling between being an act of kindness from families and a nonnegotiable entitlement for the children and obligation for the parents. Chapter 3 points to how education mobility becomes a "fate-changing" mechanism for time inheritors across the social spectrum and preempts how access to education mobility is structured across a steep hierarchy of prestige and status corresponding to these time inheritors' social origins.

Part 2 consists of five chapters. It draws on a wide range of empirical data to introduce five manifestations through which differential time inheritance perpetuates social inequalities. Chapter 4 demonstrates how differentiated time inheritance shapes educational decision making: disadvantaged time inheritors seemingly make shortsighted and self-sabotaging decisions, while their privileged counterparts enjoy their banked time through long-term strategic plans. Chapter 5 argues that inequalities in time inheritance have also predisposed the modes of living that differentiated time inheritors embodied, ranging between living in the debt-paying mode and in the mode of entitlement. Chapter 6 contends that differentiated time inheritance also shapes how social agents perceive and use time; some "squander" away their labor time, while others achieve "work-life balance." Chapter 7 contrasts two consequences of time use among differentiated time inheritors, ranging from "wasting time" to "gaining time." Chapter 8 shows how unequal time inheritance traps some in successive precarious, low-paid jobs while enabling others to make bold career moves with secure fallback options.

Part 3 comprises three chapters. It points out how time inheritance as a hidden social mechanism shapes society in complex and sometimes unexpected ways, where multiple levels of banked time and borrowed time intersect to challenge and transform existing inequalities. Chapter 9 discusses how time inheritance is not a straightforward process as there are both "unqualified inheritors," with significant bestowed banked time, and "zealous parvenus," burdened by borrowed time. Chapter 10 zooms in on how national-level time inheritance can be further nuanced through the perspective of city tiers. It also shows how when national-level time inequalities enmesh with those on the global level, time inequalities are exacerbated. Chapter 11 focuses on political time inheritance and its complex intricacies by drawing on the accounts of students from mainland China and Hong Kong who moved to study and work across the border.

The concluding chapter pinpoints the theoretical innovations and empirical contributions made by this book and outlines an ambitious research agenda revolving around a new field of "global time inheritance studies," which moves beyond China studies, migration studies, and education inequality research.

# List of Acronyms

| | |
|---|---|
| CCP | Chinese Communist Party |
| CAD | Canadian dollar |
| CSSCI | Chinese Social Sciences Citation Index |
| GBA | Greater Bay Area (Guangdong–Hong Kong–Macau) |
| HEIs | higher education institutions |
| HKCAAVQ | Hong Kong Council for Accreditation of Academic and Vocational Qualifications |
| HKD | Hong Kong dollar |
| HKDSE | Hong Kong Diploma of Secondary Education |
| ILR | indefinite leave to remain |
| MNE | moral and national education |
| PGDE | Postgraduate Diploma in Education |
| RMB | renminbi |
| SAR | Special Administrative Region |
| USD | US dollar |

# Presentation Style

In this book, when I cite works from the Chinese-language literature, I provide the Chinese character(s) of the surname of the lead author. For instance, this is how I cite the work of C. Wang [王] et al. (2018) and of G. Yan [阎] (2017). Readers can tell the Chinese-language literature apart by the Chinese characters used. In the reference list, I include both the original Chinese and the English translation of all Chinese-language literature cited.

# Part I

# Theorization of Time Inheritance and Education Mobility

Part 1 lays the theoretical and conceptual foundations for the entire book. It explicates the Bourdieusian origin, lineage, and application of the central concept of time inheritance as well as the supporting concepts such as banked time and borrowed time. It does so by evoking and contrasting empirical evidence of education mobility from participants who are of vastly different socioeconomic backgrounds in China.

# Chapter 1

# Time Inheritance, Banked Time, and Borrowed Time

Time inheritance is a social mechanism that underpins much social inequality. What, then, is time inheritance? How is it understood and constituted conceptually? This chapter explores how a linear, evolutionist temporalization has been deployed by both nation-states and dominant powers in the global West to arbitrarily create hierarchies of populations and institutions. Together, these state-level and international-level temporal categorizations and manipulations have instituted an underlying mechanism of *time inheritance* that designates unequal power and resources to states, institutions, and families.

At the familial level, individuals inherit time from past generations of accumulation or deprivation of resources (economic, social, and cultural—drawing on Bourdieu, 1986). Time inheritance grants the inheritors of these accumulated resources abundant "banked time," which enables them to have an assured, at-ease approach toward life (e.g., education and career). For those who do not benefit from the accumulation of resources by previous generations, their time inheritance from generations of deprivation subjects them to living on "borrowed time," haunted by constant time poverty and cultivating a submissive and docile approach toward life.

Importantly, in discussing the temporal experiences of individuals, *The Time Inheritors* emphasizes, following Bourdieu (2000), that time is not external to social agents but in fact is made in practice by social agents. This is what economic sociologist Marcin Serafin (2016) refers to as "*time in action*," while the broader temporal structures fostered by nation-states and dominant global countries in the West are what Serafin considers "*time of action*." Serafin suggests that time has been understood in two main different ways:

- time as either quantitative (clock time) or qualitative (subjective experiences of time passing)
- time as either linear (from past to present to future) or cyclical (e.g., seasons of a year, a woman's menstrual cycle)

Based on these two understandings, Serafin introduces a third way to understand time: "time of action" versus "time in action." By *time of action*, Serafin refers mainly to the temporal calendars that are used to structure different fields—for example, the academic year is structured in ways that are different from the religious year—and here he uses the term "temporal structures" to help clarify the meaning of "time of action." For *time in action*, Serafin engages with the notion of agency and with that of power. He writes cogently on the distinction between "time of action" and "time in action":

> Whereas time of action can be understood as "objective" time, the time of events happening and structuring social life; time in action is "subjective," or cognitive, it takes place in the minds of actors. Actors not only experience time in a certain way . . . but also direct their actions towards a certain moment in time: past, present or future. As the anthropologist Maurice Bloch argues people have the ability to "time travel": "Time travel enables us to remember, and, to a certain extent, experience past events of our lives and to imagine future events in which we may be involved." (Serafin, 2016, p. 20)

Serafin's distinction between time of action (broadly speaking, "objective," i.e., quantitative and linear) and time in action (broadly speaking, "subjective," i.e., qualitative and not necessarily linear) will serve as the foundational theoretical basis of this book and informs the structure of this chapter.

## Time of Action in Education Mobility

### THE STATE'S TEMPORAL CLASSIFICATION AND POLITICS OF TIME

A major actor in creating temporal structures or time of action for individuals is the nation-state, or, more practically, managers of the modern state. In "Temporality and the Modern State," David Gross (1985, p. 77) points out that in order to assert and achieve legitimacy to rule, modern states often resort to temporal rationales such as "continuity" and "'meaning systems' of the past in order to extract a measure of allegiance from their constituencies." This behavior is what Gross calls "a politics of time" that enables the state managers to "resuscitate powerful memories of the genealogy of the state, or of the state's place in time, in order to strengthen their authority" (p. 77).

## China's State Victimhood and Political Unification

In the case of China, the state government led by the Chinese Communist Party (CCP) arguably deploys "powerful memories" such as China's victimhood under imperialist and colonialist forces. These powerful memories include, for example, the two Opium Wars with the British Empire and the Japanese invasion in the 1930s (Vickers, 2015), which constitute China's "Century of National Humiliation" (Callahan, 2009; Garcia & Bianco, 2023). In addition to these historical narratives that emphasize how China was weakened and disintegrated by the abovementioned imperial forces, the CCP has also made analogies with how the United States and its mostly Western allies are trying to contain the now "revived" and strengthened China, thus appealing to China's contemporary "place in time" on the world stage (Chang & Yang, 2020; Ohnesorge & Owen, 2023). This essentially anti-imperialist temporal categorization is seen to have successfully evoked nationalist and patriotic sentiments among individual Chinese citizens (Weiss, 2019), whose overall orientations are, as a result, aligned with the state's seemingly neutral and "objective" political orientations.

The same can be said about the CCP's underlining of sovereignty, unity, and continuity over the disparate regions of Hong Kong, Macau, and Taiwan (P.-C. Lan & Y.-F. Wu, 2016; E. K.-W. Ma, 2012; Vickers & Kumar, 2015). By appealing to temporal construction of a unified nation from the past that should be sustained in the present and last well into the future, the CCP-led state can "plausibly affect, in almost imperceptible ways, not only the attitudes people hold, but their incentives and motivations as well" (Gross, 1985, p. 78). As such, the CCP-led government becomes the vanguard that safeguards the country's and its people's interests against malicious imperialist powers or separatist forces in Hong Kong and Taiwan alike, thereby further strengthening its governing legitimacy and political domination. Subjects of the CCP-led state thus can be argued to have embodied a politicized time inheritance in the realm of national history and discourses of unity and unification.

*China's Domestic Hierarchies of Temporal Inequalities*

Crucially, apart from deploying this anti-imperialist temporality to directly serve its political interest on the international stage, the CCP-led Chinese state also employs linear, evolutionist developmental "temporal classification" systems (Gross, 1985, p. 78) to govern its diverse population. This is manifest in the country's imposed dichotomous distinctions between the rural and the urban, between the Han majority and the ethnic minorities, and among the uneven regional developments and unequal city tiers.

PLACE HIERARCHY

As opposed to a cyclical understanding of time such as the four seasons in a year or women's monthly menstrual cycles (Adam, 1990), the teleological way of interpreting time assumes that "time is inherently progressive" and that "the direction in which [time] moves is always forward rather than backwards, and that most if not all aspects of life have manifestly improved as one travels the distance from the past to the present" (Gross, 1985, p. 70). In the context of China, this teleological interpretation of time is closely linked with what anthropologist Zachary Howlett (2021, p. 44) calls the ideology of developmentalism. Howlett suggests that developmentalism is "a distorted view of reality that justifies the status quo" in China, whereby a strict hierarchy of place (village, township, county seats, prefectural-level cities, capital cities, first-tier super metropolises) is closely pegged to a perceived hierarchy of qualities. This ideology denotes that people from the periphery are gravitated toward the center, in search of better resources and opportunities with a view to increasing "their status, reputation, and earning potential" (Howlett, 2021, p. 45). As such, "geographical mobility (movement through space)" is considered "synonymous with social mobility (increase of status)" (p. 45). According to this developmentalism ideology, the center is almost ubiquitously equated with the urban.

URBAN–RURAL DICHOTOMY AND UNEQUAL
TIME INHERITANCE

In this manner, the CCP-led state utilizes teleological developmentalism to designate power and status to the urban centers, which become symbols of development thanks to processes such as industrialization and urbanization. Indeed, as anthropologist Andrew Kipnis (2011, p. 160) notes, China's rapid industrialization induces a devaluation of the labor of farmers. Under this ideology of modernization, "peasants" are labeled as backward, and non-farming occupations are considered "advanced" and "modern." As such, the urban becomes the modern and the "present," endowed with advantageous time inheritance, while the rural belongs to the "past," lagging behind in development, and is compelled to catch up with the urban in order to enable the state to "accelerate" its "economic transition into a middle-income country of urban consumers" (Howlett, 2021, p. 49).

More crucially, the rural–urban dichotomy is further reinforced by another level of inheritance: inheritance of *hukou* (household registration) status. Since its introduction in the 1950s, the Chinese government has administered the household registration system with a view to regulating tax administration and maintaining social order. Under this regulation, every citizen must register either a rural or an urban *hukou* status at birth in accordance with their locality; this registration is inherited—children born to rural residents will inherit their rural *hukou*, while children born to urban parents will inherit their urban *hukou* (Cai, 2011; C. Chen & Fan, 2016).[1] This *hukou* system effectively divided China's population into two parallel societies. As sociologist Xiaogang Wu (2019, p. 366) aptly articulates, "the majority of the population [were] confined in the countryside and entitled to few of the rights and benefits that the socialist state conferred on urban residents, thus [the *hukou* system] creat[ed] not only a spatial stratification between the countryside and the cities but also two unequal classes of Chinese citizens."

Such unequal spatial and classed divisions are precisely evidence of the Chinese state's unequal temporal classification bestowed on the urban and rural residents. Concomitantly, offspring of urban and rural residents continue to inherit unequal treatments, and this can theoretically continue for many generations (Murphy, 2020, 2022). In this way, the rural can be said to have disadvantageous time inheritance.

By establishing this temporal and developmental hierarchy between the urban and the rural, the CCP-led state also fosters the notion of *lack* among the rural population. Kipnis (2011, p. 133) cites Deleuze and Guattari (1983), highlighting how "social organization depends on lack," or "an abject fear of lacking something." In China's constructed urban–rural hierarchy, "lack is especially marked in rural, uneducated, and impoverished persons, households, and communities" (Kipnis, 2011, p. 133). This is further rein-forced by indicators such as educational attainment and income disparity between the urban and the rural. Xiaogang Wu's (2019, p. 366) review of consolidated empirical evidence indicates that "after taking residence place into account, rural *hukou* origin was found to significantly decrease one's educational attainment and chances of joining the Communist Party (Wu 2011, Wu & Treiman 2004), and large disparities in schooling and income between rural and urban *hukou* holders remain even today (Hao et al. 2014, Liu 2005)."

Moreover, as the state-designed policies favor urban education, rural education practices have been further disadvantaged through an urban-based curriculum that is inapplicable to the rural contexts, a short supply of qualified teachers who can deliver such a curriculum to the rural students, and a general lack of educational resources (S. Xu & Law, 2015, p. 79). In other words, inheriting the rural *hukou* means inheriting a lesser access to various kinds of educational resources while being subjected to the same highly competitive national college entrance examination—Gaokao—as the better-resourced urban counterparts (Howlett, 2021; Y. Liu, 2013).

By designating the "rural, uneducated, and impoverished" as lacking (and thus of deficient time inheritance) and limiting their accesses to valuable educational and life resources, the state manufactures intense desires, wants, and needs for these populations to aspire to be urban and escape the rural. Indeed, as Kipnis (2011) observes, "Farming parents who lack both connections to urban areas and skills valuable to the secondary and tertiary economic sectors can come to *see education as the only way out of this low-status trap for their children*" (p. 160, my emphasis).

## UNEVEN REGIONAL AND CITY DEVELOPMENTS AND ETHNIC HIERARCHY

The same temporal classification[2]—in other words, teleological developmentalism—can be discerned in China's hierarchical and uneven regional developments and its strict geographical tiers of places. It is now widely acknowledged that China's eastern and southern provinces and regions tend to have higher levels of economic and social development than its western and inland regions (C. L. Xu & Y. Ma, 2023; Yin et al., 2022). This status quo is arguably the result of perpetuation over time, due to factors such as differentiated natural resources endowments, variegated degrees of remoteness, different infrastructural and financial investments by local and central governments, and contrasting economic organization and government-policy orientations (Hamnett et al., 2019, p. 253). Similarly, within China's hierarchy of places, the first-tier super metropolises like Beijing, Shanghai,

Guangzhou, and Shenzhen yield the highest concentration of resources (economic, educational, health); these are followed by capital cities, prefectural-level cities, and then the rural administrative county seats, townships, and villages. Within this strict place hierarchy, the first-tier super metropolises are considered as representing the modern and the present, endowed with positive time inheritance, while the townships and villages are undoubtedly backward and need to catch up in order to become as "modern" as possible, thus possessing negative time inheritance.

In fact, as Howlett underlines, echoing Edward Vickers's (2015) analysis, teleological developmentalism is not new in China. China has a long history of "imperial expansion and internal colonialism" (Howlett, 2021, p. 47) in which the empire enacted "civilizing missions to cultivate the populace and incorporate the periphery, which has long been regarded as the realm of uncultured barbarians" (p. 47). In China's contemporary ethnic hierarchy, the Han majority is unquestionably placed at the top, regarded as more "advanced," "modern," and "civilized," thus possessing advantageous time inheritance, while the ethnic minority groups such as Mongolians, Tibetans, and Uyghurs are often rendered as "uncivilized" and "backward" (X. Guo & Gu, 2016; Jue Wang, 2023; C. L. Xu & M. Yang, 2019; M. Yang & C. L. Xu, 2020; Yuan et al., 2017; Yuan & Zhu, 2021), thus inheriting negative temporal assets. There is therefore a civilizing mission that the state proclaims to be enforcing by helping these ethnic minority groups to modernize through various measures such as the *neidi ban* (inland classes; Y. Chen, 2008; Grose, 2010, 2015; Leibold & Dorjee, 2023).

In summary, in the case of China, the CCP-led state government has adopted a host of "temporal classifications' (Gross, 1985, p. 78) to establish its legitimacy in governing through appealing to anti-imperialist, nationalist, and patriotic sentiments among the population; it also deploys the teleological developmentalist ideology to designate a hierarchy of development between the urban and the rural and the different tiers of cities and regions as well as a strict ethnic hierarchy. Through these temporal classifications and creating the fear of lack among its disadvantaged populations such as the rural and the ethnic minorities, the CCP-led state accords differentiated temporal wealth or deficits to diverse populations, thus manufacturing sentiments (e.g., patriotism and nationalism, entitlement or contempt), desires, and wants among its population in order to accelerate its pace of becoming a "middle-income" nation of urban consumers. Intriguingly, however, this very politics of time used by the CCP-led state seems to submit to what Vanessa Fong (2011, p. 41) calls a "global narrative about the teleological, dichotomous, unilineal evolutionist division of the world." This is what I shall now turn to discuss.

## The Global Temporal Classification and China's Position

While the contemporary Chinese state uses its own temporal classifications to establish its political legitimacy and govern its populations, the global community has been dominated by a neoliberal and capitalist narrative of development for some time too. Arguably stemmed from the aforementioned teleological developmentalist ideology, the global neoliberal narrative is characterized by what anthropologist Vanessa Fong (2011, p. 41) refers to as a "dichotomous, unilineal evolutionist division of the world into developed countries that sit at the top of the global social, economic, and political hierarchy and developing countries that must, can, and should play by the rules of the global neoliberal system in order to become developed." In this global hierarchy, the developed countries are symbols of the modern, the advanced, and the desirable. In contrast, the so-called developing countries, among whom China is positioned, are relegated to the past, the backward, lagging behind in development, and should strive hard to transition into the desirable (Hou et al., 2021).

Arguably, this teleological perspective of the world's developmental hierarchy was deployed by the previous imperialist and/or colonialist powers and current developed countries to legitimize their very own dominance in the global capitalist world and the neoliberal system. This temporal classification of the world's various countries into different developmental stages thus proclaims "an evolutionist path" (V. L. Fong, 2011, p. 41) by which the current "developing" countries can one day become "developed" or "middle-income" so long as they play by the rules set out by the developed countries/former imperial and colonial powers (Bhambra, 2014; Said, 1978/2003). Through this linear temporal classification, the developed countries assert their global dominance while imposing the idea of lack on the developing countries, driving them to adopt a "catch-up" mentality (Howlett, 2021; Jokila, 2015) and willingly submit to their own dominated position. In other words, the developed countries are endowed with significant temporal wealth, while the developing countries have inherited temporal deficits. These differentiated time inheritances among countries thus not only shape national standings in developmental terms but also orient national policies and affect individuals' lives and educational pursuits, as this book will amply demonstrate.

Indeed, since China's reform and opening era, successive administrations under the leadership of Deng Xiaoping, Jiang Zemin, and Hu Jintao have all adopted this linear historicization of the modern world (Luo [罗], 2021). Under this linear temporalization, China was set to open up and embrace the market economies and developmental models of "advanced" Western countries in order to cast off its status as a "backward" nation, especially in the 1970s and 1980s (Buzan & Lawson, 2020; Meinhof, 2017). Thus, on the one hand, the CCP-led Chinese state positions itself as at the forefront of anti-imperialist struggles to safeguard its people, while, on the other hand, it willingly submits to its "lagging behind" and "backward" economic positioning on the world stage.

### Globally Classified Higher Education Arena

This lineage of global teleological temporal classification has also been amplified in the arena of higher education, which is widely acknowledged to be an unequal playing field (Altbach, 2004; Marginson, 2008). This is largely rooted in the historical domination of medieval European universities and contemporary hegemony of Anglo-American universities (Glass & Cruz, 2023). As Altbach (2004) points out, almost all the universities in the world today are modeled after medieval European universities, due mainly to the imposition by European colonial powers on their non-Western colonies' higher education systems. Curiously, though, in countries that were not colonized (e.g., Japan and Thailand) or not fully colonized by Western imperial powers (e.g., China), higher education has in all cases adopted the Western academic model (Altbach, 2004, p. 4).

Carrying on the "torch" of this historical lineage, the contemporary Anglo-American universities, which Shahjahan and Edwards (2022, pp. 750–751) refer to as "White institutions," have occupied what Marginson (2008) calls a *hegemonic dominance* in global higher education. These powerful universities have dominated the "production and distribution of knowledge" as well as setting the rules (i.e., leadership) on "all aspects of science and scholarship" on a global scale (Altbach, 2004, p. 4). From a temporal perspective, these Anglo-American, "White institutions" position themselves "as the future for which the rest of the world must aspire" (Shahjahan & Edwards, 2022, p. 751). This temporal positioning could be argued as the global-level temporal wealth of these institutions, as it controls and shapes educational imaginations and aspirations and, concomitantly, resource allocations of universities located in the Global South, or the developing countries, which are subject to following "in their wake" and playing by their rules, so to speak (Altbach, 2004; Shahjahan & Edwards, 2022).

Clearly, mirroring the world developmentalist narrative, in the higher education arena, there is arguably a similar "evolutionist path" for universities in the developing countries to catch up with their powerful Anglo-American, "White institution" counterparts. As such, this hierarchy of global universities establishes a temporality of progress and advancement (progressive teleology; Gross, 1985, p. 70), placing Western higher education institutions (HEIs) at the highest echelon, representing the future and boosting wants and desires among the families and students within developing nations (such as China) to move transnationally to acquire the credentials these powerful universities award. In this way, the global neoliberal narrative marries the capitalist logic to commodify Western higher education credentials as globally desired products, thus driving up the desires and wants among those from countries "lacking" such offerings (e.g., China; Glass & Cruz, 2023). Again, the differentiated time inheritance of HEIs in the Global West/North versus their counterparts in the Global East/South can shape differing positioning of these HEIs not only in international rankings but, more importantly, in their degrees of desirability among prospective students and employers of their graduates.

Another pivotal aspect of the West's global-level time inheritance is the dominance of the English language. English, as the language of colonial power, dominates the global scene of higher education research, publication, and teaching (P. K. Choi, 2010; Crystal, 2003; H. Li, 2020). Amano et al. (2023, p. 1) carried out a survey of 908 environmental scientists to examine the "manifold costs to non-native English speakers in science." They provide strong evidence to show how much more time nonnative English speakers require to complete the same academic tasks. For example, nonnative English speakers spend up to 90.8% more time than native English speakers in reading academic papers and 50.6% more time in writing for publication. Apart from being quantitatively advantaged in temporal terms, native English speakers benefit qualitatively due to the sense of ease, entitlement, and social recognition bestowed on them. This is vividly captured in Rebecca Kuang's (2022, pp. 141–142) novel *Babel: An Arcane History*, in which she depicts the views of Robin, an immigrant from China, about his native-English-speaker peers, such as Pendennis:

> Still, Robin could not help but envy those boys—those born into this world, who uttered its codes as native speakers. When

he saw Elton Pendennis and his crowd strolling and laughing across the green, he couldn't help but imagine just for a moment what it might be like to be a part of that circle. He wanted Pendennis's life, not so much for its material pleasures—the wine, the cigars, the clothes, the dinners—but for what it represented: the assurance that one would always be welcome in England. If he could only attain Pendennis's fluency, or at least an imitation of it, then he too would blend into the tapestry of this idyllic campus life. And he would no longer be the foreigner, second guessing his pronunciation at every turn, but a native whose belonging could not possibly be questioned or revoked.

While Robin's context was in England, where he was an immigrant, the Western-dominated and English-dominated global higher education arena could be likened to the "native land" of English speakers.

Compared with the dominated players (e.g., newer universities in non-Anglophone countries and emerging economies), the Anglo-American universities have (hundreds of years of) cultivations (thus capital) that are readily (mis)recognized as legitimate (Bourdieu, 1984; Marginson, 2008), sought after, and valuable in the global market of educational credentials; for example, multinational companies and international organizations consistently operate in the English language and recognize degrees from these universities as markers of distinction and quality (Y. Liu et al., 2022; S. Zhang & C. L. Xu, 2020). Holders of degrees from these Western universities (which are sometimes placed as the "center" of the center–periphery dichotomy) continue to reap high rewards not only in the global market but in their national and domestic labor markets, no matter whether in the West (Wakeling & Savage, 2015; Waters & Brooks, 2011) or in the Global South's emerging economies (Ren & Qi, 2024). Graduates of these Western universities are found to earn a higher premium when they return to their home countries based in the Global South (King & Sondhi, 2018; Prazeres, 2019; Tu & Nehring, 2019), while graduates with "foreign" degrees, even if they are of Western origin, still get less desirable jobs due to the employers' lack of understanding of foreign degrees other than those in the Western countries (Waters & Brooks, 2011). In a nutshell, educational credentials earned from these dominating Western universities enjoy a much higher purchase power than counterparts from the "dominated" universities situated in the Global South/East, such as those in mainland China (Altbach, 2004). As such, these graduates from Western universities can benefit temporally by spending less time seeking jobs, getting promoted more quickly, and earning higher salaries, which means that their (work) time is valued more than that of their counterparts. This is their advantageous time inheritance.

Within China, the CCP-led government's submission to the global narrative of teleological development has clear implications for its higher education scene (Ahlers & Christmann-Budian, 2023). As Rui Yang (2018, p. 39) points out, in contemporary China, "Western education is perceived as prestigious" and Western knowledge as "the real knowledge by both the educator and the general public." In higher education, a thoroughgoing adoption of the "Western style" has been rampant, encompassing aspects such as textbooks, teaching content, organization, and operation of the universities (R. Yang et al., 2018, p. 2). This complete transplantation of the Western models to China's higher education aligns with its catch-up mentality as dictated by the aforementioned global temporal classification. Meanwhile, the high regard for credentials acquired from powerful Anglo-American universities has also driven Chinese families and students to desire and pursue higher education in a transnational sphere, making China the world's largest international-student-exporting country for over a decade (V. L. Fong, 2011; Y. Ma, 2020; Martin, 2022; Miao & Wang, 2024; Xiang & Shen, 2009; C. L. Xu, 2021a).

## Time in Action

### Bourdieu's Temporalization and Capital/Time Accumulation

*The Time Inheritors* adopts Bourdieu's (2000) argument that time is not external to us but instead is produced or made in and through practice. In Bourdieu's (2000, p. 206) words, we tend to consider time as "a thing with which we have a relation of externality, that of a subject facing an object," often because of our habits in daily language. We are inclined to speak of time as if it is "something that one has, that one gains or wastes, lacks or has on one's hands" (p. 206). This positioning of time as external to us is also due to a convention of considering "history either as a pregiven reality, a thing in-itself, previous and external to practice, or as the (empty) *a priori* framework for every historical process" (p. 206). This convention aligns with the "temporal classifications" by nation-states and the global community, which impose certain grand temporal structures on individuals. However, Bourdieu advocates that we can "break with this point of view by reconstructing the point of view of the acting agent, of practice as 'temporalization,' thereby revealing that practice is *not in time but makes time* (human time, as opposed to biological or astronomical time)" (p. 206, my emphasis).

Bourdieu's argument is closely aligned with Serafin's (2016) "time in action" theorization, which emphasizes the phenomenological, subjective aspect of qualitative time, how time is lived and experienced by individual human actors. Bourdieu's attention to "human time" as opposed to "biological or astronomical time" thus allows *The Time Inheritors* to develop an understanding of the "time in action" aspect of education mobility in China. Adopting this Bourdieusian view that "practice" of human agents makes time and "of practice as 'temporalization' " thus enables this book to accentuate the central place of the social agents across data sets.

More importantly, as social agents "temporalize themselves" (Bourdieu, 2000, p. 213), it should be noted that time is made and lived only by those who are endowed with the necessary faculties and capacities to "see objective potentialities in the present structure" (Bourdieu, 2000, p. 213), for this is how they become "interested" and "invested" (i.e., Bourdieu's notion of *illusio*) as opposed to being "indifferent to" and completely out of the game. In Bourdieusian terms, a social agent has to be equipped with the right disposition (i.e., habitus) that is properly adjusted to the game (or the field) so that they are able to have the "capacity to anticipate, in the practical mode, forth-coming" (Bourdieu, 2000, p. 213). As Bourdieu (2000, p. 212) plainly puts it, "Investment or interest, which presupposes possession of a habitus and a capital capable of providing it with at least a minimum of profits, is what brings people into the game, and into the time that is specific to it, that is to say, the forth-coming and the urgencies that it offers. It is proportionate to capital as profit potential—disappearing when the chances of appropriation fall below a certain threshold."

How, then, is time felt or experienced? According to Bourdieu (2000, pp. 208–209), time is most acutely felt when our expectations (which are informed by our tacit understanding of how the game operates, the logic of the game) are broken. As such, our "subjective" disposition collides with the "objective tendency," leading to "relations to time such as waiting or impatience . . . regret or nostalgia . . . boredom or 'discontent' " (Bourdieu, 2000, pp. 208–209). Only when we have the right set of requisite habitus (dispositions) and capital and are willingly entering into the game, becoming invested in the game, can we begin to truly feel time, especially when our expectations are not (fully) met. Bourdieu's theorization helps us in vivid and nuanced ways to disentangle the intricacies of time in action.

## Capital as Accumulated Labor Time: Foundational Theorization of Time Inheritance

Due to the differentiation of power/capital possessed by different social agents when in the same game/field, the social agents' practices tend to make time differently. To articulate this clearly, Bourdieu makes a foundational argument that capital is "*accumulated labor* (in its materialized form or its 'incorporated,' embodied form)" and that it "takes time to accumulate" capital (economic, social, and cultural; Bourdieu, 1986, p. 241, my emphasis). As such, individuals born into families of substantial economic, social, and cultural wealth are in effect advantaged because they can expect to inherit a great deal of accumulated (labor) time. In Bourdieusian terms, these are people who live in a "dominant" mode, while their counterparts who are set to inherit little or no accumulated (labor) time from their families live in a "dominated" mode. Bourdieu points out that for those dominated, they are often "condemned to live in a time orientated by others, *an alienated time*" (Bourdieu, 2000, p. 237, my emphasis).

Bourdieu goes on to suggest, "This is, very exactly, the fate of all the dominated, who are obliged to wait for everything to come from others, from the holders of power over the game and over the objective and subjective prospect of gain that it can offer, being therefore masters at playing on the anxiety that inevitably arises from the tension between the intensity of the expectancy and the improbability of its being satisfied" (Bourdieu, 2000, p. 237). In comparison to the dominated, those who are "holders of power over the game" tend to exercise their power by "exploit[ing] the opportunities offered by the field," in other words through "manipulating other people's time, or, more precisely, their career rhythm, their curriculum vitae" (Bourdieu, 1988, p. 88). This power imbalance thus produces the dominated, who tend to be "docile and submissive, even somewhat infantile" toward the power holders.

As social agents, a pivotal condition for the advantaged to live a time that is not "alienated" is that they enter the "game" equipped with "the necessary assurances concerning the present and the future" (Bourdieu, 2000, p. 225), thanks to their possession of relatively more advantageous forms of capital. This capital thus endows them with the requisite dispositions "to confront the future actively," which means that they enter "the game with aspirations roughly adjusted to their chances" (Bourdieu, 2000, p. 225). In other words, to aspire to live the "dominant" time, one needs to have an active sense of agency to play by the game rules, with the ambition and anticipation that one can "win" or do well in the game, and the ultimate aim of achieving time freedom: "time used freely for freely chosen, gratuitous ends which . . . may be those of work, but work that is freed, in its rhythm, moment and duration, from every external constraint and especially from the constraint imposed through direct monetary sanction" (Bourdieu, 2000, p. 224).

Bourdieu's temporalization and capital/time accumulation theses furnish significant insights regarding the inheritance of time. That is, inheritance of time is both quantitative and qualitative. The family's passing on of economic and social capital, which themselves required time to acquire by previous generations, can be considered the quantitative bequest of time. On the other hand, the family's handing down of cultural capital, which manifests, for example, in everyday conversations, can be considered "effortless" and "natural" passing on of time wealth. Both these quantitative and qualitative inheritances are transmitted through inculcation and nurturing of high or omnivore-like culture that is to be deemed legitimate and sought after in the schooling or labor-market settings—this is the qualitative bequest of quantitative time (i.e., it took the past generations time to acquire such cultural understanding). More importantly, the family's substantial amount of time wealth (as in the forms of economic, social, and cultural capital) can cultivate a secure relation with time (Adam, 1990)—a sense of assuredness about the future, a trusted and safe understanding that there is something to fall back on, an understanding that the inheritors are deserving of the resources bestowed on them. As such, the security, assuredness, and sense of entitlement jointly constitute the qualitative aspect of time inheritance—or, in Bourdieusian terms, the facets of the inheritors' habitus that manifest time security, entitlement, and assuredness.

This qualitative aspect of time inheritance is often hidden. Throughout this book, I will unmask the various ways through which the qualitative and quantitative inheritance of time (or the lack thereof) shapes the education and career decision making of individuals and their families by examining the case of education mobility in China.

TIME INHERITANCE AND EDUCATION MOBILITY

This book argues that time plays a pivotal yet underacknowledged role in education mobility. This pivotal role manifests on three different levels: the present, the past, and the future. First, it should be noted that physically moving to pursue education itself takes time. The students have to physically embody the mobility by changing their locations, enrolling in an HEI, attending lectures, passing exams, joining excursions and sightseeing trips—all of these are embedded in the act of education mobility, take time, and cannot be carried out by another person or proxy. On this level, therefore, education mobility matters to individual students in a qualitative way in that their present and personal trajectories are altered, such as moving from one space to another, and they qualitatively experience the host of exposure brought along by education mobility in real time (i.e., at present).

Second, looking back at the "past" when examining the desires and aspirations that motivated or pushed these students to move for educational purposes, time plays a crucial role in that nation-states and global neoliberal forces exercise their "temporal classification" (Gross, 1985, p. 78) to manufacture senses of "lack" (Kipnis, 2011) and foster desires for individual families to send their children away to receive higher education.

Third, looking forward to the future, time plays an important role in that education mobility becomes an intervention to keep certain agents in the game while bringing certain new agents into the game, thus creating the coexistence of older and newer players within the same game. In this sense, the uneven and unequal power relations between these players will have an impact on how they feel and experience the game (i.e., temporal experiences), will motivate strategies and resistance among the players, and will affect the prospects of future generations. From the present, the past, and the future perspectives, time plays an important role in education mobility.

## A Framework Encompassing Temporal Structures and Agency

*The Time Inheritors*, following Serafin's (2016) insightful theorization, devises a theoretical framework of time that encompasses both time of action ("temporal structures") and time in action ("temporal orientation"). On the one hand, the time-of-action theorization pertains to the temporal order and structures that organize social spaces, thus allowing us to examine the broader *temporal classifications* conducted by nation-states and global forces such as neoliberal and capitalist powers. On the other hand, the time-in-action conceptualization draws heavily on Bourdieu's temporalization and capital/time accumulation theses; it enables *The Time Inheritors* to examine in detail how time (in education mobility) is not external to the social actor but instead is produced and lived by the social actor through practice, in an often emotional and habitual rather than "rational" manner. It also enables this book to compare how social actors of differentiated powers (i.e., time inheritance) act differently under similar circumstances. It is indeed pivotal to marry time of action and time in action in this framework:

Focusing solely on time of action (time as sequence) we end up with a mechanistic theory: a purely structural account of the social world, where social order is reproduced or transformed without anyone contributing to its reproduction or transformation. In this account there are invisible social forces, but no actors with their projects, emotions, perceptions, memories. On the other hand if we forget time of action and focus solely on time in action (time as intention) we end up with a voluntaristic or romantic theory in which the social world is purely the realization of individual wills, with no power relations, no struggles, and no inequalities—in other words no social structures. (Serafin, 2016, p. 26)

Encompassing both aspects of time (of action and in action) thus aligns with Bourdieu's (2002) long-held ambition to transcend structure and agency. Importantly, this theoretical framework is based on Serafin's broad theorization while incorporating elements (e.g., the state and global temporal classification, the distinction between borrowed time and banked time) that are unique and tailor-selected for understanding the education mobility scene in China. In this way, this theoretical framework can have potential wider applications for understanding broader education temporalities beyond China and beyond mobility issues. I will discuss these broader implications in the concluding chapter.

## Time Inheritance: A Conceptual Contribution and the Book's Central Argument

Building on the above theoretical framework, this book proposes the concept of *time inheritance* to capture an underlying social mechanism whereby unequal inherited temporal wealth and deficits accorded to countries, organizations, and population groups can shape social lives and trajectories of individual actors. As briefly rehearsed in the introduction, this book argues that there is a *time privilege continuum* when it comes to time inequalities. On one end of this continuum are the disadvantaged time inheritors, who live on "borrowed time" in three different ways and across three different levels (familial, national, and international). On the other end of this continuum are the advantaged time inheritors, who live on "banked time" in three different ways across the same three levels. This time privilege continuum is captured in figure 1.1.

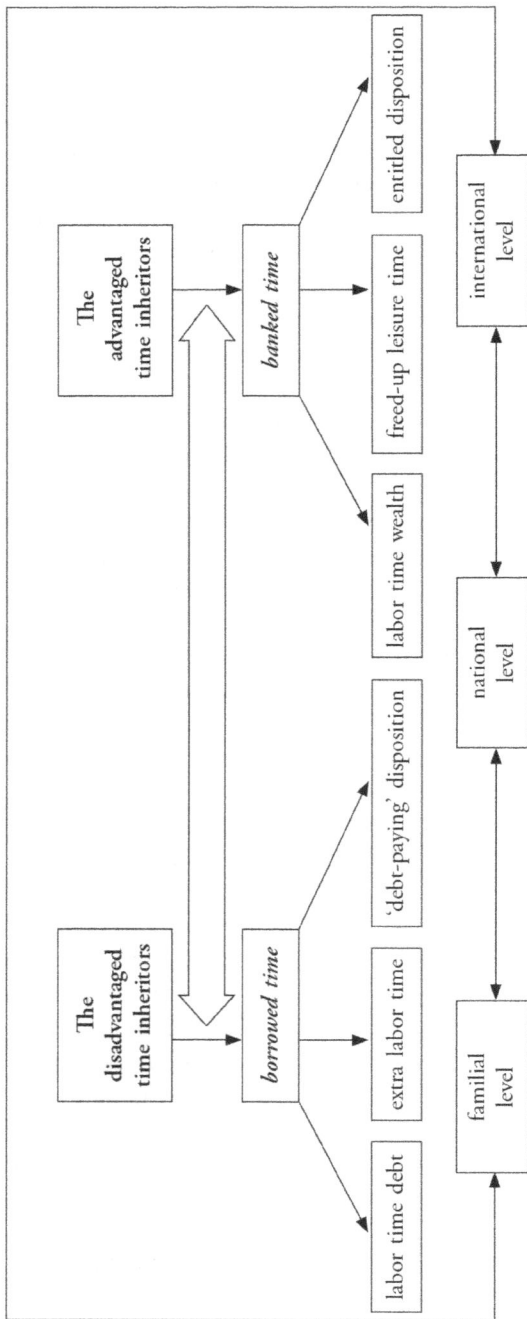

Figure 1.1. The Time Privilege Continuum.

*The Advantaged Time Inheritors and Banked Time*

Based on Bourdieu's (1986, 2002) theorizations about forms of capital and habitus (disposition), this book argues that the advantaged time inheritors live with *banked time* through inheriting (1) accumulated *labor time* from their ancestors, which manifests in different forms of capital; (2) *freed-up leisure time*, which allows them to pursue preferred life causes and consume and appreciate life; and (3) *time that feeds into their disposition and mentality*, through which they develop this secured, safe, confident, entitled, and relaxed approach to life and its vagaries, which in turn, as I shall demonstrate in part 2 of this book, enables them to make more informed decisions and end up saving more time or even gaining time. This is what they inherit at the familial level.

At the national level, time inheritors possessing state-sanctioned characteristics, such as an urban *hukou* or the Han ethnicity in China, enjoy better (or sometimes exclusive) access or entitlement to valuable resources (e.g., education, health, housing, social welfare) that would otherwise have taken a long time to acquire through labor (Cai, 2011). Thanks to these bestowed privileges, which are equivalent to substantial labor time, these time inheritors can have "freed-up leisure time" to pursue preferred life causes and consume and appreciate life. Shaped by such time privileges, they gain higher (symbolic) recognition; for example, *hukou* holders of first-tier cities tend to be favored for job opportunities and held in high regard in the marriage market (Z. Wang, 2023; C. Zhang, 2023). Subsequently, they cultivate an inherent sense of superiority and entitlement, which can enable them to make confident and informed decisions that contribute to saving time or even gaining time (see part 2).

At the international level, time inheritors possessing globally established dominant characteristics such as developed-world citizenship and the native-English-speaker identity can have better entitlement and easier access to valuable resources (e.g., highly ranked HEIs in Western countries, job opportunities due to native-English-speaker identity), which would otherwise have taken a long time to acquire through intense studying and labor time (e.g., learning to communicate in English or acquiring developed-world citizenship; V. L. Fong, 2011; Marginson, 2008). Thanks to these inherited privileges, these time heirs can have freed-up leisure time. They also gain higher (symbolic) recognition (e.g., as native-English-speaking degree holders of prestigious HEIs) and inculcate an inherent sense of superiority and entitlement, feeding into their disposition, enabling them to make confident and informed decisions that can directly contribute to saving time or even gaining time.

Often, heirs of time privileges may not be able to inherit their banked time on all three levels; for example, those from "developing" countries or the Global South may inherit banked time at the familial and national levels but not the international level; an ethnic/racial-minority working-class citizen from a globally dominant Western country may inherit banked time on the international level but may not do so at the familial or national level.

## *The Disadvantaged Time Inheritors and Borrowed Time*

On the other end of the time privilege continuum, the disadvantaged time inheritors live on what I call *borrowed time*. They do so through inheriting generations of deprivation of "labor time," which manifests in forms of debt (e.g., monetary, social, and moral debt). Therefore, instead of inheriting labor-time wealth, they inherit labor-time debt. These time debts compel them to devote extra labor time in order to pay back the various forms of debts and hopefully acquire some forms of capital; this extra labor time, as I shall demonstrate in part 2, is often at the price of their leisure time or freed-up time and can end up compromising their future plans and personal interests. Due to these inherited labor-time debts and the extra labor time demanded of them, these heirs of time debt tend to foster a debt-paying mentality and are urged to generate immediate monetary income for survival needs, thus displaying a predominant focus on the present, making seemingly short-term, self-sabotaging decisions that end up wasting even more of their time (see chapter 2 and part 2). This is what they inherit at the familial level.

At the national level, time inheritors deprived of state-sanctioned characteristics and instead possessing marginalized identities, such as holding a rural *hukou* or being an ethnic minority member in China, cannot have access or entitlement to valuable resources (e.g., education, health, housing, social welfare; X. Wang et al., 2013). Their identities become negative assets that attracted extra barriers to get things done; these characteristics of deprivation thus demand that they devote *extra labor time* to acquire the valuable resources they are denied access to by the nation-state and to tackle the extra barriers imposed on them. Due to such state-engineered hierarchies, these time inheritors tend to become stigmatized and alienated and can embody an imposed sense of inferiority; this can push some of them to seek alternative avenues (e.g., education mobility) for potential social mobility.

At the international level, time inheritors deprived of globally established dominant characteristics tend to share no or little access and entitlement to valuable resources (e.g., highly ranked HEIs in Western countries, job opportunities due to native-English-speaker identity). Instead, their identities, such as being a nonnative English speaker, become negative assets that attract extra barriers to access global (elite) higher education; these extra barriers demand extra labor time (e.g., having to pass IELTS [International English Language Testing System] or TOEFL exams to gain admission to the global universities). Due to such extra barriers, these time inheritors may experience exclusion and alienation, cultivating an imposed sense of inferiority, which can push them to invest excessive labor time to acquire valued capital (e.g., English-language capability and academic publishing capability).

Similar to banked time, not all disadvantaged inheritors experience all three levels of borrowed time. For example, the working-class citizens from globally dominant Western countries can live on borrowed time at the familial level but live on banked time on the national and international levels. Meanwhile, upper-middle-class students possessing urban *hukou* in China can live on borrowed time at the international level due to their nonnative-English-speaker identity, but they live on banked time at the familial and national levels.

## Time Inheritance: Not a Mechanistic Determinism

Time inheritance as a mechanism for reproducing inequalities does not work in a mechanistic manner. Time inheritance in its three forms and across three levels can intersect to create scenarios where disadvantageous time inheritance at certain levels (e.g., familial and national) can be turned into a source of distinction at another level (e.g., see the case of Jiao in chapter 9); meanwhile, advantageous time inheritance at a certain level is not necessarily a guarantee of success at another level (e.g., see the cases of Bing, Wang, and Mengxi in chapter 9).

While inherited time inequalities (i.e., wealth versus debt, banked time versus borrowed time) largely shape citizens' life chances and can further exacerbate existing social inequalities, there are anomalies where the individual agency of the disadvantaged inheritors trumps the structure and goes on to create capital and distinction, thanks to various acts of education mobility. To these citizens, education mobility is fate changing, as it facilitates opportunities for them to move beyond the confines and constraints imposed by borrowed time at the familial and/or national level and instead engage in global-level struggles of time privilege (or vice versa). Meanwhile, inherited time wealth (or banked time) does not favor its heirs equally and indiscriminately. Instead, to activate "past stocks" of "stored historical capital" (i.e., inherited temporal wealth), one needs to come to terms with "contemporary conditions" and exercise agency (Bourdieu & Passeron, 1979; Savage, 2014, p. 595). Part 3 will demonstrate that despite substantial banked time at the familial and national levels, some of these inheritors can still face great challenges at the international level and become in danger of "downclassing," and thus are dubbed "unqualified inheritors" of time privilege. Refer to tables 1.1 and 1.2 for a summary of how time inheritance works.

Table 1.1. How Time Inheritance Works: Advantaged Time Inheritors

| Level | Labor Time (Wealth) | Banked Time | | Time-Shaped Dispositions |
|---|---|---|---|---|
| | | Freed-up (Leisure) Time | | |
| **Familial** | Generations of accumulation of labor time, which manifests or is turned into different forms of capital. | Time freed up to pursue preferred life causes, consume, and appreciate life, thus improving quality of time. | | Secured, safe, confident, entitled, and relaxed about life and its vagaries; tend to make more informed decisions, which enable them to save time or even gain time. |
| **National** (state-sanctioned characteristics, such as *hukou* and ethnicity) | Better access and entitlement to valuable resources (e.g., education, health care, housing, social welfare), which would otherwise have taken a long time to acquire through labor. | Time freed up to pursue preferred life causes, consume, and appreciate life, thus improving quality of time. | | Higher (symbolic) recognition from others; an inherent sense of superiority and entitlement that feeds into their disposition and enables them to make confident and informed decisions, which can directly contribute to saving time or even gaining time. |
| **International** (globally established dominant characteristics, such as developed-world citizenship and native-English-speaker identity) | Better and easier access and entitlement to valuable resources (e.g., highly ranked HEIs in Western countries, job opportunities due to native-English-speaker identity), which would otherwise have taken a long time to acquire through intense studying and labor (e.g., learning to communicate in English or acquiring developed-world citizenship). | Time freed up to pursue preferred life causes, consume, and appreciate life, thus improving quality of time. | | Higher (symbolic) recognition from others (e.g., native English speakers, degree holders of prestigious HEIs), an inherent sense of superiority and entitlement feeding into their disposition and enabling them to make confident and informed decisions, which can directly contribute to saving time or even gaining time. |

Table 1.2. How Time Inheritance Works: Disadvantaged Time Inheritors

| Level | Labor Time (Debt) | Borrowed Time | | 
|---|---|---|---|
| | | Extra Labor Time | Time-Shaped Dispositions |
| **Familial** | Generations of deprivation of labor time, which manifests in forms of debt (e.g., monetary debt, social debt such as *renqing*, moral debt) | Extra labor time has to be devoted to pay back the various forms of debt and hopefully acquire some forms of capital, thus compromising future plans and personal interests; little work-life balance | Debt-paying mentality; urged to generate immediate monetary income for survival needs, thus focus on the present; make seemingly short-term, self-sabotaging decisions that end up wasting even more time |
| **National** (state-sanctioned characteristics, such as *hukou* and ethnicity) | No/denied access and entitlement to valuable resources (e.g., education, health care, housing, social welfare); instead, identities such as being rural *hukou* holders become negative assets that attract extra barriers to getting things done | Extra labor time has to be devoted to acquire the valuable resources to which the nation-state denies access and to tackle the extra barriers imposed | Stigmatization, alienation from others, an imposed sense of inferiority, pushed to seek alternative avenues (e.g., education mobility) for potential social mobility |
| **International** (globally established dominant characteristics, such as developed-world citizenship and native-English-speaker identity) | No/little access and entitlement to valuable resources (e.g., highly ranked HEIs in Western countries, job opportunities due to native-English-speaker identity); instead, identities such as not being native English speakers become negative assets that attract extra barriers to accessing global elite higher education | Extra labor time has to be devoted to acquire the valuable resources to which global forces deny access and to tackle the extra barriers imposed (e.g., having to pass IELTS or TOEFL in order to gain admission to global elite HEIs) | Exclusion, alienation from others, an imposed sense of inferiority, pushed to invest excessive labor time to acquire valued capital (e.g., English-language capability and academic publishing capability) |

# Chapter 2

# Education as Debt Accumulation or Entitlement

My mother had invested a great deal in me. She had to borrow money, and pay the debt, pay others' favor [*renqing* 人情]. It took them so much effort to support me through my university studies . . . my parents were always waiting, waiting for me to *pay it back*. Time, for the elderly, sometimes they can't wait.

—Lian, born in the 1980s, Guangdong Province

Other people think of nurturing a child as a business; they aim at having the child support them when they become old. To me, I don't think of it this way. I told Lingshan, "You belong to the whole world, where the sky is high, and the birds can fly wherever they want [*tiangao renniaofei* 天高任鸟飞]."

—Mr. Yue, father of Lingshan, 18 years old, Shandong Province

This chapter proposes that differentiated time inheritance of families across vastly different socioeconomic backgrounds fundamentally shapes how education is constructed in a temporal sense. For the disadvantaged time inheritors (e.g., the rural-origin and urban, working-class, multi-child families), education is often constructed as an act of kindness; thus to receive education is to accumulate monetary, social, and moral debt toward parents and siblings. In contrast, for single children of urban, upper-middle-class families,[1] education is construed as a nonnegotiable entitlement and an obligation of the parents. These two contrasting constructions shape how

27

education is differentially experienced and lived through by these time inheritors of differentiated social origins.

## Education as a Gift and Debt

Jing Wang (2023) interviewed 38 dyads of parents and their children at the juncture of college entrance examination, from one rural area and one urban area in China. Wang found that while rural parents of impoverished families focused more on future prospects for their children's upward social mobility and for their children to pay them back, urban parents of affluent families focused on their children's enjoyment of learning and the intrinsic value of education. Wang's research finding resonates with the argument in this chapter: that differentiated time inheritance of families across vastly different socioeconomic and geopolitical backgrounds fundamentally shapes how education is constructed differently in a temporal sense. For the disadvantaged time inheritors (e.g., the rural-origin and working-class, multi-child families[2] in this book), how to allocate limited familial resources to support the education of one certain child becomes a serious decision-making process that has notable consequences for the life chances of not only that selected child but also the other children who are not chosen (Murphy, 2020, 2022). To receive education or not, in such circumstances, tests not only the relationship between the child and the parents but also with their siblings (Xia et al., 2024).

Among these families, it was typical to hear stories of struggling to pay tuition fees and education expenditures for multiple children, with one or more children ending up not being able to pay tuition fees at all. Xun (born in the 1980s, Hunan Province) recounted, "There are three children in my family. As I was the youngest one, my parents usually gave money to my elder sisters to pay their tuition fees. When it came to my turn, they always ran out of money, so I would sit on the steps of my family house for hours, refusing to go to school, because I was too ashamed."

Vivienne (born in the 1990s, Hong Kong), whose father had passed away and mother worked as a security guard (i.e., low income), revealed that her adult elder brother was unemployed and was not contributing to her family's finances but instead needed support from her mother's meager salary. Vivienne's mother was therefore not able to provide any financial support for Vivienne's education expenditures.

Since it was always a struggle to support all of the children's education, at certain junctures, such as from junior high school to senior high school or from senior high school to university, these families had to make difficult decisions about whether to continue to support a certain child's education. Ku (born in the 1980s, Hubei Province) narrated his experience: "My mother passed away when I was one year old. My father married my stepmother after that. When I was finishing my junior high school, my father did not want me to continue to senior high school but to join a two-year teacher training program so I could get a job and begin earning as a primary school teacher quickly." However, Ku was determined to enter his senior high school and then continue to pursue his university education. This created a conflict for Ku and his parents, so much so that Ku's uncle had to intervene and Ku's elder sister, who was forced to give up her own primary education and became a migrant worker, promised to support Ku's education expenditure.

For these families, therefore, due to their limited financial resources and the needs of multiple children, allocating resources for education pursuits became a fate-changing endeavor for the selected child but also for the family. It was common among the rural-origin and working-class families to concentrate their resources on only one child, with the other children having to drop out of school and become migrant workers and/or engage in manual work. Zhen (born in the 1980s, Jiangxi Province), for instance, revealed how his younger sister became a migrant worker in Shenzhen, in part to support his education, while Xun's elder sisters both left school and started working in nearby county seats as seamstresses. Bian's (born in the 1960s, Anhui Province) and Pu's (born in the 1970s, Hubei Province) brothers all became migrant workers in Guangdong.

For these rural and multi-child families that were struggling to support their children's education, to decide to concentrate their limited resources on one specific child's education thus became a family project. In anthropologist Zachary Howlett's (2021, p. 64) discussion of family mobility strategies in rural China, he notes that some rural families adopt this strategy of having "some members go out to work while others pursue college education and a white-collar job." He especially mentions that "in large families, it is normal for an older sibling, particularly a girl, to go out for work to pay for a younger sibling's education. When these beneficiaries graduate, they are expected to return the favor by contributing financially to their sponsors" (Howlett, 2021, p. 65). Building on Howlett's observation, I argue that such arrangements often give rise to a profound sense of indebtedness for the selected child or sibling.

## Education Pursuits as Debt Accumulation

Indeed, for this selected child, their education was not an entitlement but an act of kindness and sacrifice of not only their parents but often also their siblings. Lian's (born in the 1980s, Guangdong Province) account is typical in conveying the sense of debt: "My mother had invested a great deal in me. She had to borrow money and pay the debt, pay others' favor [*renqing* 人情]. It took them so much effort to support me through my university studies . . . my parents were always waiting, waiting for me to pay it back. Time, for the elderly, sometimes they can't wait."

Ku, whose sister dropped out of school and became a migrant worker to support his education, confessed, 'I am forever in debt to my elder sister." Time and again, these rural-origin and working-class protagonists from multi-child families articulated how much debt they owed. This is consistent with existing studies on left-behind rural children (X. Gu, 2022) and on rural-origin students at elite universities, who are found to articulate this expectation of "repaying their parents" as part of their heavy ethical duty in the face of their parents' sacrifices (Meng Cheng & Kang, 2019; Y. Xu, 2022, p. 255). To receive education, therefore, was to acknowledge debt, to their parents but also to their siblings and the entire family.

The sense of debt and the need felt by the "selected" child to pay back the debt is also found among upwardly mobile individuals in Germany who come from the "bottom of the class structure" (Born, 2024, p. 395). When depicting his feelings toward his immigrant parents' sacrifice, Dario (a pseudonym) expressed his gratitude for his family's support for his private tutoring despite a lack of financial means: "At the interview he said he therefore hoped that he would soon be able to '*pay them back*.' Significantly, when I asked him at the end of the interview what goals he had in his life, he talked almost exclusively about his parents" (Born, 2024, p. 400, my emphasis). This sense of debt, in Dario's view, can be paid back through "a house for them back home" (Born, 2024, p. 400). This is strikingly similar to the rural-origin and working-class participants in this book.

In Shahrokni's (2018, p. 1175) research with second-generation descendants of North African working-class immigrants to France, these second-generation youth considered their own upward social mobility "as a powerful way of '*giving back*' to former-generation migrants whose mobility dreams often had to be relinquished." Here the notion of giving back was framed under the "immigrant bargain," whereby the second generation feels a strong "sense of moral duty" and "a collective desire to make the first generation's endurance 'worthwhile'" (Shahrokni, 2018, p. 1175).

Both Born's and Shahrokni's participants are arguably disadvantaged time inheritors given their marginalized positions as the working class and migrants. For these groups, to receive education requires their families' concerted efforts to concentrate resources and often incredible sacrifices. It could therefore be synthesized that for disadvantaged time inheritors, the process of receiving education thus becomes a debt-accumulating process. This has three implications for how they live their time in education.

First, they live on borrowed time—time that is not theirs, but is "on loan" to them, bestowed on them as an act of kindness, which creates this subjective sense of hurry, of time shortage and poverty, wanting to cherish this time and achieve as much as they can. Second, because of this time being on loan to them, they are inculcated into believing that they have to pay it back some time in the future. In some cases, their "creditors," such as their parents, moved this time of debt paying forward (see chapter 5), which can leave significant long-term psychological and social impacts on them (what I call "time interest" in chapter 5). Third, the difficult process of deciding to concentrate the family's limited resources on them also constructed these selected children as potentially "undeserving" subjects of this time spent in education or education mobility. Hence, anyone who helped them on their educational journey is *enren* (恩人) or *guiren* (贵人),[3] becoming their creditor, which turns their education or education-mobility journey into a continuous debt-accumulating process. Instead of a feeling of entitlement to such help, this undeserving positioning creates pressure and burden for the selected child to repay all kinds of debts, not only to their parents and other family members but also other creditors, such as their superordinates. All of these impacts will be demonstrated in the remaining chapters.

## Education as an Entitlement

In contrast to these disadvantaged time inheritors, single-child families[4] of middle-class and upper-middle-class backgrounds constructed education as an expectation and an entitlement for their only child. There was a complete absence of any mentioning of struggles with tuition fees. Instead, the students' well-off families expected them to not just receive education but receive a high-quality, progressive kind of education. Lingshan (born in the 1990s, Shandong Province), Nianci (born in the 1990s, Beijing), and Keqin (born in the 1990s, Guangdong Province) typically recalled their parents taking them to travel around China and abroad before university with a view to "broadening their horizons," under the mantra "Read ten thousand books, walk ten thousand miles" (*duwanjuanshu, xingwanlilu* 读万卷书，行万里路). Without exception, the parents in these families had university-level or above qualifications. They often articulated a strong desire for Western-style family education and pedagogies when raising their children. Lingshan's father, Mr. Yue, shared during an interview in 2017 that he read books by John Dewey to understand and practice Western educational philosophies in his own child-rearing. He said,

> When Lingshan was in junior high school, I recited the poem "On Children" by Khalil Gibran, and this poem has been deeply imprinted in my heart. I have been telling Lingshan that other people think of nurturing a child as a business; they aim at having the child support them when they become old. To me, I don't think of it this way. I told Lingshan, "You belong to the whole world, where the sky is high, and the birds can fly wherever they want [*tiangao renniaofei* 天高任鸟飞]." To other people this may sound like a cliche, but to me this is real.

Mr. Yue's approach to educating Lingshan resonates with that of Yu's parents, who both have PhDs and were working as university professors. Yu suggested, "My parents would never tell me what I ought or ought to not do. Instead, they would analyze the pros and cons of the options I have together with me and leave the decision making in my own hands."

Mr. Yue and Yu's parents are representative of the middle-class and upper-middle-class parents in my data. These parents typically assumed their obligation of providing the best possible conditions for their children to receive a progressive education, with no expectation for their children to pay them back. To these families, their children's reception of quality education was a nonnegotiable entitlement, while their own contribution to their children's education was taken for granted. Such an unambiguous construction of education resonates with these lines in Kahlil Gibran's (1923/2021) poem "On Children," mentioned above by Mr. Yue:

Your children are not your children.
They are the sons and daughters of Life's longing for itself.
They come through you but not from you,
And though they are with you, yet they belong not to you.
You may give them your love but not your thoughts.
For they have their own thoughts.
You may house their bodies but not their souls,
For their souls dwell in the house of tomorrow, which you
    cannot visit, not even in your dreams.
You may strive to be like them, but seek not to make them
    like you.

These urban middle-class and upper-middle-class families' approaches to their children's education contrast starkly with the rural and urban working-class families, mainly because of their better socioeconomic backgrounds and their single-child family makeup, which enables them to concentrate all their resources on their single child's education. This is in line with existing research that finds urban, single-child families devote greater amounts of time to provide higher quality educational care (Du et al., 2023, pp. 130–139) and to nurture children who have a strong sense of entitlement to the resources passed on to them, both in receiving education at home and abroad and well into their adulthood (Kajanus, 2015a; Tu, 2018).

The temporal implications of this construction of education as a non-negotiable entitlement for the children and an obligation for the parents to provide the best possible education opportunities are large and far-reaching, especially in comparison with more disadvantaged time inheritors, for whom education is constructed as a gift. First, feeling entitled to the education they receive means that these students are more at ease about taking their time to explore what they like or dislike; this, as I will show in the chapters of part 2, also shapes their pursuit of temporal autonomy. Second, instead of feeling pressured and hurried for time, their sense of ease and assuredness about time also instills in them an empowerment and capacity to plan for the long term and not get stuck by the need to address immediate necessities. Third, their well-off families and their highly educated parents' aspirations often get carried forward by these children through their education—in other words, their education pursuits become an extension of their parents' unfulfilled dreams. This has temporal significance in that they effectively live a type of time called banked time, which enables them to gain extra time and strive for their preferred lifestyles. These key impacts will be elaborated in part 2.

*The Time Inheritors* argues that these two contrasting constructions of education (1) as a gift versus (2) as an entitlement shape how education is differentially experienced and lived through by time inheritors of varied social origins. Intriguingly, one common theme that cropped up across the accounts of these protagonists of vastly different backgrounds was that, at one point or another of their education journeys, they all tried to escape their "doomed futures." And, interestingly, all of them resorted to one form or another of education mobility.

# Chapter 3

# Education Mobility as Fate Changing

This chapter notes how, despite having vastly different academic calibers and socioeconomic backgrounds, the various groups of time inheritors in this study were all keen to circumvent their "fates" or "doomed futures." These fates or futures, while they might have seemed inevitable had the students stayed in their places or fields of origin, became escapable once they strategized to move away and pursue education elsewhere—that is, engage in forms of education mobility. As such, education mobility became a "fate-changing" mechanism. However, this chapter also briefly previews how access to education mobility is structured across a steep hierarchy of prestige and status corresponding to these time inheritors' social origins.

## Escaping Differentiated Doomed Futures

All participants in this book, irrespective of their academic caliber (e.g., academically inclined or a "failure") and socioeconomic background (rural-origin and deprived, urban working class, middle class, or upper middle class), were terrified of their fates or doomed futures. What transpired as their "way out" was to move away from their places of origin (fields) through pursuing education.

As such, education mobility shouldered important temporal roles. First, education mobility allowed these participants to temporarily withdraw from the existing temporal structures and logics of their original fields and also enabled them to insert themselves into a different field where alternative temporal structures may apply. This temporary withdrawal and insertion created possibilities that were unavailable in their original fields and could therefore potentially allow them to circumvent their "doomed futures." In this sense, education mobility can be fate changing. Second, given their differing socioeconomic backgrounds as well as their relations with time in education (e.g., either living on borrowed time as "undeserving subjects" or living an entitled banked time in education), these participants' capacity to interact with the new temporal structures of their new fields differed greatly. Thus, their endeavors to change their fate through education mobility may have different degrees of success. Some may find it easier to change their fate through education mobility, while others may encounter yet more barriers in this process—these will be explicated in the upcoming chapters.

In general, this chapter will focus on addressing these following questions: What fates are the students circumventing? How are they circumventing these fates by engaging in education mobility?

## Fate One: Struggling at the Bottom of Society

By observing their own parents, siblings, and neighbors who either stayed within the rural vicinity or became migrant workers in cities, the rural-origin participants in this book became acutely aware of their likely fate of meandering "at the bottom of society [*shehui diceng* 社会底层]" all their lives. Ku, whom we met earlier, sighed, "The rural labor, like herding sheep and collecting woods for fire, which I had to go through before going to university was hard, so hard that it was bitter. I did not want to do that all my life." Su (born in the 1970s, Hubei Province) similarly recalled, "Life was hard as peasants. The agriculture taxes were high. As a girl with little natural beauty, my mother told me that my only way to escape a life of toil was to study." Bian (born in the 1960s, Anhui Province) articulated his only two options to leave the rural life, joining the army or higher education. Lacking *guanxi* (关系)[1] (Xie & Postiglione, 2016), Bian figured that he could only rely on his Gaokao result. Tian's (born in the 1980s, Shandong Province) account was typical:

> Unlike urbanites—even if they cannot get certain jobs, they at least have their families there to support them. However, for people like us, in order to climb upwards, education is perhaps the only way out. We do not have other paths to choose from. To fight and survive [*dapin* 打拼] in the city we can only rely

on ourselves. Even if we return to our hometowns, we do not have the kind of social networks [*guanxi* 关系] that classmates from the county seats possess. We still have to rely on ourselves, which can be even harder.

This shared fear of struggling at the bottom of the (rural) society was so powerful that it propelled the rural-origin individuals to work extremely hard on getting offers from higher education institutions from the cities, thus achieving their initial rural-to-urban education mobility (Howlett, 2021; C. L. Xu, 2020).

## Fate Two: Becoming Unemployed or Underemployed

Meanwhile, labeled or self-considered as "failures" in Hong Kong's education system, the working-class students wanted to escape their destiny of becoming unemployed or underemployed. In Hong Kong's highly competitive education system, only 18% of high school graduates are offered government-funded degree-level courses. This means that those who do not perform well enough in the HKDSE (Hong Kong Diploma of Secondary Education) exam,[2] who are disproportionately from working-class backgrounds, tend to be excluded from entering Hong Kong's local government-funded universities (O'Sullivan & Tsang, 2015; C. L. Xu, 2019). As such, they are faced with either dropping out and engaging in predominantly working-class jobs, as their parents do, or enrolling in self-funded subdegree or top-up degree programs, the graduates of which are found to be slighted as "lesser" by employers and the government in Hong Kong (Leung & Waters, 2013; Y.-L. Wong, 2022).

As a matter of fact, most working-class students in this book did not perform well in the HKDSE and have had to consider and even enroll in subdegree courses. Clive (father a retired worker, mother does handy jobs, family monthly income HKD 20,000), for instance, was studying in a Chinese medicine subdegree course. However, he found that the teaching provision was suboptimal and became very concerned about his career prospects. He dropped out after three months. Lawrence (father a restaurant chef, mother a cleaner, family monthly income HKD 20,000), Apple (parents' professions not disclosed, family monthly income HKD 30,000), and Stephanie (parents owned a small barbershop, family monthly income above HKD 15,000) all acknowledged that given their less than desirable performance in the HKDSE, they had to consider subdegree or foundational degree courses in Hong Kong. Lawrence, when reflecting on his decision making then, referred to these subdegree programs as "half a bucket of water" (*bantongshui* 半桶水). He explained, "The level of social recognition of such subdegree or foundational degree programs is not high. Enrolling in them is a waste of my time and money, because the outcomes of such qualifications are not promising."

Observing their friends, these working-class students became acutely aware of their own destiny. Norman (father retired, mother a homemaker, low-income family) revealed, "I have a few good friends who have become unemployed as soon as they finished their post-compulsory education. It is hard to get a job [in Hong Kong with their qualifications]. One of them studied for a top-up degree. Now he is unemployed. He attempted to become a police officer but failed. Now he works part-time in McDonald's and convenience stores."

Coming from low-income families and not having performed well in the HKDSE, these working-class students are caught in a dead end, with high probability of unemployment or underemployment. Their unflattering fate reminds us of O'Sullivan and Tsang's (2015, pp. 454–455) comment: "Many young people in Hong Kong are now faced with diminished career prospects in a job market that offers little beyond soulless service jobs with stagnant wages." To circumvent this "doomed future" in Hong Kong, these working-class students had to be creative. They chose to enroll in higher education degree courses at mainland China's prestigious universities, thus engaging in cross-border education mobility. This was thanks to the preferential treatment policy carried out by the mainland Chinese government and universities toward citizens of Hong Kong, Macau, and Taiwan (F. Gao, 2024; P.-C. Lan & Y.-F. Wu, 2016; C. L. Xu, 2019).

## Fate Three: Getting a "Worthless" Degree

Unlike the previous cases, the upper-middle-class group of students were concerned about their fate of getting a degree deemed worthless by their families, thus failing to legitimately inherit their family's wealth and power. Bing's and Li's cases are representative of this group.

In January 2019, Bing began her third year working as a representative at a pharmaceutical company in her home city of Chengdu in Sichuan Province. This was a job arranged by her parents that required a "good enough" university degree. The problem was, Bing was not an academically inclined student. After Gaokao, in which she did a "disastrous" job, Bing was faced with the likely fate of entering a third-tier university[3] (Loyalka et al., 2012; R. Yang & M. Xie, 2015) and getting a "worthless" degree that would have been deemed insufficient for her arranged job. To circumvent this, Bing's family enrolled her in a 3+1 program, which allowed Bing to join a post-92 university in the UK (Blyth & Cleminson, 2016) as a Year 2 student.[4] However, after studying for two years in that university, Bing failed her course and had to transfer to a lower-ranked university, where she eventually received a bachelor's degree.

Upon her graduation, she was urged to return home to take up a job that her parents had arranged for her through their contacts in the same company. Unlike the rural and poverty-stricken families or the working-class Hong Kong families, Bing's urban family was much better off in economic conditions and social connections. Bing was among the 284,700 Chinese students in 2010 who were family- or self-sponsored to pursue degrees overseas, mostly in developed countries such as the US, UK, and Australia (Ministry of Education of the People's Republic of China, 2011).

Similar to Bing, many other participants in this group confessed that they did poorly in their academic studies. As a "sanctuary" route (Waters, 2007), their parents decided to send them abroad to accord them foreign degrees, with a view to increasing their competitiveness and fundamentally shunning their "fates." Li, for example, is originally from Guangzhou. Seeing that he was not "study material," his parents sent him to the UK for his A-level studies and subsequently sponsored him to attend a post-92 university in the south of England. Li confessed, "Had I stayed in Guangzhou, I would not be able to get a good degree and I might end up being jobless." However, coming to the UK allowed him relatively easier access to a "decent enough" university, where he developed a strong interest in luxury sales and marketing and eventually became a luxury sales representative in London.

These upper-middle-class students resemble human geographer Johanna Waters's Hong Kong middle-class students who used study abroad in Canada as a "sanctuary" to circumvent their "failure" in Hong Kong's education system (Waters, 2006a, 2006b, 2007). Unlike their more disadvantaged time inheritors who had to engage in less prized forms of education mobility (e.g., rural to urban or cross-border Hong Kong to mainland China), these affluent time inheritors were able to access the most expensive and time-rich[5] form of education mobility, transnational mobility from China to the developed Western country of the UK.

## Different Fates, Same Strategy of Education Mobility

Clearly, although these participants all articulated a desire to circumvent their doomed fates, these fates were qualitatively different. While the rural-origin and working-class Hong Kong students were desperate to be rid of their fate of struggling at the bottom of society, living a life of toil and hard labor, and/or facing unemployment or underemployment, the upper-middle-class students were more concerned about not being able to legitimately inherit their families' wealth and power. Intriguingly, the shared fear of confronting their doomed fates propelled them to move to different places to pursue education, thus engaging in education mobility.

Given their differentiated time inheritance, these groups had different access to forms of education mobility. As discussed in the theoretical framework chapter's global temporal classifications, higher education in the developed Western countries is classified as of the highest echelon of prestige because of their rich and long time inheritance. Unsurprisingly, to access higher education provision in these countries also requires a great deal of economic and cultural resources. Statistics have revealed that only around 2% of China's population has access to transnational higher education (Q. Gu & Schweisfurth, 2015b; C. L. Xu & Montgomery, 2019), making it a highly exclusive form of education mobility only accessible to the families that are of the highest level of time inheritance.

Intriguingly, for the working-class students from Hong Kong, despite their disadvantageous time inheritance in their socioeconomic status, their political time inheritance was such that they could capitalize on the CCP-led government's temporal classification of Hong Kong as an inseparable part of China, which fostered "preferential admission treatments" toward students from Hong Kong. To them, getting admitted to mainland China's elite universities thus became a much easier form of education mobility to access in order to potentially shirk their doomed future (see chapter 11).

In contrast, the rural-origin individuals had the most disadvantageous time inheritance, due to their lack of social and cultural resources and, more importantly, due to their inheritance of the rural *hukou*, a state-constructed "backward" position. As pointed out in the theoretical framework chapter, the CCP-led government constructs the rural as needing to catch up and accords the rural populations and areas lesser social, health, and educational resources; in contrast, the urban is deemed modern, advanced, and desirable, concomitantly attracting much of China's higher education resources (J. Guo & J. Chen, 2023; Zhao, 2023). As such, these rural-origin students have inherited not only little familial temporal privilege but also little state-sanctioned temporal wealth when compared with their urban counterparts. They had to strive hard and pass the highly competitive and also deeply unfair Gaokao (Y.-L. Chiang, 2022; Hamnett et al., 2019; Howlett, 2021; Y. Liu, 2018, 2019) in order to access HEIs in the urban centers, which would only allow them to be at the baseline of their urban peers.

So far, I have established how differentiated time inheritance shapes contrasting constructions of education and access to a hierarchy of education mobility among families of differentiated social origins. In part 2, I will first discuss how students of differing time inheritance lived their time in education mobility differently, varying from living on borrowed time to living on banked time, and how these different temporal experiences further shaped their contrasting life and career trajectories. In a nutshell, I will show the roles that time inheritance plays in reproducing and exacerbating inequalities. Then, in part 3, I will turn to emphasizing the complex "anomalies" wherein time inheritance does not work seamlessly to reproduce privileges. I will demonstrate instead the individual agency (or lack thereof) among my participants in fighting the specter or spell of time inheritance.

# Part II

# How Time Inheritance Reproduces Inequalities

Part 2 draws on a wide range of empirical data to introduce five manifestations through which differential time inheritance perpetuates social inequalities. These manifestations are visions of decisions, time-shaped dispositions, time-induced consequences, time use, and shades of career.

Chapter 4

# Visions of Decisions

## From Self-Sabotage to Path Paving

This chapter demonstrates how familial time inheritance differentiated across individuals of varied social origins shapes their education decision making. It argues that participants with limited and disadvantageous time inheritance at familial and national levels tend to make less informed, seemingly short-sighted and self-sabotaging decisions about higher education. In contrast, the participants with ample inherited time privilege at familial and national levels tend to enjoy their banked time through long-term strategic plans. Typically, members of this latter group adopt strategies that allow them to buy "time" out of the competitive higher education system in China and invest their "time" into a relatively more lenient temporal sphere in the advantageous Global West. This way, they capitalize on the global-level time inheritance of degrees awarded by these Western higher education institutions (HEIs).

This chapter shows how advantageous time inheritance at familial and national levels begets further global time inheritance, while disadvantageous familial and national time inheritance subjects participants to further disadvantages at the higher education stage.

## Time Inheritance at the National Level: Rural–Urban and Higher Education Inequalities

In China, differentiated time inheritance at the national level can manifest markedly between inheritors of rural and urban origins. China's dual

45

household registration system (*hukou*), enforced since the 1950s, has arbitrarily categorized its population into those of urban *hukou* and those of rural *hukou*. It has been widely documented that this dichotomized household registration system has subjected the former to more advantageous access to resources in education, housing, health, and social care. In contrast, individuals of rural *hukou* are reduced to substandard welfare (Xiang, 2016; C. L. Xu, 2020).

In education, especially in higher education, China's suite of urban-inclined policies has resulted in an overconcentration of resources in the urban centers and underresourced rural areas. As of 2022, an overwhelming majority of HEIs are located in China's urban areas.[1] In contrast, there has been a notable void of HEIs in rural areas of the country (Xu [徐] & Hu [胡], 2017; Xu [徐] & Wang [王], 2021).

From a temporal perspective, such a void of HEIs deprives the population in rural areas of any exposure to or cultural engagement with the higher education sphere. As a result, for many rural-origin individuals in China, the first time they set foot on a university campus often coincides with the day they register for their first year of university studies (Meng Cheng [程], 2018a, 2018b; Meng Cheng [程] & Kang, 2018). Compared with their urban counterparts, especially those from big metropolitan centers where the highest-ranked and most prestigious universities are located (Chiang, 2022; C. L. Xu & Y. Ma, 2023), these rural populations are denied the time and opportunity to accumulate a feel for the "game" (Bourdieu, 2020), a sense of ease, familiarity with, and understanding of the higher education field (Y. Liu, 2018, 2019).

A further aspect of temporal inequalities resulting from the urban-biased policies is the quota system at the juncture of university entrance. This arises from the city- and province-based financing mechanism of HEIs that favors *hukou* holders of the local municipality (J. Guo & J. Chen, 2023; Hamnett et al., 2019; Liu, 2018, 2019; Zhao, 2021). A notable consequence is that students who have rural *hukou* are much more likely to be rejected access to prestigious HEIs simply because they lack the generational capital of *hukou*: their parents or grandparents were born into the "wrong" areas, so as offspring they have to pay the price for their lack of "institutionalized cultural capital" (i.e., the urban *hukou*)—they have *negative time inheritance*, or *time debt*.

Moreover, China's uneven regional developments have had substantial temporal implications for higher education students. Research has shown that rural students and students originally from areas less economically developed have fewer chances of accessing prestigious HEIs in the more developed areas than their urban peers (J. Guo & J. Chen, 2023; Hamnett et al., 2019; Zhao, 2021). However, jobs with the best career prospects and earning capacity are often located in these economically developed areas. Due to local protectionism and an incentive to increase local graduates' employment rates, public sectors including the government's civil services have often prioritized graduates from local institutions (C. L. Xu & Y. Ma, 2023). As such, these students (rural students and students from less developed areas) are further disadvantaged. Not only have they inherited negative temporal assets from their places of origin, but their institutional qualification can be negatively valued in the labor market as their HEIs belong to the "wrong" regions, which have negative temporal valuation. This is also to do with China's steep hierarchy of temporal inequalities among higher education institutions.

Generally in China, the institutions with the longest history are accorded the highest prestige; for example, the top two elite universities, Peking and Tsinghua, are also the two oldest universities. The Chinese equivalent of the Ivy League, the C9 group of China's most elite universities (Peking, Tsinghua, Fudan, Nanjing, Zhejiang, Shanghai Jiaotong, Xi'an Jiaotong, Harbin Institute of Technology, and the University of Science and Technology of China) contains also the HEIs that are among the oldest in the country. In comparison, the newer universities tend to be placed lower in the hierarchy. Correspondingly, the funding mechanisms in China are such that the HEIs on top of the hierarchy receive the highest amount and biggest proportion of funding from the country, as well as provincial, municipal, and local finances (Loyalka et al., 2012, p. 287; R. Yang & M. Xie, 2015). As such, these dominant and older HEIs tend to have a much bigger say in determining the kinds of resources to be deemed legitimate and desirable—to a great extent, these dominant HEI players determine what is valuable and what is not. Therefore, these dominant players have an added advantage, as they have had more years to accumulate such capital, such as prestige and reputation—what I call advantageous time inheritance. This then is transferred to be their graduates' advantage, so that their graduates can get better jobs, earn a higher salary premium, and have faster career progression, with their work time being rendered more valuable than their peers' (C. L. Xu & Y. Ma, 2023).

Inherited time inequalities at the national level become amplified when combined with unequal inherited time at the familial level. Together, differentiated time inheritance at these levels inclines disadvantaged time inheritors (e.g., those from rural and impoverished socioeconomic backgrounds) toward making seemingly uninformed, shortsighted, and self-sabotaging decisions about higher education. In contrast, the more advantaged time inheritors (e.g., those from urban and upper-class/middle-class backgrounds) tend to benefit from concerted, long-term, and strategic plans for higher education.

## Self-Sabotaging Decisions? Unequal Time Inheritance for the Rural-Origin Youth

Based on the results of his Gaokao (national college entrance exam), Jiao could have applied to China's elite Peking or Tsinghua University. Surprisingly, Jiao chose to enroll in a second-tier university in southern China that required lower tuition fees while also providing food compensation and monthly allowances. Considering the substantial economic and social premium that an elite university degree could have brought him (Wakeling & Savage, 2015; C. L. Xu & Y. Ma, 2023), Jiao's decision seemed almost self-sabotaging. However, looking back, Jiao revealed his considerations then: his family was always struggling to make ends meet. Neither of Jiao's parents went to school, and their primary means of livelihood was farming. However, farming was tough and agricultural taxes were high (X. Wang & Shen, 2014). Jiao's family could not afford to pay for his university tuition or expenses.

Moreover, the deal-breaker that put Jiao off applying to Peking or Tsinghua University was the one-year military training requirement. This was not because Jiao was opposed to military training but because this one-year time investment would have been a big sunk cost: it meant not only an extra year's tuition fee but also one year's delay of entry into employment that could generate income. This income was much anticipated by Jiao's poverty-stricken family as they clenched their teeth to put him through higher education.

From a temporal perspective, Jiao had limited time inheritance at the familial level. This is evidenced by his parents' low education level and little understanding of the higher education system. Jiao's parents themselves lacked the educational and cultural resources (which would have taken substantial time to acquire) that could have informed them about the implications of receiving degrees from elite versus second-tier universities (i.e., the national-level time inequalities inherited by HEIs). Jiao's family also fell short in economic resources (which could have been passed on from previous generations and also would have taken time to acquire). This constrained Jiao's options, making him decide that the one-year military training was *not affordable* and inclining him toward the choice of having food compensation and monthly allowances at the lower-tier university. Jiao's *limited familial time inheritance* thus reduced him to becoming oblivious to the long-term national-level time inequalities—that is, the prices he would have to pay for receiving a less prestigious degree four years down the line when he graduated and tried to look for a job and 10 or 20 years down the line when he repeatedly encountered first-degree discrimination (Yan [阎], 2017). Indeed, in 2018 when Jiao looked back, he marveled at how "ignorant" he was at the time about such implications.

Jiao's story is not unique. Unequal time inheritance at familial and national levels has shaped the higher education decision making and subsequent trajectories of millions of rural-origin youngsters across China. Research has repeatedly demonstrated that limited familial understandings of how the higher education system works (or discriminates) have negatively affected students with rural *hukou*. Michelle W. Cheng et al. (2023) investigated 103 rural families with a child who was about to enter university. They found these parents struggled to communicate with and prepare their children, due mainly to their own lack of knowledge about and experience with the higher education system. As a result, these young people of rural origin tend to cluster in lower-tier HEIs and less prestigious disciplines (Hamnett et al., 2019; H. Li, 2013; Y. Liu, 2018, 2019). Subsequently, given that graduates of lower-tier universities and vocational colleges in China tend to fare much worse in the labor market than their counterparts from prestigious first-tier universities (Mok, 2016; Mok et al., 2016; C. L. Xu & Y. Ma, 2023), these rural-origin young people pay a long-term price for the "uninformed" decisions they made at the juncture of university entrance.

Their stories have found resonance in other national contexts (Boliver & Capsada-Munsech, 2024). In Malaysia, where rural absolute poverty is three times that of urban absolute poverty, Nungsari and colleagues (2024, p. 79) find that rural female youth are more likely to demonstrate "self-blaming tendencies," which incline them toward choosing "careers of lower occupational prestige" and being forced into "necessity" part-time entrepreneurship. Although Nungsari et al. did not discuss such findings from a temporal perspective, the in-depth interview accounts from their rural female participants (e.g., on p. 89) are full of anxieties about the lack of time and plagued by the insufficient information that could have helped them make more informed career decisions. In France, Bourdieu and Passeron's (1979, p. 14) extensive study on the impacts of social origins on higher education students reveals severe long-term and sedimented time inequalities: "In a student population, we are dealing with the final outcome of a whole set of influences that stem from social origin and have been exerted *over a long period*. For students from the lower classes who have survived elimination, the initial disadvantages have evolved: their social past has been transformed into an educational handicap through relay mechanisms such as *early, often ill-informed decisions, forced choices, or lost time*" (my emphases).

Among the 26 rural-origin informants in this book, all reported not having sufficient information and understanding about how they should choose which university to attend. They ended up either over- or underestimating their Gaokao performance and chose either unrealistic universities or universities that were way below their mark brackets. As a result, although all did well in their Gaokao and could have entered elite, first-tier universities, only five (out of 26) managed to do so. The great majority ended up in second- or third-tier universities for their undergraduate degrees.[2] This is consistent with existing research that shows rural-origin students are "seven and 11 times less likely to access any college and elite Project 211 colleges than urban youth, respectively"[3] (H. Li et al., 2015, p. 185; L. Li, 2004).

## Familial Path Paving

Time inheritance at the familial level has been most manifestly demonstrated through concerted and calculated paving of educational paths for the single children of middle-class and upper-class urban families. Receiving high-quality education, often overseas (or at least cross-border) education, is frequently discussed as a rite of passage or "basic threshold" among upper-middle-class families.

### "It's a Family Tradition"

Man, from Beijing, intimated that many of her relatives had studied abroad before returning to work in China. In her extended family, studying abroad was a "basic threshold" (*jiben menkan* 基本门槛) that had to be met. Man counted: her mother's little sister had studied in Italy and Germany before returning to work in a foreign enterprise in Beijing; her other aunt (i.e., her father's little sister) emigrated to the US with her husband and son about 20 years earlier. In Man's own family, her elder sister[4] studied in London and settled there. When Man's sister gave birth to a baby in the University

College London (UCL) hospital, Man's family went there to take care of her. There, they witnessed how students at UCL were studying hard in the libraries in the early hours of the morning. Deeply impressed, Man's parents decided that the academic atmosphere was great in London; hence they encouraged Man to apply to universities in London for her undergraduate course (which was a 2+2 cooperated program with a London university) and master's degree. Indeed, as Man casually remarked, "Studying overseas is kind of a family tradition."

Man's case is representative of other upper-middle-class families in this book. These families typically sent their children to international and private schools in China (e.g., Dao, Chang, Jing), sixth-form colleges[5] in the UK (e.g., Li from Guangzhou in Guangdong Province and Dong from Taiyuan in Shanxi Province), or senior high schools in Singapore (e.g., Yu from Shijiazhuang in Hebei Province and Chuan from Jingdezhen in Jiangxi Province) in their preparation for an international higher education. Other equally affluent families instead opted for highly ranked key high schools within China (Chiang, 2022; S. Liu, 2020); for example, Nianci (from Beijing) went to an elite high school in Beijing before she received a full-cost scholarship to study at one of Hong Kong's top universities.

Many families had traditions of emigration. For example, Guoxiang, from Hohhot in Inner Mongolia, intimated that her family tried emigrating to Canada when she was around eight years old but came back after a little while as her father could not get used to living in a foreign country. Dao's parents had emigrated to Spain before, and Dao was born in Spain before the family decided to migrate back to Shanghai when Dao was five years old.

In families that had not had experiences of migration, the parents were usually well-traveled and had their eyes set on their children one day receiving some form of education outside of mainland China. For instance, Yu's mother was a visiting scholar at a New Zealand university for one year and was determined to send Yu to study abroad from a young age. Nianci's father has a PhD himself and had traveled extensively across the world, including attending short-term courses at universities like the Massachusetts Institute of Technology and Harvard. He was therefore keen to have Nianci attend a university in the Boston area one day.

As rightful inheritors of such long lines of familial tradition, these single children of affluent and upper-middle-class family backgrounds benefited temporally from their families' banked time in four ways.

First, having been immersed in this kind of familial experience sharing and placed under such expectations of studying abroad, these students were able to develop a sense of familiarity and ease with the idea and act of studying abroad. They were effectively "fish in water" in the Bourdieusian sense and well-acquainted with the "rule of the game" (Bourdieu, 1984).

Second, even before these students ventured abroad to study in person, other members of their families were already doing site visits on their behalf, such as Man's parents inspecting and affirming the study environment in London and Nianci's father getting acquainted with the Boston universities in the US. This, coupled with their own family members' experience of studying (and even settling) abroad, provided them with valuable firsthand information and acted as crucial familial temporal wealth acquired over decades.

Third, to prepare to ease these students into studying abroad, their families adopted various temporal strategies such as enrolling them in international and private schools within China or in various articulation programs (e.g., 2+2).[6] These temporal strategies enabled these students to ease into an all-English environment gradually. In other words, their families were carefully planning and monitoring the pace of their higher education studies to ensure an optimal experience for them. Again, such careful planning required their familial temporal wealth in being well-versed with the various secondary school and higher education options.

Last and perhaps most fundamentally, these families all had ready access to economic resources that enabled them to fund not only their single children's overseas studies but also other family members' site visits beforehand. Some affluent families even bought properties in their children's study destinations[7] so that their children would not need to worry about paying rent or looking for student accommodations and thus could focus solely on their studies (see chapter 8). This kind of economic wealth is also an important constituent of these students' overall familial temporal inheritance (i.e., "accumulated labor time" in the form of economic capital; see Bourdieu, 1986).

# Chapter 5

# Time-Shaped Dispositions

## From Debt-Paying Mentality to Sense of Entitlement

Inequalities in time inheritance also predisposed the modes of living that differentiated time inheritors embodied. While the descendants inheriting substantial temporal wealth inhabited a sense of entitlement and ease in their time deployment, their disadvantaged counterparts were subjected to debt-paying modes in which they were always short of time to generate monetary, moral, and emotional repayment of debts toward their "creditors," who were often their parents and family.

## Time Poverty and Time Interest

Xia et al.'s (2024) and Lin Gao's (2023) latest research reveals that parents and grandparents of rural-origin and of urban working-class backgrounds (e.g., rural-to-urban migrants) in China tend to value the economic and utilitarian aspects of having children. They find that children's financial and material benefits to the family are emphasized in such families, especially their ability to provide economic security for their parents' and grandparents' old-age care. In this sense, child-rearing becomes a practice of economic investment for the parents and grandparents to seek future expected economic returns as the children repay their efforts. These research findings align with what I pointed out in chapter 2, that families of limited temporal wealth tend to construct education as a gift, an act of kindness for the "selected" child. This has rendered the receiving of education as a debt-accumulation process; thus these disadvantaged time inheritors shoulder a debt-paying mission throughout their education and at work. This debt-paying burden, when combined with limited social and cultural resources to repay the debt, thus fosters a constant sense of time poverty (Adam, 1990; Lingard & Thompson, 2017). The disadvantaged time inheritors commonly articulated that there is not enough time to study and work, which would allow them to generate sufficient income to pay back their families.

## "My 24 Hours Are Not Enough": Lawrence's Story

Originally from Hong Kong, Lawrence's father had retired from his role as a restaurant chef, while his mother continued to work as a cleaner. Lawrence exclaimed, "I feel that my 24 hours are not enough for my use now" and "I feel like I cannot stop . . . I have to keep going, going forward, all the time." This sheer sense of time poverty, when probed further, clearly stemmed from his familial economic burdens and demands. Lawrence revealed,

> I have a younger brother who is 14 years old and only going to junior high school [Grade 9]. Now I have to shoulder all my family's very heavy financial burden. My father is no longer working, my mother's salary is meager [*beishuichexin* 杯水车薪], I have always been shouldering my family's insurance and financial outgoings, including my brother's study expenditure. My plan is that after a few years when my little brother has graduated from senior high school and reached adulthood and can take care of himself, I can begin to save up some money for my family's use, then I can leave this place.

Instead of inheriting economic wealth from parents, which is a positive temporal asset, Lawrence was instead tasked with shouldering his family's financial outgoings and his little brother's education expenditure. To this end, Lawrence devoted his entire income from work to his family and little brother, and even after his brother reaches adulthood in four years Lawrence would spend another few years saving up a sum of money for his family's use before his planned emigration. At the time of this interview in 2022, Lawrence had already been working for five years. To finish supporting his little brother as well as saving up some money for his family, he would need at least another seven years' work. This meant he would have spent a total of 12 years to fulfil his debt-paying mission and to embark on his own pursuit of life ideals: "My ideal life is that my 24 hours can be equally distributed and I would feel that they are enough for my use; this way it can make me feel relaxed."

Lawrence's case is typical among the working-class students from Hong Kong and other rural-origin individuals. Most of them had substantial familial obligations to support not only their parents, who were either retired or still toiling in manual labor or farming jobs, but also their siblings. For example, Vivienne (from Hong Kong, father passed away, mother a security guard) had to support both her mother and elder brother, while Xin (born in the 1960s, Shanxi Province) and Fen (born in the 1960s, Shandong Province) had to provide financial support to each of their three siblings, who were all still based in a rural environment. Lian (born in the 1980s), originally from a small rural village in Guangdong, suggested, "I feel like I am running out of time to provide my parents a life that is slightly more comfortable. Now they still live in the same mud house from my childhood. My father still does farm work day in and day out. I don't know when I can do it. I probably will never be able to do it."

## Premature Debt Collection: The Cases of Su and Meng

Coming from a small rural village in southern China's Hubei Province, Su (born in the 1970s) was among the five (out of 26) rural-origin individuals in this book who managed to enter a top university in Beijing for her undergraduate studies. Her excellent academic performance even earned her some scholarships during this period. Keen to repay her debt to her parents, Su sent most of her scholarship money back home. However, her father began to brag about her elite status to other villagers and wrote to her letter after letter to ask for more money. Merely an undergraduate student who had limited capacity to generate income other than relying on her scholarships, Su felt powerless. "My father kept thinking that I was now somebody in an elite institution in Beijing, but I was actually nobody." Her father's constant demands for money led to serious depression for Su, who said, "All I wanted to do was escape." The premature "debt collection" by Su's "creditor," her father, resulted in Su's repeated conflicts with her family; these in turn subjected her to "near collapse" during her second and third years of undergraduate studies.

Meng (born in the 1980s) is from a rural village in Hebei Province. Like Su, Meng used her scholarship money to help weather her family's financial difficulties during university. Still short of money, Meng spent a few months of her PhD studies ghostwriting an article that was eventually published in a Chinese Social Sciences Citation Index (CSSCI) journal.[1] This brought her RMB 5,000 (USD 700), which she sent home to pay off some of her father's debts. However, her father was constantly tricked in his business attempts, so she would get very worried when she heard about any issues from home. This was so serious that she often had nightmares in which she dreamed about her father asking for more money from her again, and she would cry, struggle, and wake up in tears. By the time we conducted the interview in January 2018, Meng had already finished her PhD and was working at a university. However, she still had such nightmares, as her family still had debts for her to pay back.

Compared with Lawrence and others who were allowed the time to graduate and get into paid work before they started to pay off their "debts," Su's and Meng's cases represent those whose families fast-forwarded their debt collection to a stage when they were not yet financially independent. By the time of these interviews, Su and Meng were at least 10 years out of their undergraduate studies, and yet the mental strain caused by their parents' premature debt collection remained. In all these cases, therefore, it is clear that inherited temporal debts (as opposed to wealth) not only did not help to propel these time inheritors' education or work but instead cost them substantial *time interest* in the forms of their work time (e.g., 12 years of Lawrence's work time) and their mental health suffering (e.g., at least 10 years of nightmares for Meng and years of depression for Su). This brings us back to the idea that these underprivileged time inheritors were living in time that was "on loan" to them, and they had to pay back not only the *time debt* through their economic income but also the *time interest* through the years of work time and mental strain.

## Time Entitlement and Time Freedom

As discussed in chapter 2, families with significant temporal wealth tend to construct education as an entitlement, and the parents tend to shoulder a nonnegotiable sense of obligation to provide their children with high-quality and progressive education. This has created a sense of entitlement among the advantaged time inheritors and bred their sense of ease about the time they have at hand, which is what I call *time entitlement*, as opposed to the *time poverty* experienced by their underprivileged counterparts. Instead of focusing on debt paying toward their families and siblings, the privileged time inheritors (e.g., the upper-middle-class urbanites) championed different forms of time entitlement, which eventually allowed them to arrive at "time freedom."

## "Take Your Time to Explore the World": Mr. Yue's Account

Substantial familial temporal wealth often manifests in the parents' encouragement for their children to "take their time" to explore the world. Mr. Yue, father of Lingshan, typically suggested,

> I have always preached to Lingshan about the idea that the future is not fixed. . . . My suggestion for her is, don't hurry to choose, after your graduation . . . you can travel around [zhuan yi zhuan 转一转] Europe and South America, take a look, spend around two to three years, and when it reaches a point where we can no longer afford it, or we cannot support you with the funds, then you can start to look for a job and to make a living [mousheng 谋生]. My advice for her is to not make haste to make a living.

This sense of ease that there is no need at all to hurry into a job and start "mak[ing] a living" acts as a stark contrast to the urge for debt collection among the parents of the disadvantaged time inheritors. What mattered to Mr. Yue was that Lingshan took the time, at least two to three years, to explore different parts of the world (e.g., Europe and South America) and to slowly figure out what she wanted to achieve or preferred to do. The time inheritance that Mr Yue has passed on to Lingshan included not only the funds for traveling around the world after graduation but also his own visionary advice about the relationship between work and the art of living, which he acquired through his dozens of years of experience. He said,

> Even if she has only the same level of intelligence as just an ordinary person, then whatever jobs an ordinary person can do, she too can do it. Therefore, if an ordinary person does not starve to death, she won't either. The last resort is [if she cannot get any job], then she can kenlao. We may not be able to afford luxurious food, but only ordinary food, [but we will be able to support her material needs]. To me, it is not my life's pursuit to be very instrumental, to be very keen to make

a big fortune [*facai* 发财], or being keen to buy up castles and land. Partly perhaps it is because . . . I embrace being ordinary [*ganyu pingyong* 甘于平庸].

Although Mr. Yue is from a family of wealth and intellectuals (in his own words, "fallen nobility," *moluode guizu* 没落的贵族) and has an upper-middle-class level of life provision for his own family, he considered himself as "embracing being ordinary." His sense of "being ordinary," however, has more to do with the sense of ease and poise that people with "old money" (i.e., substantial inherited time wealth) tend to exhibit, especially in contrast with the "nouveau riche," who hurry to acquire symbols of wealth or importance (e.g., castles and land) but just lack taste and ease (Osburg, 2013). This confident and at-ease self-positioning, despite some self-deprecation, typically marked the upper-middle-class parents' approaches toward their children's employment seeking. Mr. Yue mentioned the idea of *kenlao* for Lingshan, which succinctly captures the substantial familial temporal wealth available to these students from upper-middle-class backgrounds.

## KENLAO AND TIME FREEDOM

"I have classmates who say that they cannot continue to spend their family's money once they graduate from university as they want to be financially independent. However, I have a different view. I have a *kenlao* [啃老] mentality." Nianci shared her view unapologetically, with a smirk, when we met for lunch at a Japanese restaurant in London. *Ken* means chewing or gnawing, while *lao* refers to the elderly; in this case, *lao* points to the parents. *Kenlao* is used to highlight a phenomenon in China whereby children are not financially independent and instead exploit their parents' financial and labor support well into their own adulthood (W. Liu, 2017). When used to depict these adult children's behavior, *kenlao* often carries a sense of moral judgment of them, connoting that they should have relied on themselves instead of exploiting their parents.

However, in both Mr. Yue's account and Nianci's understanding, "*kenlao*" conveys a willing intergenerational transfer of wealth, which enables the children to enjoy *time freedom*—that is, time in which they are free to explore and engage in what they prefer. As Bourdieu (2000, p. 224) writes, "Time used freely for freely chosen, gratuitous ends which . . . may be those of work, but work that is freed, in its rhythm, moment and duration, from every external constraint and especially from the constraint imposed through direct monetary sanction." In a similar way, Yi, originally from Beijing, intimated that she had a "back-up plan," which made her feel fine for not hurrying to look for a job. She was assured that her family would "drag her out of the abyss (*shenyuan* 深渊)" of being a NEET (not in education, employment, or training), as they would "never allow this to happen" to her.

Students like Nianci and Yi who are among the advantaged time inheritors of substantial familial wealth commonly exhibited such a sheer sense of ease, evoking the temporal mode of protention (after Bourdieu; Hansen, 2015, p. 59), which requires a pre-reflexive familiarity with the rules of the game in career making and a confidence in being able to foresee and adapt accordingly as events gradually unfold. Having her family as a stronghold of support to fall back on, Yi exuded feelings of being at home and an assuredness regarding infinite time available to her to pursue what she desired. Such assuredness resonates strongly with the elite girls in England's and Scotland's private boarding schools (Forbes & Lingard, 2014; Maxwell & Aggleton, 2013).

Nianci emphasized further, "My parents' resources are *my* resources too." She considered it a blessing that her parents were willing to support her continuing her postgraduate studies and career pursuits; all she had to do was to enjoy it. Yi likewise reasoned, "I am my parents' only child. Who else are they going to pass their wealth to? We just have this understanding from when I was born, I think." These single children's sense of entitlement to their familial inheritance echoes Tu's (2018, p. 110) findings that single children from urban China who have studied in the UK showed "confidence in the parental capacity and willingness to fund their financial needs." Overall, Tu found among these middle-class families "a predominantly parent-to-child intergenerational flow of money and care regardless of the child's income level and age" (p. 115).

Differentiated time inheritance at the familial level thus inclines the disadvantaged inheritors toward living in a debt-paying mode. Haunted by time poverty, they are commonly hurried into generating economic income as soon as possible, or even prematurely. They were also forced to endure years of work and mental suffering as time interest amid their debt-paying mission. In contrast, the privileged time inheritors of upper- and middle-class families exhibited a sheer sense of entitlement to their parents' economic and intellectual wealth well into their own adulthood. This secure understanding of their parents' capacity and willingness to carry out the intergenerational flow of wealth and care instilled in them a sense of ease and assuredness. They had an indefinite amount of time to pursue what they desired and found enjoyable unencumbered by time constraints—that is, to strive for time freedom (Bourdieu, 2000).

# Chapter 6

# Time-Induced Consequences

## From "Squandering" Labor Time to Achieving Work-life Balance

Differentiated time inheritance also shapes how social agents perceive time and their approaches to education and work. Inherited labor-time debt can propel the disadvantaged inheritors to resort to the most accessible form of resource, their own labor time—they devote excessive diligence to work while compromising their family and personal time. In contrast, the inheritors of substantial familial, national, and global time wealth tend to have the resources and dispositions that allow them to strive for and eventually reach work-life balance when making education and career decisions.

## Diligence and Time Squandering

Faced with time poverty and the imperative to generate income immediately, the underprivileged time inheritors often resorted to the only resource they had access to, their own available labor time. It was, indeed, not uncommon for the rural-origin and working-class individuals to spend all their waking moments at work.

### "Three Shifts per Day, Seven Days a Week"

Jingpi (born in the 1960s, from a village in Fujian Province), a chief physician at a provincial capital city, PhD holder, and PhD supervisor, told his colleagues about his "philosophy" of hard work: "If you take two shifts per day, I will take three. If you work five days a week, I will work seven days." Jingpi had been working so hard that he hardly took any holidays and rarely spent time with his family. Even his wife could not understand him. She confronted Jingpi: "Other people are not working as hard as you, but they progress faster than you." To this, Jingpi replied with "not everybody is equal."

Jingpi observed that leaders need three different types of talent: "The first kind are those who have backgrounds; if you don't use them, you will find it hard to be in a leadership position; . . . the second kind . . . are those like me, who are not that smart, but are diligent [*kengan* 肯干]. The third kind are those who are full of creativity and professional capabilities." Jingpi reflected wryly, "I do not have any backgrounds, or *guanxi*, nor do I have very special talents. All I can do is to be hardworking, sincere, and diligent, and work well—this is the way to eventually gain my own foothold and realize some of my life goals." Clearly identifying himself as the second type, Jingpi said, "My conditions were so bad that it could not be any worse, so I can endure any extreme hardships no matter what." Even though at the time of the interview Jingpi was near retirement, a successful physician who had an excellent reputation, he confessed that he often reminded himself of his peers from the same village who did not change their fates and remained "rather deprived."

Jingpi's experience finds ready echoes among anthropologist Shanshan Lan's (2021) rural-origin participants who managed to pursue transnational studies in South Korea. Lan's rural participants from China typically devoted all their time to studying, working (at their part-time jobs), and resting. There was a notable absence of time spent on leisure activities. Lan (2021, p. 674) therefore argues that "leisure time has become a middle-class privilege that is sustained by some urban respondents' affluent financial status."

## "No Time to Date"; Surviving, Not Living

Lawrence, a working-class graduate from Hong Kong whom we have met before, recounted what his work week looked like: "Every week, apart from my full-time work at the school from Monday to Friday, which begins at seven in the morning until around nine in the evening, I also do extra work on either Saturday or Sunday at the school. On top of that I provide private tutorials as my part-time work on Mondays for two hours, Saturdays for three hours, and Sundays for two hours." Lawrence spent so much time at work that he confessed, "I don't have time to date right now . . . if I had a girlfriend, I would not have time to spend with her." When I marveled at how diligently he worked, Lawrence sighed: "What I am doing now is surviving [*shengcun* 生存], not living [*shenghuo* 生活], which I hope that one day I can actually do." The distinction Lawrence drew between his survival mode and his ideal living mode reminds us of his ideal life, "to distribute [his] 24 hours a day equally" to work and leisure and "feel relaxed" (see chapter 5).

These disadvantaged time inheritors' stories evoke Howlett's (2021, p. 144) depiction of diligence as "a shared cultural value": "the desire to change fate through diligent self-cultivation," which is widespread across China. Howlett notes how the Gaokao perpetuates this belief that in order to avoid failure for a lifetime later, it is crucial to exert extreme diligence at present in studying for the Gaokao. This maxim that an investment of time can be taken as a form of compensation, and also this existential belief that the cultivation of habits and bodily changes through excessive amounts of work will produce outputs and results, is well-practiced by working-class and rural-origin individuals.

In fact, diligence is a commonly found trait among working-class and rural-origin students at elite universities in China. In He Li's (2013, p. 842) research with 30 "wonder" children from rural areas who entered the elite "Stone University" in Beijing (a pseudonym), she observes, "When other forms of capital seemed inaccessible, academic capital became the only form [they] could accumulate and scholastic success the only route to change [their] disadvantaged position and rural identity." Li's rural participants spent long hours studying instead of joining extracurricular activities to acquire other forms of capital deemed useful for future employment prospects. Jin and Ball (2021) likewise depict working-class students who exerted incredible efforts and diligence in their academic studies compared to their middle-class counterparts. Similar observations have been noted in other research on disadvantaged students from rural and working-class backgrounds in elite higher education institutions (Meng Cheng [程], 2018a; Liao [廖], 2016; Xie [谢], 2016; Xie & Reay, 2020). While this existing research focuses on what it is like to be disadvantaged inheritors at the undergraduate stage, stories like those of Lawrence and Jingpi show that at the postgraduate and later stages in life, they too have adopted overcompensation through time—that is, resorting to "squandering" their own (labor) time as a way to compensate for their negative familial time inheritance. For them, time and efforts were the most accessible resources at hand, which they invested in great quantity in order to accrue the academic and technological currency deemed valuable in their respective fields.

Such excessive diligence[1] evokes Howlett's (2021, p. 135) discussion of social constructions of differentiated diligence in China. He notes how "people of rural origin are said to exhibit an excessive form of *low-quality diligence*, like women" (p. 135, my emphasis). Howlett (2021, p. 144) furthermore observes that rural-origin individuals, women, and ethnic minorities in China are often portrayed as lacking quality due to "an excess of the wrong kind of diligence or to a lack of this virtue [i.e., quality] at all."

These underprivileged time inheritors' obliged diligence is clearly a necessity rather than a desire. The stigmatization of their diligence as of "low quality" demonstrates the structural discrimination against them. This perception of so-called "low-quality diligence" can also be linked to the fact that their work time often attracts lower economic compensation, which will be illustrated in the section "Trapped in Precarity" in chapter 8.

## Balance

Substantial inheritance of temporal wealth, on the other hand, not only instills in the advantaged inheritors a sense of ease about job seeking but also empowers them to strive for work-life balance and preferred lifestyles fearlessly and relentlessly.

### "Paddling Water": "No Desire, No Striving"

Originally from a middle-class family in Shanghai, Fei described his life and work philosophy as of "no desire, no striving" (*wuyu wuqiu* 无欲无求). He depicted how his course mates in the PhD programs in Hong Kong would think about getting promoted to associate professor or professor after a certain number of years, or about getting funded research projects. He would not think about such issues. He reflected, "Over the past few years, I have been feeling that there is not much meaning in doing research, either; I have other things to do, e.g., reading some books, or things that I fancy doing; I would not have to worry about making a living, so there is no fundamental difference." For Fei, his principle has been to "paddle in the water" (*huashui* 划水) and live a comfortable life. *Huashui* is a popular Internet term that points to the behavior of individuals who do not pull their weight or make a contribution to their employers and instead seek comfort in doing nothing and being "lazy." Fei decided not to "waste time" on networking, either. The notion of "wasting" here also implies that he prioritized other more worthy causes, such as reading books or practicing his Chinese calligraphy, over striving for earthly rewards in academia or at work (*yingying gougou* 蝇营狗苟). When I asked Fei if he "preferred" a postdoctorate or part-time research jobs, he laughed and then sighed, looking straight into my eyes, "I prefer not to work at all, but one cannot just stay home and not work, so I have to do a bit of work."

Fei's peculiar understanding of work in academia and his attitudes pointed to a preferred lifestyle that demands minimum effort and allows maximum enjoyment of his delights in life. This approach is consistent with a host of other privileged time inheritors.

No Overtime Work, Ever!

Li, whom we have met before, revealed his ideal career and lifestyle. "I feel that I should have a good job, a satisfactory and fulfilling [*chengxin* 称心] job; apart from making money I should be able to feel happy about what I do. Then I should have some rich personal life; that is, you cannot keep having overtime work and end up not having time to spend the money you make; in addition, you should also have a property and a car [*youfang youche* 有房有车]." Li's emphasis on not doing overtime work is unanimously echoed by other students from upper-middle-class families. Qie (who is originally from Shenzhen and completed all his degrees in the UK) went as far as rejecting three job offers in China and opted for a lower-paid job in the UK, just to avoid the possibility of having to do overtime work. He said,

> My classmates who have returned to China are in a pitiable position . . . some of them entered some good companies, e.g., Huawei, Tencent, and Baidu—but they find it very stressful. In Huawei, they have compulsory overtime work, and some have lost all their hair. . . . All these are quite scary. . . . Your salary will surely be very high, but you may not be able to live long enough to spend the money that you make [*youming zhuanqian, meiming huaqian* 有命赚钱, 没命花钱]—this feels horrific.

The implicit expectation of overtime work is an aspect of work culture that is common among major companies in China (Q. Wang & Shane, 2019), captured in the 996 model. This model became a contested topic on social media when the founder of the successful e-commerce platform Alibaba, Jack Ma, publicly defended the necessity of having his staff work from 9 a.m. to 9 p.m. for six days a week (Q. Wang & Shane, 2019). This 996 model evokes what Snyder (2016, p. 6) pinpoints about the greedy nature of "flexible capitalism" (a form of social production that has emerged in major capitalist societies such as the US) and its demands placed on the workforce: "Putting in long hours is often seen as a sign of commitment and dedication to the job. As a result, core employees are often both over-employed and overworked. They tend to work more hours than they would like and feel rushed." For Qie, such overtime work presented a "scary" and "horrific" prospect, as he would have to concede control of his personal time to his work time, submitting his "individual time" to "the employer's time" (E. Thompson, 1967). The health implications, such as hair loss, may mean that he would also have to compromise his health and shorten his biological time, thus be deprived of the time to consume the fruits (e.g., of goods and services) earned as the price of his overwork. Through the control of work patterns and timing, the 996 model could potentially dominate the temporality of Qie's life.

Qie's attitude toward overtime work is commonplace among his similarly privileged peers, who vowed to avoid overtime work with all they could. Lingshan, who in 2022 was working as a programmer in Canada, confessed that if one day the IT sector in Canada started to adopt the 996 model, she would "definitely jump ship" to get another, more relaxing job. Chang, who worked in London for one year at an international accountancy firm, left her job because "I was working in London as a fresh graduate with only £30K per annum. After paying for rent, tax, food, and some enter-tainment, I basically could not have any savings. Besides, this job was all about auditing, and I did not find it interesting. I often had to work until late, with no money and no personal life; what was the meaning of all this?"

BEING IN CONTROL OF WORK TIME

Intriguingly, while Qie's rejection of the overwork culture in China was further confirmed during his three years' work experience in the UK, at the time of interview he revealed that he was considering returning to work in China, only that this time he was intending to establish his own start-up research lab by entering one of the attractive talent schemes of China: "There are many high-end talent schemes like A Thousand Talent Scheme. If I join this scheme, my development in China would be fast. . . . Basically they have all kinds of money to give me convenience." Qie has now acquired several patent rights and become a seasoned researcher and innovator in his field, and his career ambitions have evolved. He confided that once he set up his own research lab with the abundant funding and policy support available, he would be able to set his own rules at work, thus allowing him to protect his personal and family time while rapidly advancing his career. This way, he could continue to strive with his time freedom, unencumbered by any external demands of overtime work. Similarly, Chang relocated to Switzerland, where she was now able to land a well-balanced job in finance. Chang exclaimed, "Now every day when I wake up I cannot wait to get back to work—this is an ideal life in my view!"

## Time Freedom and Work-Life Balance

These affluent time inheritors' persistent pursuits of time freedom in their work life manifests through their uncompromising attitudes toward overtime work and their "carefree" philosophy, such as Fei's "water paddling" and "no desire, no striving" principles. The fact that they have their families' substantial temporal wealth to fall back on empowers them to reject job offers and to relocate to parts of the world where better work-life balance can be achieved. It can be seen that their time inheritance at the familial level has enabled them to also tap into the global level of time privileges (e.g., being able to study and work in the UK or relocating to Switzerland). As such, they were better able to strive for their time freedom compared to their working-class and rural-origin counterparts, who were forced to work at all waking hours.

Chapter 7

# Time Use

## From Wasted Time to Gained Time

This chapter contrasts two consequences of time use among differentiated time inheritors. For the disadvantaged time inheritors, although they are often short on time, their inherited time debts and the demand of debt paying further subject them to "wasted time" as they are often compelled to focus on tasks that yield no return; in contrast, the beneficiaries of notable temporal wealth typically experience what I call "gained time." Such gained time manifests in their gap years, gap semesters, or leaves of absence: periods of life when they buy their time "out" of the normative temporal structure or expectations to enrich their life and increase their competitiveness. This chapter points out how unequal time inheritance at the familial level often leads to further widened time inequalities through this wasted time for the disadvantaged time inheritors and gained time for the advantaged time inheritors.

## Wasted Time

In a paradoxical sense, the disadvantaged time inheritors, who have always been haunted by time poverty, can also often end up wasting time. This often manifests in their getting involved in endeavors that yield little or no material or symbolic return. Typically, such "time-wasting" endeavors often pertain to what I call the "qualification trap" and the "survival trap."

## THE QUALIFICATION TRAP

Jiao, who, despite his excellent Gaokao results, chose a second-tier university in order to save time and money, ended up "wasting two years' time," as he sighed. Jiao recounted that his degree from that second-tier university was not helpful at all when he began to look for a postgraduate job. Although he managed to get a position at a company in his hometown, the company went bankrupt after one year. Out of a job, Jiao managed to secure a position as a temporary English teacher, which was precarious and lowly paid. He was anxious to get out of this situation and figured that the only way out was to get a master's qualification. Determined, he sat the postgraduate entrance exam, which has been extremely competitive, with only around a 20% success rate (Song & Zhang, 2022). To Jiao's dismay, he failed the exam not just once but twice in two consecutive years. By this point, Jiao was exhausted and disillusioned. He felt that he was worse off than before he started to prepare for his exams because he had wasted not only two years' time but also a substantial amount of money on the test preparation.

This curious paradox, where the more pressed students were for time, the more they ended up wasting time, was like a universal formula that could be applied to the urban students from low-income families of Hong Kong. Christine, a working-class student from Hong Kong who completed an undergraduate degree in law in Beijing, similarly "wasted" one year sitting the postgraduate entrance exam, which she failed. She then spent another year and a half preparing to sit the National Uniform Legal Profession Qualification Examination (*fakao* 法考), which she passed, and she could then qualify as a lawyer. However, at this juncture, the COVID-19 pandemic broke out, and she was unable to leave Hong Kong to look for a job in mainland China. Since the legal system in Hong Kong is completely different from that of mainland China, Christine's legal training from Beijing, which she spent four years pursuing, and her lawyer qualification from the mainland became irrelevant as she tried to look for a job in Hong Kong. As such, Christine effectively wasted six years of her life pursuing legal training and sitting exams that were of no use to her at all.

Norman, originally from Hong Kong, regretted wasting three years of his time pursuing his master's degree when I interviewed him in 2022. Prior to that, Norman completed his undergraduate degree at an elite university in Beijing. Determined to be a litigating lawyer from day one, Norman, however, realized too late that he actually did not need a master's degree in law for his career pursuit. When asked why he decided to pursue a master's degree in the first place, he said, "everybody around me was going to graduate school, so I thought I had to do it as well."

The cross-border qualification recognition challenge also severely affected those who trained to become teachers. In November 2016, when I spoke with Stephanie (whom we have met briefly in the introduction) for the first time, she had just graduated from her four-year education program at a prestigious university in Beijing. She was trained to become a teacher, but she experienced great difficulty in securing a teaching post in Hong Kong. Instead, she was working as a teaching assistant at a Hong Kong school. Stephanie revealed,

> When I studied in Beijing, I learned that once I received my degree from the BNU [Beijing Normal University], I could submit it to the Hong Kong Council for Accreditation of Academic and Vocational Qualifications [HKCAAVQ]. So long as my degree is recognized, I would not be required to study for a PGDE [Postgraduate Diploma in Education][1] to qualify as a teacher. However, after I submitted my degree to the HKCAAVQ, they replied that I did not study educational psychology, so I did not meet the requirements. When I returned to Hong Kong, it was too late to apply for the PGDE program. So now I can only get a job as a teaching assistant, work for one year, and wait for next academic year to apply for the PGDE program.

In 2022, when I spoke with Stephanie again, I found out that in the end, she did not pursue a PGDE, but she enrolled in a course on educational psychology in a part-time mode while working as a teaching assistant. Once she passed that course, she submitted her request for degree recognition again, and this time she was considered as having met the requirements. However, this took her altogether three years' time before she managed to get a position as a teacher in Hong Kong.

Lawrence, who was training to become a physical education (PE) teacher in Beijing, had an internship at a Hong Kong secondary school in 2016 when I first interviewed him. Lawrence revealed that although there is said to be this mutual degree recognition in Hong Kong, many of his peers who graduated from the same university in Beijing returned to Hong Kong but were not able to get a job as a PE teacher. Instead, they took up completely irrelevant jobs such as those in the police or firefighting forces. After his graduation, Lawrence returned to Hong Kong and obtained a job as a teacher, but, similar to Stephanie, he had to go through a process of qualification recognition, which identified a lack of certain training in his degree structure in Beijing. It took him an extra two years, during which he worked as a private football coach to pay his bills, before he eventually managed to secure a teaching post.

Generally, for those who trained to be teachers, because of the different education systems and teaching focuses, their training in Beijing had to be adapted when they sought teaching posts in Hong Kong. More importantly, although they were promised mutual degree recognitions between the mainland and Hong Kong when they began their studies, in practice this was much more difficult. They generally spent at least two to three years' extra time in order for their teaching qualifications to be properly recognized in Hong Kong. This can be considered the socio-career costs to these Hong Kong students. True, they were able to get a prestigious degree from Beijing, but, as many of them chose to return to Hong Kong, they had to pay a higher "time tax" (Gasparini, 1995, p. 32) and make an additional financial investment. These "detours" in their postgraduation stage meant that their career development was also negatively affected, such as having to take up jobs that were tangentially relevant, and at a lower earning capacity.

In a similar fashion, those who had legal training in Beijing, such as Christine and Norman, were uninformed about what was required to pursue the kind of legal careers they desired, either in mainland China or in Hong Kong. In the case of Norman, he realized too late that in mainland China one only needs a bare minimum of an undergraduate law degree to be a litigating lawyer and that experiences of handling cases at court were much more important. Instead, he "wasted" three years pursuing a master's in international law, which proved "useless" when he looked for a job. In the case of Christine, she was uninformed about the fact that legal employers in Hong Kong do not recognize any legal training or qualifications received from mainland China and thus wasted six years to be treated by Hong Kong's employers "as if [she] knows nothing" (Christine's words).

Indeed, it was typical among these rural-origin and Hong Kong working-class students to have wasted time because of a lack of understanding about the temporal inequalities across higher education systems and the labor markets.

## THE SURVIVAL TRAP

Chunpu (born in the 1970s) comes from a rural village in Zhejiang Province. At the time of our first interview in 2017, she held an academic post at a university in Shanghai. Having had to make a living in the pricey city of Shanghai, Chunpu and her young family have had to live in substandard accommodations and constantly keep an eye out for goods on sale at supermarkets. Chunpu sighed, "I cannot tell you how exhausting this is. I wish I did not have to wait until there are discounts to buy a bag of rice. I wish I did not have to spend all this time every day thinking about the most basic daily goods. I hope that one day I can shop in the supermarket whenever I want." Not only is this mode of survival energy consuming, but it also detracts time from Chunpu that she could have used for her research. Chunpu frowned, saying, "It is only when you do not have to worry about your daily necessities can you afford to do research without worrying about where the next meal lies." She recognized the pertinence to spending substantial time on her academic research and publication work that would bring her the "hard currency" in academia (B. Li & Y. Shen, 2022). However, her survival needs took over and forced her to "waste" her time every day on getting discounted goods.

Ku (born in the 1980s) comes from a small village in Hubei Province's Jinchun County. As he was an "extra" child not permitted by the one-child policy (Kipnis, 2011), his parents were given a hefty fine after Ku was born. This fine drove his cash-strapped family's economic situation to the ground. After Ku's arduous journey to entering academia, Ku's ideal preference was to work on research that fit his research interest and could benefit his career in the long run. However, Ku found himself unable to say no to any requests of work on research projects that bore no relevance to his own interest. He confided this burning need to "make more money" to support his family and "survive in this city" while realizing that "resources that fit [his] need will almost never be accessible to [him]. [He] can only get those that nobody else wants and that need to be done urgently." As many of these projects were urgent, he had to manipulate his own temporal arrangements in such ways that he could only deal with the urgent and the immediate, and not his passion, where his long-term research interests lay. As such, Ku ended up putting his own research and career pursuits on hold and wasted considerable time working on projects that brought him income but no long-term career benefits.

Both the "qualification trap" and "survival trap" subjected these working-class and rural-origin participants to *wasting time* because they saw no clear prospect of improving their life circumstances. Instead, they often ended up worse off than before. It can be seen clearly that in both circumstances, the rural-origin individuals' weak familial economic wealth and the working-class Hong Kong students' lack of understanding about temporal inequalities across higher education systems and the labor markets inclined them to further time wasting. Their disadvantageous time inheritance at familial and national levels exacerbated further temporal inequalities as a result.

## Gained Time

Inherited temporal wealth can facilitate further acquisition of "extra" time, which manifests in gap years and gap semesters or leaves of absence for the privileged time inheritors. A significant role of these extra time periods pertains to how they effectively "buy" these inheritors' time out of the normative temporal expectations, grant them an alternative and usually enriching experience, and enable them to return to the original "time track" even better equipped than before, thus increasing their competitiveness.

### Leave of Absence: A Bought Time Vessel

It was common practice for the upper-middle-class participants to have experiences of a gap year or a gap semester during their higher education journeys. Such gap periods were usually deployed to accrue temporal advantages, which could benefit those seeking employment or pursuing a better job. According to Nianci, whom we have met before, this "has become a fashion" among her equally elite undergraduate peers in Hong Kong. She said,

> Many people have done that. I know at least four to five peers, most have worked during their leaves of absence as they want this work experience. In my department [art history department], within my cohort of around less than 20 students, two have taken a leave of absence [*xiuxue* 休学] . . . one is working in an NGO and the other is doing some marketing work. He does not want to pursue postgraduate studies so he feels that it is better to gain some work experience during his undergraduate period . . . I have another high school classmate who is doing his BSc in engineering in the same university. He too has taken a leave of absence for half a year, during which he worked in a Japanese company, and now he has received a full-time job offer from this company.

Nianci's account is echoed by Yu, whom we have met before as well. Yu confessed that he deferred his own graduation by half a year as he undertook an internship at an actuarial firm. This internship was "hugely beneficial" for his success in securing a position in a pension fund immediately after graduation. "This is a known secret among my peers, to be honest," Yu intimated.

Well-versed with the most sought-after currency in the postgraduate labor market, work experience, these upper-middle-class students like Nianci's peers and Yu took leaves of absence during their undergraduate studies with a view to accruing exactly such experience, so that they could gain a competitive edge in the job market. As such, the leaves of absence effectively served as *time vessels* they bought to shield them out of the otherwise well-regulated temporal structures of their undergraduate studies, such as when to graduate. Because these students had inherited substantial temporal wealth from their families, they were in no hurry to enter the job market and start generating an income, which contrasts sharply with the underprivileged time inheritors mentioned previously. Instead, they momentarily withdrew themselves from their undergraduate studies and inserted themselves into a more "productive" arena, the actual workplace, where they accumulated hands-on work experiences that would yield much bigger financial returns in the labor market, a coveted job offer that could bring potentially bigger income and better social status. This way, these time vessels manifested as leaves of absence were time well spent. As such, their rich time inheritance begot further extra productive time.

## Gap Year(s)

Originally from Beijing, Yi did not do so well in her Gaokao and was not able to get into her desired university in Beijing.[2] Instead, she got an offer in Tianjin, studied there for one year but found the teaching methods "too outdated" and disliked her major. So she dropped out. Instead, her family supported her to apply to an elite Australian university using her Gaokao marks, where she switched her major to economics. Yi described this one-year stint in Tianjin as her gap year. She smirked, saying, "It was not time wasted. I used it to figure out what my favorite subject was and what type of teaching I preferred." Coming from an upper-middle-class family,[3] Yi tapped on her inherited temporal wealth to turn her otherwise "not so successful" year in Tianjin into an "extra year" in her life. In this gap year, Yi sorted out her preferred subject of studies and teaching methods. Her family's economic and cultural readiness to support her to drop out and apply to Australia bred her confidence and self-assuredness about the role of this gap year. Indeed, following Yi's reasoning, if she stuck with her studies in Tianjin, she would have wasted another three years of her life[4] studying and living in an environment that was not suitable for her. Yi's inherited temporal wealth thus also prepared her for acting decisively to cut her potential "temporal loss" in this sense.

Xian, originally from Tianjin, undertook her master's degree studies at one of the UK's most elite universities. However, she took some gap years to enrich her life. She noted, "BB University was too much like an ivory tower. When I was there, everybody was very similar, coming from very distinguished senior high schools and prestigious undergraduate institutions. Most people were from very well-off backgrounds. They had never had to worry about their livelihood. And we all gathered in BB University. What we discussed and our life circles were all very similar. And it felt so boring." Coming from a privileged background, Xian felt stifled by the elite and yet homogeneous environments that she had always been placed in, all the way up to her master's program. Xian cried out, "I hoped to live in a completely different place and a completely different life." Eventually Xian decided that she "wanted to understand what life is like at the bottom of the society, how the poorest live." Therefore, immediately after her master's graduation, Xian volunteered for 18 months in a nongovernmental organization (NGO) at a remote rural county in China's southwest (Jue Wang, 2023; J. Wu, 2016) that helps rural children get more diverse educational provisions. Without an income, Xian relied on her family's financial support during her entire 18-month stint. In 2020, Xian contacted me to indicate that she was applying for PhD programs in the UK by drawing on her experience of working with disadvantaged populations in China.

Referring to her NGO volunteering time as "gap years," Xian benefited substantially from temporarily withdrawing herself from the privileged and yet homogeneous surroundings. Instead, she gained alternative exposure to the "miseries" of the "poorest" and those "at the bottom of the society." Her enriched perspectives constituted her newly acquired temporal wealth, which were made possible by these gap years, her family's financial support, and an assuredness that she was in no hurry to enter the job market and generate an income (Forbes & Lingard, 2014; Maxwell & Aggleton, 2013). In 2021, Xian received a doctoral program offer from another of the UK's most elite universities on a topic that would enable her to "tackle educational inequalities in China." Xian's gap years clearly yielded notable cultural and symbolic returns (Bourdieu, 1986). With her abundant time inheritance, Xian was therefore better able to beget further temporal wealth than her less privileged peers.

No matter the leaves of absence or the gap year(s), these privileged time inheritors gained extra, more productive and worthwhile time that yielded substantial returns culturally and symbolically. Unencumbered by the urge to graduate as planned and generate income, these students of upper-middle-class backgrounds were able to temporarily withdraw from the normative time track of higher education studies and instead inserted themselves into more "lucrative" temporal arenas and acquired coveted currencies in the labor market. Their existing temporal wealth thus facilitated their confidence and decisiveness to beget further temporal advantages. This phenomenon evokes Matthew's principle, "To him that hath shall be given" (Szydlik, 2004, pp. 41–42). The temporally wealthy received even more time wealth. Those endowed with time gained even more time.

Chapter 8

# Shades of Career

## From Being Trapped in Precarity to Making Bold Career Moves

This chapter shows how unequal time inheritance subjects disadvantaged inheritors to being trapped in successive precarious, low-paid jobs. Meanwhile, it enables their more advantaged counterparts to try out different career options with a secure fallback option and eventually arrive at their ideal career choice and lifestyle.

## Trapped in Precarity

In addition to wasting time, many of the disadvantaged time inheritors also tended to spend substantial periods of their postgraduation work life in precarious jobs. This is usually a consequence of their uninformed decision making at the juncture of entering higher education and during their higher education journeys. Among the rural-origin participants, 21 out of 26 entered second- or third-tier universities despite their strong Gaokao results, due to their lack of familial inheritance in understanding about the temporal inequalities of higher education systems. For this majority of participants, their first jobs after university were mostly poorly paid and precarious.

We learned of the case of Jiao in a previous chapter and understood that he had two temporary jobs after graduation. Ping, originally from Hubei, went to a university in the northwestern part of China and only managed to get a low-paid position at a Japanese company in Tianjin. A typical commonality of such jobs is that they are not only poorly compensated but also require long work hours, making the economic value of the work time even less. Chen, who became a fixed-term contract high school teacher after his first degree, recounted his life:

> On one hand, I had administrative duties. On the other hand, I had to prepare for teaching. I still remember vividly: I had to get up at 4:40 every morning. After that I had to visit the students in their class for their morning self-study period. . . . On a normal day I had to teach English classes, prepare for my teaching, prepare for homework, mark homework, until the evening. In the evenings there was also the evening self-study period. Usually the last self-study period was for English and lasted until 11 p.m. So my work time was from 4:40 a.m. to 11 p.m. This was the sort of work intensity.

Chen's account evokes Lawrence's in the "Diligence and Time Squandering" section in chapter 6. In the case of Lawrence, he was caught in a series of low-paid and precarious fixed-term contract jobs for six years (2016 to 2022) before he finally managed to get a permanent position. His experience was shared by many of his working-class peers from Hong Kong.

Norman, whom we have met before (see the "Wasted Time" section in chapter 7), managed to land a job as a litigator in 2021, but the pay was so low (RMB 4,500 [USD 653] per month) that he was not able to survive on that salary (CEIC, 2021).[1] He only worked there for three months before he quit this job. Following that, in June 2021 Norman began his job at a law firm that was cofounded by partners in Hong Kong and in Guangdong. This position qualified him to join the Greater Bay Area Youth Employment Scheme, which stipulated that "the participating enterprises shall engage the eligible graduates under the Hong Kong Law, offering them a monthly salary of not less than HK$18,000 and shall station the graduates in GBA [the Greater Bay Area][2] to work and receive on-the-job training. The Government will grant a monthly allowance of HK$10,000 to the enterprises for each graduate engaged up to 18 months" (Interactive Employment Service, 2020). As part of this scheme, Norman was qualified to receive a total of RMB 3,500 from his law firm and HKD 10,000 (around RMB 9,131) from the scheme every month. This made his salary income (RMB 12,631, around USD 1,834) close to the median salary income in Guangzhou in 2021, which stood at RMB 12,024 per month (CEIC, 2021). The problem was that Norman was only eligible for this scheme for up to 18 months, which meant that by March 2023, he would no longer be able to receive the HKD-10,000-per-month subsidy from the Hong Kong government.

Norman's low pay and precarity were symptomatic among his fellow working-class peers. Shane, also from Hong Kong, is a trained engineer who graduated in 2015 from an elite university in Nanjing. Between 2015 and 2022, Shane worked in Guangzhou, Hong Kong, Shenzhen, Shanghai, back to Shenzhen, and then Guangzhou again across industries in real estate, insurance, a public relations start-up, stock brokering, and shadow education. All the jobs were either short-term and then the business failed or more stable but lowly compensated and lacking long-term career development prospects. In 2022, Shane had been working as a tutor at a tutorial centre in Guangzhou, teaching HKDSE supplementary classes to Hong Kong students who were stationed in Guangzhou. He exclaimed, "It feels good that now when I go to the supermarket, I don't have to keep staring at the price tags of the goods. I can buy whatever I want."

While Shane was now able to make a decent enough income to support his daily living expenditure in Guangzhou, he was often exhausted because his income now depended on the hours and numbers of classes that he taught. In some weeks, he had to teach up to 45 classes. His constant exhaustion also reduced his time to pursue any further studies he would have liked (e.g., he wanted to learn more advanced finance skills). Shane was also constantly worried about the future of his industry given the uncertain policy environment around shadow education in mainland China.[3]

Christine, whom we also met previously, was forced to look for jobs in Hong Kong due to the outbreak of COVID-19. Because of the different legal systems between Hong Kong and mainland China, she was only able to get a series of paralegal positions, which were lowly paid and presented "problematic" work environments for her.[4] She quit these jobs one after another and eventually got a position as a contract writer/editor, still precarious but with a better pay. Christine smiled wryly, saying, "It has been a bumpy road so far." When asked if she had considered studying for a Juris Doctor (JD), which would qualify her for a legal career in Hong Kong, she confessed that she did not because she felt "too exhausted." She said in exasperation, "I have just spent four years doing a law degree and another two years on and off sitting the postgraduate entrance exams and the *fakao* [法考]. I don't want to start all over again to read another law degree from scratch!" However, without a JD, she was just "a university graduate with effectively no legal qualification." Christine was therefore severely disadvantaged in the labor market in Hong Kong.

Looking forward, Norman stayed hopeful that one day, when he would have accumulated enough experience and reputation, he would be able to handle cases that would bring him an income of RMB 700,000 each (around USD 101,626). The problem remained, however, that Norman was unclear on how long this would take, nor was he confident that this would be the case. He was also unsure that he would be able to survive with the low salaries until that day. Norman's desired career-progression prospect did not have a clearly delineated path that could sustain him until the stage when he would finally "make it," nor could he draw on his familial financial resources to support himself.

The bumpy paths among these working-class students were the joint effects of their lack of socioeconomic resources as well as their difficulty in converting their mainland university degrees and experience into recognized institutionalized cultural capital and social capital. This was made worse by the difficulty in combining their Hong Konger identity with their mainland university degrees in the labor market in mainland China, apparent in all the inconveniences that Christine, Norman, and Shane depicted about seeking jobs and working in the mainland and Hong Kong. In other words, in their postgraduation career paths, they continued to experience this "caught in between" dilemma, no matter whether they went back to work in Hong Kong or sought work in the mainland.

A key characteristic of these precarious situations that these rural-origin and working-class students encountered was that they had no clearly delineated end point or prospect of a way out of such precarity. They could not see any light toward the end of the "precarity tunnel." In contrast, their more advantaged time-inheritor counterparts always had the familial support to ensure their transition from one job to the next. This provided them with more confidence and assurance to make bold career moves.

## Bold Career Moves

The advantaged time inheritors mostly either had stable and high-income jobs arranged for them (see the case of Bing in chapter 3) or entered professional jobs that their overseas or cross-border higher education credentials qualified them for. However, in the few cases where these privileged time inheritors could not access their ideal jobs, they seemed to be able to afford to try out different careers and eventually select one that aligned with their overall lifestyle and career preference.

## FROM KITCHEN HAND TO PROGRAMMER: LINGSHAN'S STORY

Lingshan, whom we have met a few times already, studied social sciences during her first degree in Hong Kong (2013 to 2017). During this period, she took various internships in the finance industry (e.g., insurance), but she disliked those. She was very confused about what she should do after her graduation. One evening, she made some noodles for her roommate who returned late. Her roommate enjoyed the noodles very much and asked if she had thought about becoming a chef. This inspired Lingshan, who started to research culinary programs in the West. After much hard work, she found that Canada's migration policy seemed the most friendly and she had a much bigger chance of getting work after her studies there compared to in the US, the UK, or Australia (Lomer, 2018; Y. Ma, 2020; Robertson, 2022). She thus enrolled in a two-year culinary program (2017 to 2019) in a big city in Canada, determined to make her own name through combining Western and Chinese cuisines. Lingshan felt that her decision brought much disappointment to her father, Mr. Yue, who wanted her to be another "Harvard girl." However, when I spoke with Mr. Yue himself, he suggested that he would support whatever career she chose for herself. Indeed, Lingshan's two-year study and living expenditure in Canada was all covered by Mr. Yue.

Lingshan was well aware of the perceived lower status of working in a kitchen, as opposed to the white-collar jobs that most of her peers went into. However, determined to get out of the fierce competition that she loathed in Hong Kong, Lingshan placed great hope on her culinary career in Canada. Her familial support and her readiness to grasp this opportunity both benefited her career-decision making.

In 2018 when I spoke to Lingshan during her culinary studies, she was very happy with the friendliness and nonjudgmental nature of her peers and other people around her in the culinary program. However, in June 2021 when I interviewed her again, she had become a programmer instead.

Lingshan revealed that her initial love for culinary work was stifled mainly because of the poor labor compensation in the culinary industry. She was paid minimum wage, which meant that she was not able to trade her labor for a decent level of monetary reward. Worse still, the lack of stable work hours meant that she either had too little (e.g., no work at all or only three to four hours per day) or too much work (12 to 13 hours per day), depending on the business. Due to the uncertainties about work hours, she was constantly living a precarious life, not sure about her income level and unable to make any meaningful plans about her life. Precarity bred insecurity and resentment. Lingshan confessed that she was "utterly unhappy" working as a kitchen hand.

The long work hours during peak days also did damage to her health. As she was standing up for 12 to 13 hours on a daily basis, she suffered from a lower back injury, which followed her even into 2021, two years after she changed her job in 2019. The long-lasting effects of the culinary work became registered in her bodily sphere and constantly reminded her of that period of time in her life.

Apart from these more immediate factors, Lingshan was put off by the prolonged and yet slow career progression in the culinary world. She observed that it usually took 10 years of work in the kitchen for a chef to be able to start taking charge of menu design or engage in some more creative work. Before this point, all she could do was "repetitive manual labor" like dish washing and salad prepping. Lingshan found this career prospect "dire" and felt that she could not survive another 10 years of such work. She became distressed as she saw no possibility to realize her initial ambition of having her own kitchen and creating her own menu combining Western and Chinese cuisines.

As Lingshan started to look for other jobs, she accidentally came across an advertisement for a boot camp that trained programmers. Lingshan was initially skeptical, considering it "too good to be true" as the ad suggested that after two months' training enrollees could go on to get a high-salary job. However, after attending a taster course and contacting some of the graduates of this boot camp, Lingshan started to see some hope. She signed up for the boot camp, which cost her over CAD 12,000 (USD 8,871). She spent two months studying full time and took another month to look for a job. She managed to successfully land an offer working as a programmer at a financial-technology company.

Lingshan reflected that she was "lucky" as she knew she could count on her parents' financial support to pay for the boot camp and for her bills during the two months' full-time studies. This is a perfect example of how economic resources can be readily turned into temporal capital to enable a career shift. The fact that Lingshan could afford to switch course and decided to train as a chef in a Western developed country testifies to her financial and temporal privileges as she was unencumbered by any imperative to generate an income immediately after graduation. Her family's continuous readiness to support her career pursuits, "whatever it was," demonstrates a level of temporal luxury that her less privileged peers could not dream of. Indeed, her rural-origin and working-class peers in the previous section had no such resource to support their full-time further studies or such temporal confidence and sense of security about parental financial support.

## From Boring and Repetitive Jobs to Dream Careers: "Timed" Gratification

Man, whose parents bought her a house before she came to study in London, joined a university-wide entrepreneurship competition during her master's program. She unexpectedly won an award that granted her GBP 3,000 (USD 3,932) for her start-up and the university's sponsorship for her Graduate Entrepreneur visa application. Keen to grasp this opportunity, Man persuaded her parents to invest in her destination-wedding-planning business on the grounds that she wanted to gain more work experience in the UK: "I must invest £10,000 [USD 13,106], which I needed to prove to be held in my personal account before applying for that visa. I could not have that amount of money by myself." Man's readiness to embrace this Entrepreneur visa route was clearly backed up by her family's abundant financial resources. Man's financial privilege had now enabled her to imagine further career-wise: acquiring indefinite leave to remain (ILR) in the UK.

> If my company can generate profits . . . or even allow me to speed up my application for the ILR, then I might do other things after that. . . . Now my visa has imposed constraints on me; e.g., I cannot do any business in real estate, but I am quite interested in it. Once I do not have these constraints, I may do something else. But I might well return to China even after I have the ILR. (Interviewer: Why?) What I am doing now . . . is not that profitable, and is repetitive.

For Man, the constraints imposed by this Entrepreneur visa could be likened to obstacles on her way to freedom of time deployment. She repeatedly emphasized what she would be able to do once those restrictions were lifted. This sense of burden during her current stage as a visa holder thus contrasted sharply with the anticipated state of ease and of being in control: the freedom to do business in real estate that she was interested in and not be trapped by wedding planning that she found repetitive. In order to acquire the ILR, Man had to commit a minimum of five years' time to her current wedding-planning work. This protracted period of "waiting" could be considered as a "time tax" (Gasparini, 1995, p. 32) on the anticipated UK citizenship status that would facilitate her career time autonomy.

Li (whom we have met several times by now) was further down the line of citizenship acquisition. Arriving in the UK in 2005 for his sixth-form studies, Li entered a post-92 university, where he developed a strong interest in luxury goods retail. When he graduated in 2012, he was "lucky" to be among the last batch of international students to qualify for a post-study work visa. He spent two years working as a luxury brand sales representative in London. By 2014 he had already been in the UK for nine years; he persuaded his parents to invest in his milk-tea business so he could eventually obtain the ILR in 2016 and "get whatever jobs [he] wanted."

Li's milk-tea business was instrumental to his successful acquisition of the ILR status and his new capacity to freely choose jobs that he fancied: another luxury goods sales representative job, where he could meet "all kinds of different people" and enjoy "the excitement and surprise of not knowing who the next customer is." In comparison, he described the clientele of his start-up milk-tea shop as "more predictable" and with whom he "ha[d] less time to develop a relation." He recalled painful lessons such as being coerced into paying a hefty fine to the city council for litter that his shop did not throw. Therefore, the period between 2014 and 2016 was Li's "waiting" period, during which he endured unfavorable work conditions with an anticipated reward of the ILR and the subsequent freedom to pursue his favored career.

Li's and Man's cases have demonstrated how the temporal structures of national migration governance intimately intersect with individual international graduates' personal career-planning and temporal experiences. Their respective periods of waiting and the work that they did during this time became instruments of a delayed gratification of time autonomy.

Notably, no matter Lingshan's foray into the culinary industry and then eventually becoming a programmer, or Li's and Man's patient "waiting" before they could pursue their favored careers, they all benefited from an assured security inherited from their familial temporal wealth. Li's and Man's waiting was timed with a clearly delineated expected outcome. Such a "state of anticipation," following Gasparini (1995, p. 30), gave Li and Man "control over the situation" (p. 31), facilitated by their unproblematic access to resources, such as their parents' financial support and clear immigration rules specified by the UK border agency, which favors the "socio-economic elites" (Lomer, 2018, p. 318). Therefore, Li's and Man's waiting status was characterized by "waiting in control" with an anticipation of reward: taking control of their career time. Their cases, together with Lingshan's successful career shift, are undergirded by their class privilege, as orchestrated by their dispositions. This class privilege allowed them to quickly grasp opportunities presented to them (e.g., to acquire the Entrepreneurship visa or to migrate to Canada) and to remain hopeful for a favorable anticipated-migration outcome.

The economic imperative for the disadvantaged time inheritors (including the rural-origin and working-class students) to generate an income immediately postgraduation, together with their lack of a sense of temporal security, inclined them toward jobs that tended to be poorly compensated and precarious in nature. The working-class students in Hong Kong, in particular, also suffered from their lack of cognizance of the different temporal rules across mainland China and Hong Kong. Hence, graduates with legal training in mainland China were rendered as "without any legal qualification" in Hong Kong due to the completely different legal systems across the border. Similar cases can be found among those who trained to become teachers in mainland China (e.g., the case of Stephanie discussed in the introduction). Such cross-border temporal discrepancies thus also contributed to the precarity that these working-class students often got trapped in.

In comparison, the privileged time inheritors had their secure temporal dispositions thanks to their substantial familial temporal inheritance. This enabled them to take bold actions to explore alternative careers (e.g., Lingshan) or grasp opportunities that came their way (e.g., Man's Entrepreneur visa and Lingshan's uptake of the programming boot camp). Such substantial differentiated time inheritance thus further exacerbates temporal inequalities, which manifest in career outcomes and lived experiences.

# Summary of Part II

## Observed Mechanisms of Inequality Reproduction Through Time Inheritance

So far, over the space of five chapters in part 2, I have introduced five manifestations through which differential time inheritance continues to perpetuate social inequalities. These mechanisms include visions of decisions from self-sabotaging to path paving, time-shaped dispositions from debt-paying mentality to sense of entitlement, time-induced consequences from labor-time squandering to work-life balance, time use from wasted time to gained time, and shades of career from being trapped in precarity to making bold career moves. Curiously, these mechanisms together create this phenomenon: The more time you inherit, the more, better, and more productive time you gain; the less time you inherit, the more time you waste and the less valued your time becomes.

To be more specific, the aggregated effects of inequalities in time inheritance have been such that the more privileged you are in your time inheritance, the more time you save, as you are able to foresee "traps" in future careers and circumvent them (e.g., by avoiding enrolling in lower-tier universities) through your long-term planning and vision; you are also better able to gain "extra" time by inserting yourself into a more "productive" temporal sphere (e.g., taking leaves of absences during undergraduate studies to engage in unpaid internships or Xian's foray into seeing "how the poorest live," which enriched her insights into her PhD application). Better still, the more temporal wealth you inherit, the more secure and assured you are about the education and career decisions you make, which in turn allows you to make more informed, "less hurried" decisions that eventually enable you to achieve time autonomy and your preferred lifestyle, which means the quality of your life time can be improved as a result.

In contrast, the more disadvantaged you are in time inheritance, the more time you waste, as you do not have the requisite familial temporal resources to help you see through the obfuscating temporal inequalities across higher education systems at home and abroad. As such, you make more "uninformed," seemingly self-sabotaging education and career decisions, earning less-prized university degrees, which in turn incline you toward getting precarious and underpaid jobs and thus struggling to survive and ending up wasting even more time trying to make ends meet. This is not helped by your obligation to pay off the "debt" that you accumulated throughout your education journey. As you feel undeserving of the borrowed time that is on loan to you, you are more pressed to quickly generate an immediate income, which inclines you to get into less fulfilling, more time-consuming, and less well-compensated jobs. You are also more likely to have to pay extra time interest or time tax in the form of years of work where you retain no economic benefit for yourself and accrue long-term physical and mental health suffering.

Together, these foster a vicious cycle, as the less you are paid and the fewer social connections you have (another form of familial- and national-level time inequalities that deal a heavy blow to those from rural and working-class backgrounds), the more time you must spend surviving; thus, you are more likely to accept whatever money-making opportunities come your way and end up putting your preferred career on hold. The more you put your preferred career pursuits on hold, the less likely you are to achieve time autonomy and the worse the quality of your life time becomes.

As such, time inheritance as a hidden mechanism of social inequalities reproduces privileges and disadvantages in a full circle. This mechanism demonstrates that time inheritance accumulated in the past tends to not only reproduce but often magnify and create even wider temporal inequalities, because privileges beget further privileges, while disadvantages lead to further disadvantages.

Crucially, time inheritance at the familial level (e.g., generations of cultural understanding and economic wealth among the upper-middle-class families) and national level (e.g., the urban *hukou* holders) tends to allow these advantaged time inheritors to better tap into the global-level time inheritance of highly ranked Western higher education institutions (e.g., sending children to Western countries for secondary school and university education). In contrast, negative time inheritance at the familial level and national level (e.g., the time poverty and debt-paying mode of the rural-origin individuals) tends to exclude these underprivileged time inheritors from partaking in such struggles for global-level time inheritance.

Economist Thomas Piketty (2014) writes in his renowned *Capital in the Twenty-First Century* that inherited wealth plays a significant role in shaping the distribution and concentration of wealth across the globe in the 21st century (see his chapters 11 and 12). However, Piketty was focusing on inherited material and monetary wealth transmitted across generations. When it comes to the transmission of human capital, Piketty (2014, p. 420) acknowledges that this is "always more complicated than the transmission of financial capital or real estate." Through this exposition of the mechanisms for time inheritance, part 2 of this book demonstrates how differentiated time inheritance and the inequalities it creates and exacerbates begins at birth and continues to shape every disposition, step, and decision of an individual's education and career journey. Inherited time inequalities are thus arguably one of the most fundamental social mechanisms of human inequalities across societies.

However, as powerful as time inheritance may seem in determining an individual's life chances and trajectories, it does not work as a seamless and mechanical determinism. Instead, time inheritance works in messy and sometimes obfuscating ways. This is what part 3 of this book will now demonstrate.

# Part III

# How Time Inheritance Transforms Inequalities

Part 3 points out how time inheritance as a hidden social mechanism that shapes society is not mechanistically deterministic but has complex manifestations in empirical contexts where multiple levels of banked time and borrowed time intersect.

# Chapter 9

# Not a Mechanistic Determinism

## From Unqualified Inheritors to Zealous Parvenus

This chapter discusses how time inheritance is not a straightforward process as there are both "unqualified inheritors" with significant banked time bestowed upon them and "zealous parvenus" burdened by borrowed time. I draw on empirical accounts to demonstrate how, when familial- and national-level time inheritance encounters "global"-level time inheritance, inadvertent "future orientation" and distinction can be cultivated among the so-called shortsighted disadvantaged time inheritors; meanwhile, the advantaged yet "unqualified" inheritors can become lost and trapped by their own temporal privilege.

## Zealous Parvenus: Field-Dependent Time Inheritance

Time inheritance does not work in a rigid and mechanistic way. Instead, when time inheritance at various levels (i.e., familial, national, and global) comes into contact, unexpected results can be engendered. As such, stigma can become distinction, "shortsighted" present focuses can inadvertently yield future orientations, and perpetual marginal positions can turn into long-term career wealth.

### WHEN NATIONAL-LEVEL STIGMA TURNS INTO GLOBAL-LEVEL DISTINCTION

Jiao confessed how he often felt inferior (*zibei* 自卑) when he was in mainland China because of his rural background. He would never volunteer the

95

information that he was from the countryside. However, when he was in the UK pursuing his master's degree, he gradually realized that his rural background turned out to be an asset. He was pleasantly surprised: "My rural experience cast me in a positive light: they thought of me as special, that is, my ways of thinking, stories, or sharing were different from other Chinese students, who were stereotypically thought of as from privileged and affluent backgrounds."

As revealed previously (see chapter 1), the state-sponsored teleological developmentalist temporal classification constructs the rural as backward, lagging behind, uncivilized, and by default inferior. In contrast, the urban is viewed as a symbol and embodiment of development, civilized and superior. Jiao's stigmatization about his rural identity is consistent with what has been portrayed in the existing literature about rural-origin university students (J. Chen, 2022; Meng Cheng [程], 2018a, 2018b; Meng Cheng [程] & Kang, 2018; H. Li, 2013). Jiao's transnational education mobility lifted Jiao out of this temporally linear and toxic rural–urban dichotomy in mainland China and placed him in a society with a rather different temporal frame. In the UK, the rural is represented by idyllic landscapes and resided in by mainly middle-class occupants (Batel, 2020, p. 2; Bhopal, 2014). More importantly, in this temporal frame, there is an oversupply of privileged and arguably "spoiled" Chinese international students from urban upper-middle-class backgrounds (S. Lan, 2021; C. L. Xu, 2021a). In comparison, students from Jiao's rural and deprived background are in short supply (C. L. Xu, 2020). In this very different temporal structure, Jiao's rural perspective curiously became a source of distinction. As such, his national-level time deficit became temporal wealth at the global level.

## INADVERTENT FUTURE ORIENTATION: PRESENT FOCUS AS A TEMPORAL MERIT

A further example is from Jiao as well. Having failed the postgraduate entrance exam twice, Jiao thankfully received a partial tuition scholarship from a Russell Group university in the UK for a master's program. However, still short of money to cover his living expenses, he worked as a cleaner from 6:30 to 9:30 a.m. on weekdays and all morning on Saturdays. He did not have time to make friends with his peers from China, who were mostly from families that were *feifu jigui* (非富即贵, "if not rich then powerful," Jiao's own phrase). Neither did he have time to sightsee, apart from visiting Oxford and Cambridge as part of a university induction tour and London for a physical checkup exam. To ensure his immediate survival in the UK as an international student, Jiao's time use was geared toward attracting immediate income. This was at the expense of time that could have been dedicated to building up social connections with his affluent peers or developing his exposure to the British cultures, both of which could yield potential long-term effects (Zhang [张], S. 思. Q. 齐., 2018; S. Zhang & Tang, 2021; S. Zhang & C. L. Xu, 2020).

However, as he looked back, he realized interacting with the working-class cleaners in the UK allowed him to gain in-depth, firsthand accounts and understanding of the fabric of British society, which can be rare insights not shared by other Chinese students. Siqi Zhang and I, for example, show how the Chinese international students in our study demonstrated considerable ignorance about the class and racial makeup of the UK (S. Zhang & C. L. Xu, 2020). Jiao's perspectives became inadvertently enriched, yielding long-term benefits for him as a social science researcher who started to build an international reputation and lead a transnational life. Indeed, Jiao went on to build his career in Europe, the Greater China area, and the Asia–Pacific regions. In this sense, Jiao's temporal focus on the present and the urgent yielded unforeseen long-term benefits. Such chancy gains are mirrored in the accounts of Shanshan Lan's (2021, p. 674) rural-origin participants in South Korea whose "ethic of hard work" helped cultivate their "positive qualities such as independence and perseverance."

In his discussion about the seemingly universal diligence among the Chinese people, Harrell (1985, p. 216) proposed the notion of an "ethic of entrepreneurship." By "entrepreneurship," Harrell focuses on "the investment of one's resources (land, labor, and/or capital) in a long-term quest to improve the material well-being and security of some group to which one belongs and with which one identifies." He suggests three crucial elements in this notion: long-term quest, the idea of security, and group orientation. Regarding the first crucial element, he explains, "There is the matter of a long-term quest or effort. The kind of entrepreneurship I have in mind is aimed not so much at short-term gain as at establishing something secure and enduring. The entrepreneurial ethic, in this sense, is future-oriented" (Harrell, 1985, p. 216).

Paradoxically, the disadvantaged time inheritors in this book are found to be compelled to focus on the present due to their lack of material, social, and cultural resources. However, their tactics, which involve such single-minded focus and obliged diligence—what they deemed as the only way out of their time deprivation (see chapter 6)—seemed to have a long-term effect or orientation. In other words, out of no or little choice, these underprivileged time inheritors ended up being future oriented—not by deliberate long-term planning informed by information and cultural capital but by a sheer lack of immediate options.

Admittedly, Harrell (1985, p. 223) recognizes that in the modern industrial era, the entrepreneurial ethic can be overridden or superseded by factors such as "political *biaoxian* or personal *guanxi*, not through hard work or industriousness."[1] This kind of unintended consequence could be to do with the nature of the kinds of work that these participants are drawn to. In such jobs (e.g., teaching and researching in higher education), these rural-origin or working-class individuals can be relatively independent, relying on their own excessive hard work and sheer determination to "sit on the cold bench" (*zuo lengbandeng* 坐冷板凳; Cang's words—female, born in the 1980s, Jiangxi Province), to produce and accumulate valued outputs (e.g., academic journal articles) that can be recognized and accorded distinction (e.g., in key journals; Bourdieu, 1988; B. Li & Y. Shen, 2022; W. Xu & Poole, 2023). This is probably why these protagonists felt drawn to or able to "gain their foothold" (Jingpi's words—male, born in the 1960s, Fujian Province), knowing that they do not have "political *biaoxian* or personal *guanxi*."

## WHEN PERPETUAL MARGINAL POSITIONS TURN INTO CAREER WEALTH

Bian, a humanities scholar, told an equally intriguing story about how his perpetual marginal positions through his transnational education mobility had unexpectedly turned into his source of distinction and formed his scholarly identity. Born in the 1960s in a small village in Anhui Province, Bian is from an extremely poor peasant family. Being the eldest child, he had only two options to escape the rural environment, either through higher education or through joining the army. That was in the late 1970s. He could not join the army due to a lack of *guanxi*, which left him with only one option, the higher education route. He got into a second-tier university in Anhui and then furthered his master's studies in a first-tier university in Tianjin. Upon graduation, he was immediately offered a position to teach in the same university, and he could have become an associate professor in his late 20s had he decided to stay in that university. However, he was disillusioned by the sociopolitical environments in the country then (He, 2014).

Bian eventually left for his PhD studies at a prestigious university in the US sponsored by a full-cost scholarship. After graduation, he gained a faculty position and rose to the rank of professor in a regional American university. However, more recently he moved to work in a prestigious university in the Greater China area. Bian reflected that he has always been "at the margin" throughout his academic career: first his rural background compelled him to a lower position in China's rural–urban dichotomy (Meng Cheng [程], 2018a; H. Li, 2013; Liao & Wong, 2019), then studying and working in Western academia has continued to reduce him to being at the margin (Chu, 2023; Ford, 2011). He suggested that his decision to go to the US meant that he abandoned the already-well-built academic connections back in China; meanwhile, beginning to use English as his working language in the US meant that he was using his weaknesses to compete with other people's strengths (*yijizhiduan gong tarenzhichang* 以己之短攻他人之长).

Moreover, as a racialized and ethnicized individual, to survive in the White-middle-class-dominant American academia again meant that he was subjected to various types and degrees of marginalization, which can be supported by studies such as E. M. Lee (2017), Waterfield et al. (2019), Bhopal et al. (2016), Bhopal (2019), and T. Kim and Ng (2019). At the time of the interview in 2019, he was working in the Greater China area,[2] where tensions between mainland China and the local residents had been intensifying over the past decades (T.-H. Wong, 2023; C. L. Xu, 2015). He was again positioned at the margin.

Such perpetual marginalized positions had, for a long time, confused and infuriated him. However, now he considered it a blessing. He reflected, "To be a proper academic, you need to be always at the margin, instead of being in the mainstream; because if you were in the mainstream, you may not be able to think and write independently and critically." He went on to comment that some of his peers who received PhDs from Western countries had managed to get distinguished faculty positions in HEIs in mainland China. However, he felt that this was more like submitting to a "golden cage" because these peers can no longer say what they truly think (Guiheux & Wang, 2018; Marginson, 2014). He concluded, "To me, these peers are no longer proper academics as they become engrossed in power and lose their capacity to say what they think." He added, "This is especially true for those in the humanities and social sciences."

Bian's case vividly demonstrates how his rural background and his education mobility within China, to the US, and across the world have choreographed his perpetual state of being at the margin, which understandably engendered considerable hardships along his academic trajectory. However, his scholastic disposition has now transformed his perception of such perpetual marginalization as the necessary and crucial conditions for maintaining his independent and critical scholarly integrity and identity, especially as a scholar in a humanities discipline.

Indeed, education mobility had enabled these rural-origin and deprived scholars to appreciate that despite their lack of financial resources, they could enjoy "poems and distant lands," as Xun (male, born in the 1980s, Hunan Province) articulated:

> Perhaps receiving education cannot bring you a guarantee of financial security, or of a massive increase of income, but I feel that education can change your state of being [*shenghuozhuangtai* 生活状态]. I feel that individuals with rural backgrounds who have received education have a different state of being from those who have not . . . for the educated person, even if you have the same kind of job and family, would have a different sort of mentality [*xinxing* 心态] and sentiments [*qingdiao* 情调]. Also, those who are educated and those who are not have differing impact on their children. The children of rural individuals have different cultivations/qualities [*suyang* 素养], whether or not they can change their financial status very much . . . getting education allows us to have more options, you can see how to "live a more than desultory life, open arms to poems and distant lands" [*shenghuobuzhiyanqiandegouqie, haiyoushiheyuanfang* 生活不止眼前的苟且, 还有诗和远方].

The idea about living "a more than desultory life" and instead opening one's arms to "poems and distant lands" is from lyrics of a massively popular song performed by singer Xu Wei (许巍) and written by Gao Xiaosong (高晓松). These lyrics depict a desire and pursuit of the poetics in life and not being limited by the "trivial" challenges and tedium of daily life. It has often been used to show such intellectual pursuit among Chinese citizens (L. Qian, 2022, p. 214). In his account, Xun underlined the crucial intellectual transformation that education, and especially education mobility (i.e., rural to urban) in his own case, had enabled him to achieve. Crucially, such gains in terms of transformed perspectives were often unwitting, unanticipated, chancy, and opportunistic; these were gains that could not have been foreseen. They were not planned, but due to these individuals' time spent living on various kinds of margins, they accumulated lived experiences and perspectives that eventually allowed them to turn their "time living on margins" into valuable resources.

Moreover, the *suyang* of rural-origin or working-class individuals should be recognized as worthy and of value (S. Lan, 2021). It might be true that their lack of substantial temporal wealth inclined them toward a present focus. However, as these empirical data have demonstrated, their present focus, stoicism, and humility are all important constituents of their dispositions (*suyang*). In the literature, such orientations have often been relegated to a source of "lack," or deficiency (Bourdieu, 1984; Kipnis, 2011; Lehmann, 2023). However, from a temporal perspective, their dispositions are precisely the strong suits that enabled them to succeed against all the odds stacked against them.

## English: A Temporal Accelerator?

An important common element of "success" among the rural-origin and urban working-class participants in this book is their mastery of the English language. Being able to use English well for academic purposes enabled 13 out of the 26 rural-origin participants and five out of the 14 working-class participants to partake in transnational education, either for shorter-term exchange programs during their undergraduate studies (e.g., Lawrence went to Denmark and Japan for exchanges) or master's and PhD studies (for the 13 rural-origin participants). In all of these cases, a commonly heard remark was "thanks to my English proficiency." Indeed, thanks to their English proficiency, Jiao was able to pick himself up from his two failed postgraduate entrance exams and instead venture abroad to study in the UK, Qin was able to secure a government-funded master's scholarship in Singapore and then another fully funded doctoral program offer in the Greater China area, Chen went to New Zealand, and Ming went to Finland.

Although disadvantaged in their time inheritance at the familial and national levels, these rural-origin and working-class youth in this book leveraged their English proficiency to partake in transnational education mobility and achieve upward social mobility. As such, although English is known for being a tool of colonial power and bestows unequal temporal wealth to native speakers (see chapter 1), its dominant position provides inadvertent temporal advantage to these otherwise disadvantaged participants. This supports David Crystal's (2003, p. 24) argument that English can play "a central role in empowering the subjugated and marginalized." This is another vivid example where time inheritance at the global level (in this case, English-language proficiency) can trump familial-level and national-level time disadvantages. In this context, English is akin to a temporal-wealth accelerator for the rural-origin and urban working-class students.

Admittedly, the lack of economic and cultural resources for rural-origin and working-class youth in general means that not many of them can attain a high level of English language proficiency. As sociologist He Li (2020, p. 9) points out, in her research conducted between 2007 and 2008, many rural children in China tended to struggle with anxiety and fear and viewed English as "a source of flight and disempowerment." As a matter of fact, it has been reported that some elite universities in China have scrapped English tests and some secondary schools are planning to remove English as one of the three core subjects, which normally comprise Chinese, math, and English (Gan, 2023). If this happens at a larger scale, then the disadvantaged time inheritors would effectively be denied any possibility to accelerate their global-level time inheritance; they would therefore be doomed to mire in the "abyss" of time poverty and deprivation.

These empirical accounts above thus contribute to a more nuanced understanding of the messiness of how time inheritance works. Time inheritance does reproduce inequalities, as part 2 has shown. However, our understanding of time inheritance should be enriched by how different levels (e.g., national and global) of time inheritance can intersect to generate unexpected and inadvertent effects. These effects can manifest in ways wherein certain time inheritance (e.g., the rural identity and associated dispositions [*suyang*] and the opportunity to acquire English-language proficiency) can be accorded different values and significance in different temporal structures. In other words, time inheritance is field dependent.

Moreover, time inheritance at the familial level should also take into account individual dispositions and sheer effort. As Bourdieu and Passeron (1979, pp. 25–26) suggest,

> although subjects from the most disadvantaged classes are those most likely to be crushed by the weight of their social destiny, they can also, exceptionally, turn their excessive handicap into the stimulus they need to overcome it. Would the sons of workers or petit-bourgeois who have made it to higher education evince so strongly and so generally the energy of a Julien Sorel or the ambition of a Rastignac if this were not precisely what had enabled these students to avoid the common fate of their class?

As zealous "parvenus" (Bourdieu & Passeron, 1979, p. 91), the disadvantaged time inheritors in this book have demonstrated that the value of their time inheritance cannot be simplistically dismissed as "inadequate" or "shortsighted." Rather, their inherited time wealth may be recognized by the society in general as less valuable at present, yet the stoicism and the sheer dedication to improvement of their crafts (be it doing academic research or writing journal articles), which are underpinned by their time-deprived disposition (e.g., living on borrowed time), unwittingly furnished them exposure and access to perspectives and resources that have long-term benefits. This was especially the case for those who have moved into and through global-level temporal structures (S. Lan, 2021). True, they encountered various forms of marginalization across different temporal fields (e.g., the rural–urban dichotomy in China, the colonial and imperial domination of whiteness in Western academia, the mainland China–local political tensions in the Greater China area); however, the stoicism and determination as well as sheer hard work rooted deep in their dispositions enabled them to get through all these and triumph in cultivating their unique perspectives that constitute their distinction. Traversing these multiple local, national, and transnational temporal structures thus became a pivotal impetus for these initially disadvantaged time inheritors to acquire new temporal wealth. What distinguishes them from their more privileged time-inheritor counterparts is that such self-choreographed education mobility (as opposed to paved by the family) required extra layers of self-made resourcefulness, determination, and might; these may be lacking in the more privileged peers. I call these an important *activation mechanism* of time inheritance, which the "unqualified inheritors" may not possess.

## Unqualified Inheritors: Conditions of Time Inheritance

As Bourdieu and Passeron (1979, p. 25) point out, "inheritance always implies the danger of squandering the heritage" and "it would be a mistake to suppose that cultural heritage favors all its recipients automatically and similarly." Instead, there are what Bourdieu and Passeron (1979, p. 91) call "unqualified inheritors" who may not have fully exploited the substantial (labor) time inheritance made available to them and could be at risk of "downclassing."

### UNQUALIFIED TIME INHERITORS: ACADEMIC "FAILURES"

As discussed in chapter 3, "Education Mobility as Fate Changing," some of the upper-middle-class students in this book, despite their substantial time inheritance, may not fare well in academic studies, especially in the competitive education system in mainland China. This presents a challenge, as they may lack the cultural recognition and symbol (e.g., a degree from a first-tier university in China) that will enable them to legitimately inherit their family's wealth and power. We have learned about the cases of Bing and Li, who were both sent to the UK to pursue higher education as their families attempted to circumvent their lack of academic capital. These upper-middle-class students could be considered "unqualified inheritors" in that they were at risk of "downclassing" had they remained in mainland China.

These unqualified time inheritors are reminiscent of human geographer Johanna Waters's (2007) upper-middle-class and middle-class students who failed in Hong Kong's local education and used transnational education in Canada as "roundabout routes and sanctuary schools" to accrue coveted transnational qualifications and subsequently became professionals back in Hong Kong. They are also comparable to some of Yi-Lin Chiang's (2018) elite students in Beijing who, despite their parents' high cultural capital, still failed to gain entrance to top-tier universities in China. In these cases, substantial time inheritance in their fields of origin (i.e., in mainland China for Bing and Li and Chiang's participants and in Hong Kong for Waters's research participants) did not guarantee them outstanding academic performance. Rather, they were on the verge of being excluded from elite higher education.

Crucially, even after they had moved abroad, it did not mean their studies all went smoothly. Bing, for example, found her courses at her first UK university challenging:

> I was studying accounting, but it was way too difficult. I could not understand what I was studying, so I failed my courses; I just could not get it; I failed so many modules that I had to change my subject of study. However, at this university it was too hard to switch to another subject, so I moved to another, lower-ranked post-92 university to study international management. I had to learn human resource management, and strategic management, and similar modules. In the end, I graduated with a 2:2.

Because of switching both the subject of study and the university, Bing ended up spending a total of four years in the UK to finish her undergraduate degree. This was on top of the two years she had already spent studying in the Chinese partner university for her 2+2 program prior to moving to the UK. In other words, Bing spent two more years than planned.

Bing's case is indicative in suggesting that time inheritance does not work in a straightforward manner. Rather, the inheritors' capacity and efforts devoted to exploit the social, economic, and cultural resources endowed by their families still played a pivotal part. Bing was fortunate that her family put her through her challenging and somewhat winding higher education journey with their abundant economic and cultural resources. However, compared with her peers, Bing was feeling rather anxious, stressed, and ashamed of her lack of academic achievement. She described her status in the UK as forlorn (*luomo* 落寞). Because she only barely graduated with a 2:2 degree, she had to give up her initial plan of studying for a master's degree in the UK, as this would normally require at least a 2:1 degree.

These cases evoke Yi-Lin Chiang's (2018) observation that although parents of elite students in Beijing may activate their abundant cultural capital to help their children navigate elite university admission, such efforts may not always work. In other words, the inheritance of (labor) time wealth (in the form of cultural capital here) does not automatically translate into successful higher education admission and graduation results. The time inheritors' own capacity to exploit such inheritance also plays a pivotal role.

## Urged to Return: Expiry Date and Location Limits of Time Inheritance

As soon as they finished their studies abroad, many of my upper-middle-class participants were urged by their parents to return home. Man, whom we have met, revealed that her parents had arranged a job for her at the legal department of a publicly listed company in Beijing, her home city. She said, "My parents just want to get me in there before they retire." As her parents' relations with their friends who could make hiring decisions in this publicly listed company may "expire" once they have left their jobs, this clear expiry date thus created the temporal urge for Man to return "in time."

Bing similarly was hurried back home to take up the position of a pharmaceutical sales representative, which brought her a good income, employee benefits, and job stability. All of these were based on her parents' intimate knowledge about this pharmaceutical company through previous dealings at work.

Mengxi and Wang, too, both returned to Chongqing to become civil servants. They hinted that although they had to pass the civil service test and interviews through their own merit, their parents were keen to mobilize their social networks to ensure they got more desirable job postings. Mengxi intimated, "The relations are there, but they are my parents', and if you don't use them, they will vanish in no time."

These cases were representative of the students from upper-middle-class families who often were hurried back home and shoveled into either prearranged jobs or pre-paved career paths, which were deemed to be secure and stable for them. These families' attempts to ensure intergenerational inheritance of privileges were clearly punctuated by time limits, which were mostly linked to the parents' retirements. It thus becomes clear that time inheritance in the forms of social and political power is "time sensitive" and potentially fragile. Such time endowment is threatened by the likelihood of its "vanishing" if the time inheritors do not grasp the opportunity during the right time "window."

A hidden condition of this type of time inheritance is that it has to be supported by at least a threshold of degree qualification. Bing, who became a pharmaceutical sales representative, suggested that although her arranged job did not need to use much of the subject knowledge she learned in the UK, the degree from the UK institution was a "symbolic requirement" (*xiangzhengxing de yaoqiu* 象征性的要求). Man spoke of her UK qualifications (bachelor's and master's) as a "basic threshold" to even be considered for the position at the publicly listed company her parents targeted. In other words, in order for these inheritors to fully exploit their parents' time inheritance in this way, they needed the hard currency of recognizable academic qualifications to legitimize the inheritance.

A third characteristic of this type of time inheritance is that it is limited to the families' local networks, which is partly why these students usually spoke about returning to their home city to inherit the arranged jobs. Bing revealed that she had considered working in some other cities in China, but her parents would not "let her" because in other cities her parents would not be able to arrange decent jobs for her. This aspect of time inheritance is also related to the unequal time inheritance across different city tiers and across the urban and rural dichotomy, which will be focused on in the next chapter on "city-bound time inequalities."

A caveat for this type of time inheritance is that although these jobs are considered by the parents to be decent, the time inheritors themselves may not think so. Many reflected that they were "lost" (*mimang* 迷茫) or found such arranged positions "not very meaningful" (*meishenme yiyi* 没什么意义) after a few years on the job (Bailey & Madden, 2017). Bing confessed that she had developed a strong interest in luxury goods sales work during her time studying in the UK but had to give up this pursuit to assume an arranged job. In 2018 Bing intimated that she wanted to open a florist or pet shop instead of doing the pharmaceutical sales rep work but could not. These respondents were often trapped in a "comfortable cocoon" but lost their passion or meaningfulness in the work that they did. In this sense, the "quality" of their time at work may have been compromised. Their cases also evidence that time inheritance works in complex ways. Despite their substantial familial time inheritance and their capacity to capitalize on their UK institutions' global time inheritance, when they lacked the space and time to try out different careers, they may still be trapped in a relatively low quality of time spent at work, and quite possibly their overall quality of time in life may suffer too (Bailey & Madden, 2017; Snyder, 2016).

To conclude, time inheritance for these unqualified inheritors works in complex ways: not only does it have a clear "expiry date," but it also requires a legitimate form of academic qualification and is location-specific. The location-specific nature and the clear expiry date of such time inheritance thus often resulted in allowing little to no room for free career explorations for these time inheritors, and they might end up compromising their quality of lived time. More importantly, compared with the sheer determination and stoicism of their less-time-endowed counterparts, these advantaged time inheritors seemed to lack the extra layers of self-made "activation mechanism" (which constitutes their dispositions, or habitus) that could enable them to fully exploit their inherited time advantage. As such, this book proposes that for time inheritance to work, there needs to be activation mechanisms that can encompass a certain type of disposition (e.g., the disadvantaged inheritors' sheer determination and stoicism), the right kind of timing in inheriting cultural and political power, the required qualification threshold (e.g., a good university degree), and location-specific conditions. If one or more of these conditions are not met, then, despite the sheer volume of temporal wealth inheritors may be bequeathed, they may still not be able to maximize the benefits of such time inheritance.

# Chapter 10

# City-Bound Time Inequalities

This chapter demonstrates the complex nature of the mechanism of time inheritance by zooming in on how national-level time inheritance can be further nuanced through the perspective of city tiers. In the case of China, the amount of resources that *hukou* holders from first-tier cities have access to is unparalleled by *hukou* holders from lower-tier cities. This implies that familial-level time inheritance in urban China is often place- and city-bound. Meanwhile, when global-level time inheritance comes into play, these Chinese citizens from lower-tier cities often find that global cities such as London and New York can be as "oppressive" and "alienating" as the first-tier cities of Beijing, Shanghai, and Guangzhou in China. In such a context, time inequalities on the national level enmesh with those on the global level. This leads to a widened gap in terms of time privilege enjoyed by heirs of first-tier city *hukou* holders and their counterparts in lower-tier cities, let alone their rural-origin peers.

## China's City Tiers

There is no official definition or agreed-upon classification for city tiers in China. However, there are some commonly accepted categorizations of city tiers in business research and everyday use. Social science researchers have variously adopted different categorizations. For example, Jipeng Zhang et al.'s (2019) quantitative analysis of China's *hukou* reform between 2006 and 2016 adopted a categorization of five tiers of cities. In Bilby et al.'s (2020) research on the impact of city tiers on consumer response to creative advertising, they identified six city tiers in China. In contrast, Xiao and North's (2017) study on China's technology business incubators across cities categorizes three tiers of cities.

These variations notwithstanding, Beijing, Shanghai, Guangzhou, and Shenzhen are universally recognized as belonging to the first-tier cities. This is due to their high level of economic development, advantageous economic position relative to the country and region, and historic and cultural significance (Xiao & North, 2017, p. 622). For example, these four were among the first cities to host special economic zones during China's initial economic opening-up attempts in the 1980s (Starmass, n.d.).

The second-tier cities typically include the provincial capital cities of the most developed provinces (e.g., Chengdu, Dalian, Hangzhou, Kunming, Nanjing, Suzhou, Qingdao, Wuhan, Xiamen, Xi'an) plus Tianjin and Chongqing, two municipalities directly under the central government (*zhixiashi* 直辖市). This is due to their developed economic status, significant infrastructure development, and important political and cultural status relative to the country and regions (Xiao & North, 2017; J. Zhang et al., 2019).

The third-tier cities are of a middling development status. As Bilby et al. (2020, p. 335) argue, "although less developed and more traditional in terms of cultural values and lifestyles than higher tier cities, they are considerably more sophisticated and cosmopolitan than the lower tiers." Typically, these third-tier ones include big cities in developed provinces such as Zhuhai, Wuxi, and Ningbo and provincial capital cities in the less-developed regions such as Guilin, Guiyang, Shijiazhuang, and Lanzhou.

The fourth- and fifth-tier cities are typically less developed and smaller cities with relatively smaller population sizes and slower economic and infrastructural development. For example, some of the participants in this book come from cities such as Linyi (in Shandong), Jingdezhen (in Jiangxi), and Mianyang (in Sichuan). These can be considered as belonging to the fourth and fifth tiers of cities.

Clearly, such a city-tier system subscribes closely to the linear teleological developmentalism critiqued in the theoretical framework chapter. It establishes a steep hierarchy based on these cities' history and degree of economic and infrastructural development. As such, cities that are on the top (i.e., first-tier cities) are those with the longest history of development since the opening-up era in the 1980s and have the highest levels in indicators of economic and infrastructural development, including gross domestic product (GDP) and industrial structure (Yin et al., 2022). Conversely, cities that are at the bottom (i.e., fourth- and fifth-tier cities) are those with the shortest history of development and that have the lowest levels in indicators of economic and infrastructural development. The tiered positioning of cities, then, positively corresponds with the resources that they and their residents (including *hukou* holders and migrants) have access to (C. Chen & Fan, 2016, p. 25), which aligns with a developmentalist ideology and orientation adopted by the Chinese state (Howlett, 2021). As a result, students from different origins of tiered cities, even when they are of similar upper-middle-class backgrounds, may encounter differentiated social and educational inequalities when it comes to pursuing higher education and seeking employment.

## Unequal Time Across City Tiers

Guoxiang, whom we have met before, comes from the third-tier city of Hohhot, a provincial capital city of the Inner Mongolia autonomous region. In October 2016, Guoxiang had been working in Beijing for two years as a journalist after graduating from her undergraduate program in Hong Kong. She intimated, "If I did not want to have any change in my class position, then I should have stayed home in Hohhot after my undergraduate studies and just be a civil servant." This was thanks to her family's "roots" (*gen* 根) and "social resources" (*shehui ziyuan* 社会资源) in her home city. While Guoxiang's father is a businessperson who has his own independent enterprise, her mother is "part of the government establishment" (*zhengfu jigou deren* 政府机构的人). Guoxiang revealed, "You know in small cities, jobs in government establishments are better. Unlike cities like Beijing where you can have many business opportunities, in smaller cities such opportunities are fewer. Therefore, if you belong to the government establishment, you have a lot of resources."

Guoxiang's account is echoed by Ting, who is from Fuzhou, a third-tier city that is the provincial capital of Fujian in southern China. When asked about her plan after completing her master's and undergraduate studies in the UK, Ting confessed,

> In fact, there are only two options: one is to depend on myself and fight for my living, no matter in the UK or in cities like BeiShangGuang [a shorthand for the first-tier cities of Beijing, Shanghai, and Guangzhou]. The other option is to use the help that my father can provide for me and use my hometown as a

starting point, and then in the future perhaps I can continue to go to cities like BeiShangGuang, but I do not plan to fight for my own living in BeiShangGuang right from the start, because if I go to those cities I would be like beginning from scratch [*baishouqijia* 白手起家].

Guoxiang's and Ting's accounts resemble the experiences of Bing, Wang, and Mengxi in the previous chapter. While students like them are from upper-middle-class families with access to substantial social and political resources (i.e., time inheritance), such endowment is contained within their cities of origin. All of them are from second-, third-, or even lower-tier cities, which enjoy fewer developmental resources and provide fewer career opportunities for the young and educated (C. Chen & Fan, 2016; Yin et al., 2022).

As Guoxiang figured, if she returned to Hohhot, she might not be able to get a job that would render her skills useful. This is because her home city may not even have the industry that required her skill set. She lamented, "You just feel that the entire city is stagnant, and there is no sense of development." The core reason underlying her hesitance to return lay in a mismatch between the skills and credentials that she developed in first-tier cosmopolitan cities like Beijing[1] and Hong Kong and the lack of corresponding industries in her home city.

However, as Ting commented, if they chose to seek work in the first-tier cities of BeiShangGuang, then they would have to "begin from scratch," in Ting's case because she did not have a flat, or a car, or any social relations to rely on there. More importantly, she would not have the *hukou* of these first-tier cities of BeiShangGuang, the absence of which would most likely subject her to discriminatory treatment in the workplace and in daily life, as is revealed in the extant literature. Chuanbo Chen and C. Cindy Fan (2016, pp. 11–12) note that "certain government jobs in Beijing recruit only employees who have 'Beijing Proper' hukou." Chen Zhang's (2023) research on Chinese returnees with UK degrees, for instance, has shown that for students from second- and third-tier cities, to get a job and make a living in the first-tier cities like Beijing, Shanghai, Guangzhou, and Shenzhen can become highly problematic due to their lack of the local *hukou*. Chen Zhang's participants experienced discriminations such as not getting hired by employers because of a lack of local *hukou*, despite the high level of education qualification they obtained overseas. They also were excluded from accessing the city's public health and social welfare provisions such as state-sponsored childcare. This kind of city-based *hukou* advantages and discriminations against non-*hukou* holders are particularly salient in first-tier cities and have been well documented in existing literature (Z. Wang, 2023).

Meanwhile, Chen and Fan (2016) cite the 2010 Floating Population Dynamic Monitoring Surveys (FPDMS) data to suggest that small and medium-sized cities are perceived much less favorably by internal migrants due to their lack of employment opportunities and resources. A great majority of internal migrants favored large first-tier cities, but such *hukou* remain out of reach for most. In general, the lack of a big city *hukou* can be considered as a temporal deficit in inheritance terms.

For Ting, if she ventured to look for work in the BeiShangGuang first-tier cities, she would immediately lose the temporal advantages that her family had accumulated for generations in Fuzhou, especially the paved entry to a stable and well-paid job in a state-owned enterprise where her father was working. Instead, she would have to compete with millions of other well-qualified internal migrants and be subjected to high levels of discriminations in the first-tier cities (C. Chen & Fan, 2016). The location-specific nature of her time inheritance is thus made apparent here.

The underlying reason behind Ting's hesitance to venture into the first-tier cities, therefore, is to do with the uneven development across different tiers of cities; this has seemed to place these participants from lower-tier cities in a plight where they face greater difficulties to ensure intergenerational inheritance of privileged resources, such as social connections and political influence, which are all localized and confined to their cities of origin.

In contrast, those from first-tier cities had no problem inheriting and exploiting their family's temporal wealth. For instance, Man (whom we have met before) confessed that she did not even consider the salary factor when imagining her career back in China. "My parents want me to get more experience, because my family does not expect me to make money. Also, because the job is in Beijing, I would not need to rent a place to stay. Therefore, salary is not a priority to consider." Yi and Nianci, also from Beijing, similarly expressed an assuredness about not having to worry about rent if they returned to work in Beijing. Such accounts resonate with Chen Zhang's (2023) aforementioned research in which his participants with Beijing *hukou* derived a natural sense of superiority and recognition over immigrants to Beijing. In other words, a pivotal condition of intergenerational time inheritance is that it is city-based and place-based. If those from lower-tier cities like Ting and Guoxiang decided to build their careers in one of the first-tier cities, there would be a disruption of their *intergenerational time continuity*, as the social and economic resources that their parents had accumulated would be canceled out due to the geographical changes. The place-bound nature of such intergenerational time continuity seems to work on city-based terms instead of country-based terms. This is an important finding of this study that challenges the existing literature's country-based understanding of career decision making of Chinese international students (Tu & Nehring, 2019). Intriguingly, such unequal time inheritance is closely linked to the global-level time inequalities at city levels.

## Global Time Inequalities Across Cities

### NEW YORK: THE PULSE OF OUR TIME

After two years of work as a journalist in Beijing, Guoxiang moved to New York to study at a prestigious law school. Guoxiang kept interrogating herself as to why she had to make her family pay all that money for her to study law in the very expensive New York and was not even sure if she would get a job after that. It finally dawned on her:

> I cannot tolerate the idea that I am abandoned by the steps of our times [*shidai de jiaobu* 时代的脚步]. I cannot accept the idea that I sit and read amid some ancient piles of papers [*jiuzhidui* 旧纸堆] while technology and finance are developing at a high speed out there. I cannot accept such a role. This is because I want to be closer to the place where I can feel the *pulse of our time*, the more mainstream place, and to participate in it, this is perhaps an understanding reinforced by my internship in New York. When I realized that I am able to connect with the *pulse of our time* [*shidaide maibo* 时代的脉搏], I found it quite cool. (my emphases)

Guoxiang depicted a broader place hierarchy according to how cutting-edge and mainstream such scientific, technological, and commercial developments are across different places. In Guoxiang's striving to keep up with "the steps of our times," she and her family were willing to spend a great deal of money for her to "participate in" such "cutting-edge" and "mainstream" endeavors in the US. As such, her family's abundant resources (especially economic resources) became instrumental in ensuring her membership in this desirable place of development, which is on the top of the place hierarchy that Guoxiang constructed.

The expression "the pulse of our time" signifies Guoxiang's equation between cutting-edge technological and commercial developments and the steps of our times. It connotes this idea that the most advanced developments should be considered as the leading force of our generation: an understanding that is central to the teleological developmentalist discourse typical in China's state-sanctioned temporal classifications (Howlett, 2021) and the global temporal classifications often engineered by previous and current colonial and imperial powers (refer to chapter 1).

## UK versus Singapore: Opting for the World's Finance Center

Chuan, originally from the fourth-tier city of Jingdezhen, received a full-cost scholarship to pursue senior high school studies in Singapore. After that she came to the UK to pursue her undergraduate studies with her family's generous financial support. Looking back at her experience in Singapore, Chuan commented,

> I think the Singaporean society is relatively small. I feel that in that kind of an environment, everybody's similarity is quite high, so their trajectories and paths are quite similar, their horizons are not that broad: these would make it relatively more depressing [*yayi* 压抑], not as inclusive and open as here in the UK. This kind of openness means it can absorb many diversities—I don't think Singapore is this kind of a place. But this is what I have felt after I have come to the UK.

Chuan's critiques can find ready echoes among human geographer Elaine Ho's (2011, p. 126) highly skilled Singaporean transmigrants in London. For example, one of Ho's participants, Irene, commented, "I would rather live in England than in Singapore. . . . I really liked my time in university here. . . . There is more variety of people and they have a different outlook from the people you have grown up with, especially if you grew up in Singapore. . . . Everyone knows everyone. After a while it seems like a little village! . . . It is really cosy, but for me, it makes my skin crawl." In fact, such a sentiment about the "smallness" and high level of similarity among peers in Singapore was also mentioned by Yu, who similarly secured a full-cost scholarship to study in Singapore before he moved to Hong Kong to pursue his undergraduate studies. Importantly, Chuan considered the UK "the world's finance center," where more opportunities for her career development were accessible given that her major was in business. Chuan's construction of the UK as an international financial center resembles Guoxiang's account above in which she considered the US, especially New York, as at the forefront of technological advancement and representing the pulse of our times. In both cases, they developed a hierarchy of countries and cities on a global scale and gravitated toward the "most advanced" global cities. This is in line with the global-level dominance of Western, especially Anglophone, countries, which has shaped these participants' subjective perceptions and constructions (V. L. Fong, 2011; Y. Ma, 2020). Their subscription to this hierarchy also implies that the global-level time inequalities that we have discussed in the theoretical framework chapter have been "bought" and internalized by these participants in an unquestioning manner.

## UNEQUAL TIME ACROSS GLOBAL WESTERN CITIES AND FIRST-TIER CITIES IN CHINA

Pan, who was working as a postdoctoral researcher at Glasgow, commented on the high tax and low savings for her work in the UK. However, she added that an advantage in Glasgow is that unlike London or first-tier cities (e.g., Beijing, Shanghai, and Guangzhou) in China, the property prices in Glasgow are much more affordable. Originally from Qingdao, Pan preferred smaller-scale cities like Qingdao or Loughborough in the UK, where property prices are low and she can live a quieter life. In comparison, she felt that Beijing, Shanghai, Guangzhou, and London are big cities where there are too many people with competition that is too keen.

Different from Guoxiang and Chuan, who constructed Western global cities such as New York and London as the world's most advanced cities, Pan considered Western big cities like London in conjunction with China's first-tier cities in terms of the level of competition and property prices. Pan's view is representative among the participants from other lower-tier cities. To these students, in these global (Western) and first-tier Chinese cities they have to rely entirely on themselves or begin from scratch (*baishouqijia*) because they do not have any family socioeconomic and cultural resources to draw upon in these cities. They also lacked the inherited *hukou* privilege or citizenship rights that would enable them to access the public and social welfare in these cities (V. L. Fong, 2011; Z. Wang, 2023; J. Zhang, 2023). In comparison, if they returned to their home cities, or if they choose to settle in smaller cities in the West, such as Loughborough in the UK (according to Pan), they could either rely on their family resources or enjoy a quieter life, face much less competition, and take advantage of lower property prices.

This shared sentiment is evidenced in political geographer Chenchen Zhang's (2018) global comparison between Chinese first-tier cities' points-based system, where internal migrants can acquire the precious *hukou*, and the immigration points-based systems of Global North countries such as Australia and Canada. Chenchen Zhang (2018, pp. 858, 871) argues that China's first-tier cities occupy "national positioning" that "resembles the status of Northern countries in the global hierarchy" and such a positioning "gives them privileges and incentives to implement strict internal migration policy." Moreover, Zhang (2018, p. 871) notes that these first-tier cities also "aspire to move up in global hierarchies and become China's first global cities." In this sense, it can be argued that the global time inequalities across countries are closely enmeshed with the city-tier time inequalities in China. Together, they further advantage time inheritors of first-tier-city origin and disadvantage those from second- and lower-tier cities of China.

Chapter 11

# Political Time

## Different Inheritances, Similar Prices

This chapter demonstrates the complex mechanism of time inheritance by drawing on the case of "political" time inequalities across mainland China and Hong Kong. It argues that China's state temporal classifications have clashed with Hong Kong's previous Western-style, colonial temporal classifications in the political sphere. This has shaped the differentiated political time inheritance of the students born and bred across the border. When these students crossed the mainland China–Hong Kong border to study and live on the other side, they paid comparable political prices, including being subjected to political suspicion and surveillance. In this political temporal sphere, familial time inheritance is overridden by national-level and global-level time inheritance.

## Political Time Inequalities and Time Inheritance

In the theoretical framework laid out in chapter 1, I establish how state governments routinely deploy techniques of temporal classification such as iterating "powerful memories of the genealogy of the state" to strengthen and maintain their legitimacy in governing (Gross, 1985, p. 77). In the case of the CCP-led government in China, the state evoked the temporal construction of a unified nation from the past that should be strengthened in the present and sustained well into the future. As such, historically disparate regions such as Hong Kong, Macau, and Taiwan are accorded the position of being "inseparable" parts of the Chinese nation (P.-C. Lan & Y.-F. Wu, 2016; E. K.-W. Ma, 2012). Specifically for Hong Kong, informed by this temporal construction, since Hong Kong's return from its British colonial master to China as a Special Administrative Region (SAR) in 1997, the People's Republic of China (PRC) has been actively establishing a state-sponsored unification narrative. This narrative underlines that Hong Kong is an unbreakable part of China, with a view to setting Hong Kong as an example for Taiwan (E. K.-W. Ma, 2012). To this end, the Chinese state has made possible "exceptional membership" (P.-C. Lan & Y.-F. Wu, 2016, p. 742) status to Hong Kong's citizens, such as its preferential treatments of Hong Kong's students who were willing to study in universities on the mainland. These preferential treatments, which include lowering admission scores, provision of generous state- and institutional-level scholarships, and better accommodation conditions (F. Gao, 2024; C. L. Xu, 2019), could be argued to be manifestations of the temporal wealth accorded to students from Hong Kong within China's temporal classification. In fact, the working-class Hong Kong students in this book capitalized on this state-sponsored political temporal wealth to circumvent their own disadvantaged socioeconomic backgrounds in Hong Kong.[1]

Meanwhile, as an "exceptional" and "unbreakable" region of China, Hong Kong saw its HEIs given preferential treatment, which enabled them to "cherry-pick" (Shive, 2010, p. 6) elite students from some of China's top universities in the late 1990s and early 2000s. At that time, the chief executive of the Hong Kong SAR, Chee-hwa Tung (1998, para. 103), underlined that these mainland students were to "inject . . . an element of healthy competition for local [i.e., Hong Kong] students and broaden . . . [local] students' outlook on the Mainland and the region as a whole." Under this agreement, the Hong Kong universities were able to recruit from some of China's most elite institutions its most outstanding first-year students (including Peking, Tsinghua, and Fudan Universities).

It should be noted that these elite students are targets of a fierce competition for top talent among mainland China's most prestigious HEIs. Every year there are news reports about how the most prestigious universities like Tsinghua, Peking, Fudan, and Zhajiang deployed various tactics and resources to gain the favor of top-performing students in Gaokao. In 2019, Zhejiang University was ordered to stop offering as much as RMB 500,000 (USD 72,670) in the race to attract the country's top Gaokao scorers (A. Yan, 2019). Being able to admit such elite students becomes a symbol of distinction and enables these institutions to sustain their institutional legacies by having outstanding alumni in the future. There is little wonder, therefore, that normally the most prestigious HEIs with the longest history win out in this yearly competition for the brightest in Gaokao. It can be argued, then, that having access to admitting these elite students is an indication of these elite HEIs' temporal wealth in the national field of higher education in China (see chapter 1).

Within this context, the fact that the Hong Kong universities could simply be granted such "VIP" access to "cherry-pick" (Shive, 2010, p. 6) top-performing first-year students within mainland China's top HEIs suggests an advantageous temporal positioning. This is because the Hong Kong HEIs effectively inserted themselves into the top echelon of this highly competitive battlefield for elite students without exerting any effort or deploying any tactics and resources like the other mainland universities have. As such, they can be said to enjoy the same, if not higher, degree of temporal wealth as the elite HEIs on the mainland. Such unique access was made possible because of the intention of the CCP-led government to underline political unification messages (P.-C. Lan & Y.-F. Wu, 2016; C. L. Xu, 2019). In this way, the Hong Kong universities were effectively "cashing in" their national-level political advantage in the form of institutional temporal wealth at that time.[2]

Moreover, in the 2010s, Chinese students began to be able to apply to Hong Kong HEIs at the juncture of Gaokao. On such occasions, the global-level time inheritance of the Hong Kong HEIs has played a significant role. This is because the government-funded Hong Kong HEIs generally were ranked highly in international university league tables. As we have established in the theoretical framework chapter, the continued dominance of former imperial and colonial powers has translated into the "hegemonic dominance" (Marginson, 2008) of HEIs based in the Global West. As a former British colony, Hong Kong also saw its HEIs benefit from the colonial legacies in significant ways and fare strongly in international university league tables such as the QS and Times Higher Education university rankings (QS, 2014; Times Higher Education, 2014). As such, Hong Kong HEIs became competitive contenders for elite and academically inclined students from the mainland and beyond. As a matter of fact, of the 31 students in this book who chose to study in Hong Kong for their undergraduate studies, 28 received offers from mainland China's elite institutions but chose to accept the offers from Hong Kong instead. For these middle-class students from the mainland, their elite academic status and middle-class backgrounds (familial-level time inheritance) coupled with their political positioning as students from mainland China (national-level time inheritance) facilitated their access to the highly ranked universities in Hong Kong.

On the other hand, Hong Kong's history as a British colony for over 150 years (1840 to 1997) has left a suite of legacies such as the rule of law, an understanding of and striving for democracy, and a strong higher education sector (Tse, 2007). More specifically, Hong Kong's rule of law, freedom of speech, and its people's pro-democracy tendencies have manifested in various successive protests and occupy movements. These include the 2014 Occupy Central movement, the 2019 Anti-extradition Law protests, and others (Kong et al., 2023; Lai, 2024; C. L. Xu, 2015). Having been built up during over 150 years of British rule, these colonial legacies can be understood as Hong Kong's and its people's colonial time inheritance (i.e., global level).

When such colonial time inheritance clashed with its national-level time inheritance, however, as dictated by the CCP-led Chinese government, drastic political actions began to take place. For instance, as a response to these successive political movements and arguably "unrest" in Hong Kong, the Chinese government promulgated the National Security Law in June 2020, which "cleared the way by demolishing constitutional protections for the regime's critics" (Vickers, 2024, p. 141). This law has arguably curtailed Hong Kong's media freedom and political autonomy, leading to the dismemberment of pro-democracy parties and entities such as the Civic Party and the Hong Kong Professional Teachers' Union, as well as the exiles, arrests, and imprisonment of outspoken critics (Guinto, 2023; Thomas-Alexander, 2023).

As a response, in January 2021, the British government, as Hong Kong's previous colonial master, introduced an immigration scheme for Hong Kong's British Nationals Overseas (BNO) passport holders and their dependents, who can now migrate to live and work in the UK. This is an immigration privilege not previously accessible to them. Also known as the Hong Kong UK Welcome Program, this scheme was to reflect the "UK's historic and moral commitment to those people of Hong Kong who chose to retain their ties to the UK by taking up BN(O) status at the point of Hong Kong's handover to China in 1997" (Department for Levelling Up, Housing and Communities, 2021, summary, para. 2). Under this scheme, Hong Kong residents with BNO passports and their dependents enjoy new transnational migration rights to the UK. In temporal terms, such migration privileges could have taken them considerable labor time to acquire, perhaps through years of planning and applications plus paying tens of thousands of migration consultancy fees and/or investment budgets (A. K. W. Chan et al., 2022; Chau, 2023; L. Lui et al., 2022). As such, this Hong Kong–UK welcome program is arguably a continuation of Hong Kong's colonial time inheritance.

Given these complex interplays of national-level and colonial time inheritances concerning Hong Kong and its people, the question arises of how the individual students who have crossed the mainland China–Hong Kong border to study in universities on the other side fared in their higher education and subsequent career making. This chapter will argue that in the face of political time inheritance (both at the national and global levels), individuals' familial-level time inheritance plays a less significant role. Importantly, it will demonstrate how no matter what socioeconomic class these students are from, in the face of political tensions and identity politics, their national-level and global-level political time inheritance trumped their other identities, such as class-based time inheritance.

In what follows, I will begin with discussing the respective political experiences of both groups of students. I will identify how both groups of students experienced political suspicion due to their "outsider" political identities, which was arguably their political time "deficit" (as opposed to wealth). I will show how these political suspicion and alienation have subjected them to a range of survival strategies, such as complete political rejection, antithesis, deliberate hiding of certain identities (e.g., of their Hong Konger identity or their CCP membership), and political transformation over a long time. I will demonstrate how in this process, political time wealth can turn into deficits and political temporal debts, which in certain cases caused a great deal of pain and effort for these unwitting time inheritors to pay back. For example, for the working-class Hong Kong students, the initial preferential treatment could be considered a "time loan" they took out from their creditor (i.e., the mainland Chinese government) with an implicit "time tax" (i.e., for them to act as political unification tokens).

## Political Time Wealth:
## A Vanishing Colonial Legacy in Hong Kong

What characterizes the Hong Kong students' political time inheritance could be summed up as a rapidly "vanishing legacy." During my focus groups conducted in late 2013 with 12 Hong Kong students who were studying at a Hong Kong university, there was a clear sentiment that the colonial legacy inherited by Hong Kong was quickly disintegrating due to the impending "full integration" between Hong Kong and the mainland. Ingrid, a third-year law student (21 years old in 2013) said,

> I remember I once took a module about the legal system of the HKSAR; at that time a senior barrister gave two guest lectures in which he kept asking us this question for five to six times: When Year 2047 approaches, i.e., when the 50-year period has come to an end, how can jurors [*falvjiederen* 法律界的人] position ourselves? What can we formulate to deal with this situation? In fact, when the time comes, many things have to be integrated. Quite possibly even before year 2047, most things would be all set. At least we won't find it odd during the transition. I kind of feel that now Hong Kong is slowly becoming more and more like the mainland; I don't know why. However, I really truly want Hong Kong to keep its uniqueness, because if a city loses its uniqueness, it has no reason to exist anymore, Hong Kong no longer should be an SAR, it can only be a province or even a prefecture-level city [*dijishi* 地级市], and the kind that is quite small in size.

This colonial temporal inheritance culminated in the SAR status of Hong Kong, which was a marker of the city's "uniqueness." As such, Ingrid's anxiety over Hong Kong's potential loss of its uniqueness and its probable fate of becoming just another "province" or "prefecture-level city" could be argued to stem from a desire to cling onto its temporal wealth inherited from its previous colonial days. What, then, are the manifestations of Hong Kong's uniqueness and its colonial temporal wealth? Second-year medical student Linda's (20 years old in 2013) account below provides a glimpse.

> I think Hong Kong's current position is quite contradictory. On the one hand, you want to get some benefits from China. However, in the mainland there are many institutions, such as culture and values, [that] are completely different from Hong Kong's. In Hong Kong now on the one hand we want to fight for greater democracy, to have universal suffrage by 2017. However, when you think about it, by that time you might be fully integrated with the mainland so such things will never happen. We will never have democracy, or freedom of expression

and many other things—we will completely lose out. I mean if mainland–Hong Kong integration is the trend, then I guess before that final moment, Hong Kong would be in an extreme state of turbulence and many people would find it hard to accept such a reality. For me, I am a university student now; I am also worried about my future job, about the economy of Hong Kong in the future. Will it get worse, because Hong Kong's many competitive advantages are losing out to Shanghai or some other Chinese cities that have opened up their ports? I kind of feel that this will happen sooner or later, and what I am more worried about is really the societal turbulence, and what the entire Hong Kong population will do to accept it.

Hong Kong's unique temporal wealth inherited from its colonial legacy included, as depicted in Linda's account, democracy, desires for universal suffrage, freedom of expression, and its world-class trading ports—these all distinguished Hong Kong from the other cities in the mainland. And yet, this inherited temporal wealth was on the verge of being extinct, due to the ongoing "mainland–Hong Kong integration." Looking back in 2023, Linda's concerns were justified. Hong Kong's pro-democracy movements never reached fruition: no universal suffrage was arrived at in 2017; there was a great deal of social turbulence and upheavals in Hong Kong society, such as the anti-extradition protests that began in 2019; Hong Kong's freedom of expression has been curtailed after the introduction of the National Security Law in 2020 (S. Y. P. Choi, 2023; Woo & Wang, 2024). This very anxiety about the disappearance of Hong Kong's unique status as grounded in its colonial temporal wealth induced an urge to act among the city's youth.

From data collected in the student-led Occupy Central movement, scholars have reached a consensus that the contemporary youth in Hong Kong "are different from the older generations of Hong Kong citizens, who are said to be 'only interested in making money'; young people set great store in non-material values such as democracy, freedom, and constitutional government. They are more worried about the future, and they have an extremely pronounced tendency to criticize the government" (Kurata, 2015, pp. 31–32). Macfarlane (2014, para. 3) observes further that the Hong Kong students attending local universities "come mainly from ordinary local families. Unlike the wealthier, who send their children to study abroad . . . these undergraduates have no Plan B. They need to make their future here. This is why many feel that they must make a stand for democratic freedoms before . . . it is 'too late.' One banner at the university plaintively asks: 'If not now, when?' "

The sense of urgency and exasperation among the Hong Kong youth from "ordinary families" who cannot afford to "escape" (by studying abroad, for instance) is deeply temporal. These Hong Kong students were caught in a state of temporal limbo: they wanted to cling onto Hong Kong's colonial temporal wealth but were utterly unsure about Hong Kong's future under CCP rule. There was a danger of a sudden severance of their colonial temporal wealth. This sense of having their fates tied closely with Hong Kong's, which was keenly felt among the focus group participants, as represented by the accounts of Linda and Ingrid, was perceived as instigating a highly "politicized" environment in Hong Kong that my participants from mainland China felt (Lam et al., 2023; A. Ma & Holford, 2023; C. L. Xu, 2018a). It also has become part of the assumed "political characteristics" of the working-class Hong Kong students who moved to study in Beijing and Nanjing, which catalyzed a host of political suspicion and surveillance.

## Political Time Wealth:
## An Apolitical Environment in the Mainland

Across the border, my urban middle-class participants confessed to being raised in an environment where being "apolitical" is the best protection one can ever have. Miusi (from Xi'an, Shaanxi), for instance, noted,

> Having grown up in the mainland, both schools and parents have educated us to stay away from . . . protests and demonstrations, to keep ourselves away from such political movements in order to protect ourselves—this way we can stay safe. We should not stir up troubles [*reshi* 惹事]—they all say so. They . . . will depict politics or political events as extremely dangerous, and once you get involved in politics, it will [negatively] impact your future development and prospects, apart from your academic results.

Not only did they listen to such stern advice or indeed warnings from their parents and schools, but their own witness also resonated with these warnings. Xifeng (from Dongguan in Guangdong) pointed to the often-murky consequences of political activism, which seemed to engender self-censoring:

People in the mainland won't discuss the 4 June event[3] because people are afraid that once you stand out to join a rally about this event, you may end up having the same fate as those taking part in 1989. In Guangdong, I sometimes see some people demonstrating in front of the municipal government, but they are immediately taken away by some people. You have no idea where they are taken or what for. What happened to them after they are taken away? We don't know. Like this, who would even want to demonstrate anymore?

Apart from the fact that the environment inclined these students to be "apolitical," the lack of exposure to ideas and practices related to democracy was apparent. In December 2016, Keqin (from the Greater Bay Area in Guangdong) recalled, "We grew up in a place where there is no democracy in [the] Hong Kong sense or in any Western sense, in any non-Socialist Chinese sense, so we can more readily see that democracy has many different forms and for the feeling, the roles and missions that democracy was just one of the means and there are many other alternatives as well." Arguably, this contrasting "apolitical" and "no democracy" environment has sedimented in an understanding of political time among these participants in mainland China that is markedly different from their counterparts in Hong Kong or other Western democracies, as aptly captured in Hail's depiction (2015, p. 3): "China's education system ensures that all students are well-aware of China's historical conflicts with 'the West.' In response to the mass protests of 1989, in the early 1990s, the Chinese government launched a nationwide 'patriotic education campaign' . . . that was intended to instill national pride as well as show why China's unique 'national conditions' make it an unsuitable place for the propagation of so-called 'universal values' or 'Western style democracy.'"

This CCP-inculcated understanding of political time, together with the temporal classification of Hong Kong as an "unbreakable" part of China, when etched into their dispositions, characterized the political temporal wealth inherited by my urban middle-class participants from across mainland China. When they crossed the border to study in Hong Kong, they therefore encountered a great deal of conflicting views and behavior. Similarly, the working-class Hong Kong students who crossed the border to study in universities in the mainland (including Beijing and Nanjing) were confronted with drastically different political arenas.

## When Political Time Wealth Turns Into Deficit 1:
## Hong Kong Students in Mainland China

Hong Kong's highly unequal and hypercompetitive local education system has meant that working-class students often lose out as they are largely denied access to the city's publicly funded universities (Waters & Leung, 2013, 2014; Y.-L. Wong, 2022). To find a way out, the working-class students from Hong Kong in this book capitalized on their identity as citizens of Hong Kong to enjoy preferential treatment proffered by the HEIs in mainland China, including lower admission scores, better scholarships, and accommodation provisions. Norman, whom we have met before in previous chapters, confessed that it was a dream come true for him to be able to study law at a prestigious university in Beijing. Had he stayed in Hong Kong, he would not have been able to access this exclusive discipline. He said, "In Beijing I am at least a university student. Once I graduate, I can get a more dignified job [*timian* 体面]: becoming a lawyer. This is a ladder that can allow me to achieve upward mobility and pursue my dreams, but in Hong Kong this is hard to achieve because there is much less room to develop."

Among the 23 students from Hong Kong, 17 could not access any degree offer in Hong Kong at all, and six could not secure an offer to study their favored subjects. Having access to some of the most prestigious universities in the mainland and studying their favored subjects thus could be argued as these students' cashing in on their inherited political temporal wealth, which aligned with the CCP-led government's preoccupation with underlining the country's unification and sovereignty integrity over Hong Kong and its populace (P.-C. Lan & Y.-F. Wu, 2016, p. 757; C. L. Xu, 2019).

What these Hong Kong students did not anticipate, however, was the tacit political expectations of and assumptions about them in the mainland. As their higher education journeys in Beijing and Nanjing gradually unfolded, they realized that they were implicitly expected to perform certain political duties and were also subjected to heavy political surveillance and suspicion.

### POLITICAL TIME CARRIERS AND TOKENS

As one official from the PRC's Ministry of Education articulated in a speech delivered during the 2016 mainland Chinese higher education exhibition in Hong Kong, "the Ministry of Education actively improves policies, and works hard to create better study and living conditions for Hong Kong students, so as to *convey the care and love of the central government to Hong Kong youth* . . . our youth is the future of our country, the hope of our nation.

It is mainland universities' unshakable responsibility to cultivate the reserve talents for the development of the country and the long-term prosperity and stability of Hong Kong" (fieldnotes from 2016, my emphases). As discussed in chapter 1, the CCP-led state has been consistently underlining the temporal unification of the Chinese people across mainland China, Hong Kong, Macau, and Taiwan by emphasizing a shared history and a shared passage of time as one nation. By taking part in this special HEI admission scheme offered by the mainland, these working-class students became the embodiment and what I call "political time carriers" to "convey the central government's care and love for Hong Kong youth"; moreover, their individual future development effectively became vehicles for sustaining "the development of the country and the long-term prosperity and stability of Hong Kong." As such, these students unwittingly subscribed to serving the CCP-led government's temporal classifications in which the government became the vanguard that safeguards the country's sovereignty integrity and long-term prosperity.

In line with this temporal political mission, these working-class students quickly noted their functional "display value" while on campus. Nancy (22 years old, father a businessman, mother a homemaker) recounted the unease she felt on such occasions: "Usually the Propaganda Office at my university would organize tours that attract Hong Kong students . . . they typically would get a banner and take some group photos . . . I don't like such activities, because I don't think I need to proclaim my Hong Konger identity this way." Although students like Nancy found it unnecessary to "proclaim" their Hong Konger identity in such "crass" ways (Nancy's own words), other students like Vivienne (whom we have met before) were more adept with the intentions of their universities or indeed the mainland government. Vivienne revealed that every year her university would have student organizations, such as the Hong Kong Cultural Society, which she chaired, put on activities to share Hong Kong's cultural practices. "The key," Vivienne winked, "is usually in the photos." They would make sure to take pictures that could be used for "communication purposes." Vivienne intimated, "This is the deal; we benefited from the special admission scheme, so we have to 'payback' by performing these 'functions.'" Indeed, acting as political tokens was a tacit expectation for these students to help justify the CCP-led government's temporal unification messages.

## POLITICAL THREATS?

If serving as political tokens was an "appetizer" of a temporal political feast, then the amount of political surveillance and suspicion rendered on these working-class Hong Kong students was arguably a "main dish" that could be hard to stomach. As discussed above, Hong Kong's colonial legacy has left its youth a host of temporal wealth in relation to an earnest pursuit for democracy and a fervent desire for freedom of speech and expression. These, when confronted with rising political control from the central Chinese government, evoked successive, high-profile political protests in the city. This political unrest was portrayed in the mainland Chinese media as often led by "uninformed" and "ungrateful" Hong Kong youth, thus fostering unflattering assumptions among the mainland university lecturers and students.

Christine, whom we have met before, recalled how "shocked" she was when she learned that a mainland classmate told their Hong Konger classmates to "get out" because they disliked Hong Kong and disliked Hong Kongers. She had also witnessed a Hong Kong classmate who had an uncomfortable argument with a lecturer who expressed some biased and derogatory views about Hong Kong. Catherine (24 years old,[4] father a retired engineer, mother a homemaker, low-income family) confessed her attempt to alert her lecturers of her own presence as a Hong Konger when these lecturers verbally abused Hong Kong in class.

Given such uncomfortable or even hostile confrontations with lecturers and students on campus, some of these working-class Hong Kong students resorted to hiding their identity. Frances (20 years old, father a restaurant owner, mother a restaurant waitstaff worker) confessed, "I often tell them that I am from Guangdong to avoid unnecessary troubles."[5] Some others, such as Christine, Shane (both of whom we have met), and Laura (father a marketing manager, mother a homemaker), concealed their Hong Konger identity by relying on their Putonghua proficiency.

What was even more challenging, other than the above confrontations, was the level of surveillance exercised upon these students. A group of these students (e.g., Catherine, Emily, Sandra, Honesty, Clive, and Charles) were part of the Hong Kong Student Association of Beijing Higher Education Institutions, which was a joint student organization involving members from more than a dozen universities in Beijing. When this student society began to organize activities, they encountered a great deal of constraints. The National Security Agency (*guo'an* 国安) routinely "checked on" them, for fear that they would "carry out political activities." Catherine, who was one of the main organizers, intimated, "In the end, we had to get support from the Chinese Liaison Office in Hong Kong and get lots of support from the government; we had to ensure that *there was at least one government official attending every single activity that we organized*" (my emphasis). While Catherine and her colleagues have been able to continue to organize activities since then, this intense level of political surveillance left an unpleasant aftertaste for these students. "We are treated differently, as potential troublemakers," Christine sighed.

As such, the colonial temporal legacy has been turned into these students' "original sin," as they are assumed to be political threats and potential troublemakers in mainland China. Their inherited temporal wealth as Hong Kongers (which enabled their preferential access to elite universities on the mainland) thus clashed with the colonial temporal legacy, engendering considerable conflicts and confrontations. While they enjoyed the temporal premium of accessing elite higher education on the mainland, they were also unwittingly engulfed into a debt-paying mode where they had to perform political-tokenistic roles while also being subjected to intense political suspicion on campus.

## When Political Time Wealth Turns Into Deficit 2: Mainland Students in Hong Kong

As urban middle-class heirs of substantial familial- and national-level temporal wealth, the participants from various cities of mainland China were able to access Hong Kong's elite HEIs. Having grown up in and been inculcated with the "apolitical" disposition, when these students crossed the border to study in Hong Kong, they encountered significant challenges in reconciling the two contrasting political environments.

Admittedly, many of these urban middle-class students articulated a brief period of fascination about how taboo political topics on the mainland such as the 4th June Incident could be discussed or protested in broad daylight or commemorated in vigils. Many participated in the annual Victoria Park Vigils of the 4th June event, while some, like Guojing (25 years old, engineering major) and Yu (whom we have met before) even took part in political rallies. They typically celebrated a sense of novelty and expressed admiration for such political freedom among the Hong Kong citizens to express their views in public. Guojing could hardly contain his excitement when he described his experience at one rally as "boiling his blood" (*rexie feiteng* 热血沸腾). However, this initial curiosity and excitement was quickly confronted with unpleasant political hostility from some Hong Kongers. Qingwen (19 years old, science major) recalled a distressing encounter with a taxi driver who started to vent his anger on Qingwen and her friends upon learning that they were from the mainland. Qingwen said, "I took a taxi with a few friends from [Victoria] Peak [. . . and] the driver suddenly became extremely outraged [. . . as it turned out] that . . . before he drove us, he picked up two mainland Chinese tourists and they argued over the 'anti-national curriculum' issue. . . . In the end, the driver ditched them, calling them communists."

This incident took place in September 2012, which was during the period when the people of Hong Kong were campaigning against the government's proposed moral and national education (MNE) curriculum; thousands of people took to the street with a view to opposing the "brainwashing" of this proposed MNE curriculum. Although the Hong Kong government shelved this curriculum due to opposition (J. Liu, 2012; Vickers, 2024, p. 140), sentiments against the mainlanders' infiltration became notable among the Hong Kong public. Unaware of such political disputes, Qingwen and her peers were dragged into this because of their identity as "mainlanders." As such, amid the increased political tension between Hong Kong and mainland China, these students' political time inheritance at the national level turned into deficits and negative assets.

While Qingwen was able to dismiss the taxi driver's anger as hostility displayed by a stranger, Keqin (19 years old, law major) was disheartened when her close Hong Kong friend Popo stopped talking to her after their visit to a site where the Umbrella Movement took place.[6] Keqin reflected, "I can certainly imagine why because she would see I am, although her friend, still an outsider because I do not have a permanent Hong Kong residency; I would not be trapped . . . if Hong Kong would be a mess . . . and she might even think that I was being condescending, being a mainland Chinese and saying that 'oh, you are doomed.'" Popo's unilateral decision to sever the friendship dealt a heavy blow to Keqin, as she found this completely unexpected. She recalled, "We were the best of friends; we would confide in each other secrets that we never share with others." However, burdened by her "apolitical" and "no democracy" political time inheritance from the mainland, Keqin revealed her rather different views on the democratization appeals of the Hong Kong people to Popo during this visit.

On the other hand, Popo was among the concerned Hong Kong youth who felt that their destiny was tied closely to Hong Kong and would do whatever they could to prevent Hong Kong from losing its "uniqueness," especially its democratic pursuits (Kurata, 2015; Macfarlane, 2017). What Keqin perceived as her sharing about her skepticism toward the Umbrella Movement was taken as an indication of her disloyalty to Hong Kongers' political cause. This political difference was so drastic that Popo found it hard to reconcile and decided to desert their friendship. Popo distanced herself from Keqin for one and a half years before she confessed her thinking and apologized to Keqin. Over this period, Keqin experienced her initial confusion and sense of feeling abandoned, but, most importantly, she pointed out the alienation she felt and the political suspicion that she endured. Her political temporal inheritance from the mainland became a temporal catalyst for the "destruction" of her cherished friendship with Popo.

## WHEN POLITICAL CAPITAL BECOMES POLITICAL LIABILITY

It is widely acknowledged that the Communist Party membership commands considerable political currency in mainland China. Goodman (2014, p. 178) notes that in contemporary China, while the market economy coexists with elements of a "redistributive economy," the party-state and its redistributive economy are "always politically superior to the market economy." This has meant that being part of the ruling Chinese Communist Party confers significant temporal privilege and power at the national level, as almost all government cadres must be CCP members. Inheritance of political privileges is thus a most valued and effective means of intergenerational power transfer on the mainland (Marginson, 2014).

However, having moved to Hong Kong, my urban middle-class participants quickly realized that their CCP membership became a factor that invited political suspicion. A few of them voluntarily commented on a controversy that took place in 2014 to 2015. At that time, a mainland student, Lushan Ye, participated in a student union election at a Hong Kong university. During her campaign, her opponents uncovered that she was a Communist Youth League member (*gongqing tuanyuan* 共青团员) and thus alleged her to be a CCP "proxy" infiltrating the Hong Kong university (Baldwin, 2015). When my participants saw these accusations in the media, they confessed feeling their "spine chilled." Yingying (19 years old, business major, from Shanghai) said, "Ye's affiliation with the CCP Youth League is nothing special. As students growing up on the mainland, we all have this Youth League membership." However, this membership became a point of contention in the politically sensitive environment in Hong Kong. Witnessing these accusations against Ye, Miusi (24 years old, social sciences major), whose parents are both civil servants and CCP members in Xi'an, revealed her emotional encounters with Facebook posts from her Hong Kong friends: "They all post things about . . . their issue with the CCP and suggest that they are upset if anybody has a relationship with the CCP—when you see such things, you naturally will activate your self-protection mechanism."

Contrary to the coveted political capital that the CCP membership commands on the mainland, here in Hong Kong Miusi detected a sense of political suspicion surrounding her connection with the CCP. Miusi's concerns were shared by Yuhan (19 years old, business major from Wuhan) and Xiang (18 years old, business major from Guangzhou) who decided to pause their applications to be full CCP members while concealing their probationary CCP-member identities. Guojing (24 years old, engineering major from Shenzhen) abandoned his CCP membership application after he passed on this legacy by serving as a recommender[7] for his little brother's CCP membership application. Asked why he did that to make sure his brother joined the CCP, Guojing confided, "There are 80 million CCP members in China: this is an enormous group! If you do not join them, you will be oppressed by them." Guojing's strategy is a clear example where he ensured that his political temporal privilege as an "insider" CCP hopeful could be inherited by his little brother. This was built on his acute awareness of the symbolic power of the CCP affiliation back in the mainland and also his recognition that in Hong Kong such political capital turns into deficit.

POLITICAL OUTSIDERS: COMPLETE REJECTION OF POLITICS

A typical response to the negative reception of the "mainlander" identity and CCP affiliation is a sense of alienation. Longnv (originally from Shanghai), who after graduation continued to work in Hong Kong as a financial analyst, recalled how she felt that she was an "outsider" during the Umbrella Movement when her Hong Kong colleagues would discuss in secret their political concerns and would readily disperse upon seeing her. She lamented, "It felt like I was a complete outsider to them. There was no trust whatsoever, and I had better excuse myself to avoid further inconvenience." Longnv also recounted incidents where certain Hong Kong colleagues wrote anti-mainlander political slogans in the men's toilets at her company, which invoked intervention from her company's management. She confessed, "I felt as if I had done nothing wrong, and yet I had to be responsible for everything that was wrong."

Longnv's sentiment about the negative political atmosphere due to her identity as a mainlander in Hong Kong during that period was echoed by Guoxiang, who confessed finding it unbearable that her entire life in Hong Kong was highly politicized. After working in Hong Kong for five years after graduation, Miusi decided to pursue a master's degree in the UK. When recounting her experience as a student in London, Miusi exclaimed, "It felt great because I was no longer in the center of political conflicts." She giggled a little and said, "Sad, isn't it? I had to come to London to reignite my interest in politics. In Hong Kong, I could not . . . I avoided politics completely."

These accounts from Longnv, Guoxiang, and Miusi were typical among this group of urban middle-class students from the mainland who unwittingly became engulfed in the conflictual political whirlpool of tensions between the two entities. As their inherited political temporal wealth from the mainland became devalued and turned into political temporal deficits, they chose to "flee" Hong Kong as a means of self-protection and preservation.

## Political Time Inheritance: A Complex Mechanism

In Serafin's (2016) depiction of the "political time" embodied by Polish taxi drivers, he highlighted how these taxi drivers organized as a group to fight structural impositions and constraints by the society. In the cases of the Hong Kong and mainland students in this study, their political time was lived through mostly as struggles at an individual level. There were few organized activities except the Beijing Hong Kong Students Association's attempts to host activities, which were placed under heavy surveillance. This chapter, instead of focusing on participants' organized political time, has demonstrated how these two groups of students embodied their differing political time inheritances amid their cross-border moves.

The data reveal that while state-sanctioned political identities such as being "Hong Kong citizens" can yield seemingly positive political temporal privilege (e.g., preferential admission treatment for the working-class Hong Kong students), tacit political expectations (e.g., performing as political unification tokens) can be interpreted as political "temporal interest"; in other words, the political temporal privilege that these Hong Kong students received came with an implicit "price tag" attached. Meanwhile, these Hong Kong students' inherited colonial temporal legacies were deemed their "original sin" when placed in their mainland universities. These Hong Kong students as a result experienced a host of hostile encounters and were placed under intense surveillance as their colonial temporal inheritance equated them as "politically suspicious."

The mainland students' data show that their political temporal inheritance such as the CCP membership became a source of political suspicion;

their inherited identity as "mainlanders" induced hostility and alienation from both strangers and close friends—all of these were due to the increasing political tensions between mainland China and Hong Kong.

Intriguingly, these two groups of students were from differentiated class backgrounds. They both, however, were subjected to political alienation, suspicion, and even surveillance. They both were involuntarily engulfed in political contentions and contestations when studying on the other side of the border. Amid their shared political plights, their respective political time inheritances (at the national and global levels) overrode their familial-level time inheritance (i.e., class-based differences). This is an important manifestation of how time inheritance as a mechanism of social reproduction works in complex ways.

Crucially, this attention to political time inheritance presents as an important factor to consider when discussing education mobility and access. It was true that both groups were able to physically access cross-border education mobility, thanks to government and institutional-level policies and conveniences. However, their subsequent experiences of political alienation and exclusion became heavy prices for them to pay at an individual level. There was little, if any at all, awareness or support of these students, who were arguably walking embodiments of the "political integration and unification" of the two entities across the border. This presents an alarming ethical issue, which critical scholars such as Clare Madge and her colleagues have alerted us to. Writing about international education, Madge et al. (2009, 2015) argue that in order to develop truly "engaged pedagogy" and "responsibility," it is pivotal to focus on the ethics and care rendered to mobile students, including international students. Echoing this, human geographer Johanna Waters (2018) urges more focused attention to the "politics" of international and transnational education, especially in regard to how the students are treated. This chapter's conceptualization of "political time inheritance" and empirical evidence regarding the discrepancies and exclusion experienced by these border-crossing students thus make critical contributions to this scholarship.

These political exclusions and alienation notwithstanding, the latest statistics reveal that the number of students from the mainland who enrolled in Hong Kong's universities hit a record 8,600 in 2022, which was a 9% increase from 2020–2021 (Lem, 2022). This enrollment is forecast to increase in the coming years due to growing tension between China, the UK, and the US as well as Hong Kong's recent policy in 2023 to double its publicly funded universities' intake of "nonlocal students" with a view to attracting more talent to the city. Meanwhile, the number of Hong Kong students enrolled in mainland Chinese universities stood at 4,890 in 2022, which was an increase of 2.2% compared with the previous year (Deng, 2022). These numbers demonstrate an increasing number of students who continue to find such cross-border higher education pursuits attractive and worthwhile. It could be that such political prices are not made publicly known to new students, but it could also mean that considerations about potential gains (e.g., preferential treatment) outweighed political prices. In other words, these new students may continue to reap greater rewards over the political prices that they potentially have to pay. Further research in these areas would therefore be beneficial.

# Summary of Part III

In his attempt to empirically assess the "inheritance" effect, Piketty (2014, p. 50) utilizes national statistics that allow him to measure capital that represents the fixed "stock" of value from the past, which he compares against the current tax that represents current "flow" of capital. Albeit in an imperfect way, Piketty enables us to "get some kind of assessment of the relationship between the past, historical forces as opposed to the role of current forces over different periods" (Savage, 2014, p. 595). An intriguing, tongue-in-cheek finding derived from Piketty's analysis is a six-to-one ratio of assessing the relationship between the past and the present. In other words, "six times structure to one time agency" (Savage, 2014, p. 596) is roughly the "inheritance" effect. I have demonstrated in part 2 of this book how time inheritance operates in ways that enable the advantaged time inheritors to reap greater, long-term rewards in their higher education and subsequent career trajectories. However, while the time inheritance may, as a structural mechanism, shape individual life and career trajectories six times, there is a one-time chance that the individual heirs can exercise their agency to counteract the structural forces of inheritance. Part 3 of this book has shown precisely that.

In part 3, over the course of three chapters, I have illustrated how time inheritance does not work in a mechanistic and deterministic way. In part 2, I showed how advantaged time inheritors have better inherited wealth, enabling them to make long-term plans, while their disadvantaged counterparts tend to be reduced to a focus on the present. In chapter 11, I revealed how, out of no or little choice, the underprivileged time inheritors ended up developing a future orientation (see the case of Jiao). This insight alerts us to not too readily relegate the "present" focus of the underprivileged heirs of time to a "doomed future." Instead, through the cases of Jiao and

Bian, I have demonstrated that their experiences and their subsequent successes were a joint effect of the multiple levels of time inheritance. In Jiao's case, especially, he capitalized on what I call the "exchange discrepancy" of inherited temporal wealth across national and global levels. In other words, Jiao's rural background and identity are relegated to be stigmatized as "backward" at the national level in China, subjecting him to inferior access to resources; thus he was arguably in a temporal deficit mode, yet when he ventured beyond the Chinese border and entered the transnational education sphere in the UK, his temporal deficit inherited from China turned into temporal wealth in Britain. His decades of accumulated rural dispositions, as manifested through his perspectives, unique experiences, and stories of rural life in China, reaped reward and became his inherited temporal wealth. What was crucial was that Jiao moved across national borders and placed himself in a completely different temporal structure. This field-dependent nature of temporal inheritance is thus pivotal to recognize.

In Bian's case, his inherited temporal deficits (e.g., as a rural-origin individual in China, as a nonnative English speaker in the US, as a racial and ethnic minority in the US, as an "outsider" and politically suspicious mainlander in the Greater China region) subjected him to repeated positioning at the margins. However, these lived experiences of being always at the margin turned into inherited temporal wealth when measured against the yardstick of academic production, which values the possession of a nonmainstream view. In this case, it could be argued that Bian managed to place himself in a unique temporal sphere where his aggregated and accumulated temporal deficits became temporal treasures.

Crucially, both Jiao and Bian were able to achieve these temporal transformations through their successive rural-to-urban and transnational education mobility. The role of education mobility as fate changing is thus clearly demonstrated through their cases.

Jiao's and Bian's cases are good examples to show that while inherited temporal advantages or disadvantages in a specific field or temporal sphere play a big part in shaping an individual's life chances and career trajectory, the heirs of such temporal wealth or deficit also have a part to play. When the heirs of disadvantageous temporal inheritance grasp opportunities to move themselves to a different temporal sphere or field whereby they can turn their temporal deficits into wealth, they can achieve upward social mobility. Needless to mention, all of these feats could only be achieved through sheer determination and effort by these disadvantaged time inheritors, which constitute facets of the "activation mechanism" for exploiting and even transcending temporal inheritance.

Likewise, for the advantaged time inheritors, their families' substantial temporal wealth imposed specific conditions for legitimate inheritance. These conditions include, first and foremost, that these heirs should have an acceptable level of academic qualifications. As such, their families have had to deploy their substantial economic, social, and cultural capital to circumvent their otherwise "doomed future" in China's higher education sphere. Instead, they inserted them into the advantageous and much revered transnational higher education field (in the UK or elsewhere) so that they could gain a "basic threshold" of academic qualification to legitimately inherit their parents' arranged jobs or career paths in China.

The second condition of legitimate time inheritance has to do with the "expiry date" of such temporal wealth, which typically manifests in the heirs' parents' retirement, which would block their inheritance. In order to fulfill this condition, these heirs of substantial social and political time wealth are often hurried back to China and ushered into careers that may not align with their personal interests. As such, these temporal inheritors can often find themselves "trapped" in well-paid and stable jobs that were boring or meaningless to them.

The third condition has to do with the location-specific nature of their time inheritance. We found this to be shared by the cases of the disadvantaged time inheritors, too. Specifically, the social and political temporal wealth that families possess are often city-based or field-dependent. Therefore, for the advantaged time inheritors, they can only reap the biggest benefit if they returned to their home city in their home country. This is especially the case for heirs of first-tier city *hukou* holders, as their inherited *hukou* status can enable them to enjoy better job opportunities and better access to education, housing, and social welfare provisions. On the contrary, for the disadvantaged time inheritors from rural-origin or working-class backgrounds, the major way out of their inherited temporal deficit was to escape their original temporal sphere and instead move into a different one in order to have a chance of turning temporal deficit into wealth. For the somewhat-advantaged time inheritors from lower-tier cities, their better way out was to return to their home city and capitalize on their parents' location-specific temporal wealth.

Importantly, when assessing such city-based or location-specific time inheritance, these participants readily bought into global city hierarchies that are typically aligned with the dominance of the Global West; cities and countries such as New York and the UK were positioned at the top of "developments" and desirability for realizing these participants' life ambitions. This kind of place and city hierarchy has found ready echo in existing literature, where citizens of China are found to desire and actively pursue "developed world citizenship," especially those of countries in the Global West (V. L. Fong, 2011). Their internalization of the Global West's dominance reflects what I argued in the theoretical framework chapter of this book—that global-level time inequalities perpetuate through these participants' decision making and life pursuits.

Intriguingly, though, some other participants from lower-tier cities tended to equate the dominance of global cities such as New York and London with the dominance of first-tier cities in China. This demonstrates that in terms of temporal inequalities, the *hukou* temporal inheritance of first-tier cities in China can be as significant as citizenship in the "developed" world. This equation is significant in its own right in that it shows how China's domestic time inequalities, as manifested through *hukou* inheritance, can exercise the same level of symbolic violence on those disadvantaged time inheritors as the other global-level cities. In this sense, the national-level time inequalities and global-level time inheritance are similarly destructive.

In chapter 11, I demonstrate how political temporal wealth inherited on one side of the border (either mainland China or Hong Kong) can yield added advantages over the other side when such inheritance aligns with the ruling regime's temporal classification (such as the Hong Kong students capitalizing on their Hong Kong citizen identity to benefit from the preferential admission scheme of mainland universities). However, it also shows how such inherited political wealth can inadvertently turn into deficits when it clashes with the hosting society's temporal classification. This is evidenced through the various types of political suspicion, surveillance, and exclusion that both groups of students encountered and endured. In such a context, these students' respective political time inheritances (at the national and global levels) overrode their familial-level time inheritance (i.e., class-based differences). This adds a further level of complexity to the mechanism of time inheritance.

Overall, the three chapters in part 3 together add nuanced facets to time inheritance as a complex mechanism that underpins social inequality. While time inheritance generally ("six times") exacerbates social inequality by benefiting the advantaged inheritors, who enjoy and gain time, it has its strict conditions such as an expiry date, field-dependent, and city-based. While time inheritance generally benefits those with stronger familial temporal wealth, when it comes to political inheritance, the national and global levels of temporal classifications trump familial-level class differences. In other words, irrespective of one's class backgrounds, when it comes to political tensions and contestations, the political suspicion and exclusion may be similarly experienced.

As such, part 3 demonstrates how time inheritance does not work automatically to benefit or punish the heirs or recipients of temporal wealth or debt. Instead, various inheritors have to actively exercise their agency to ensure a smooth (or not) intergenerational transfer of privilege and power. On occasions where the inheritors are "unqualified" and do not fully exploit their inheritance, they can be in danger of "downclassing" and being declined access to the privileges that they family have accumulated over the past. Equally, for inheritors who are zealous and determined, their sheer hard work and inadvertent changes of fields can bring them opportunities for upward social mobility.

Agency aside, when in the face of political contestations and tensions, political time inheritance can go both ways, either benefiting the time inheritors in substantial ways, or subjecting them to indiscriminate political suspicion and alienation, regardless of their familial-level time inheritance. On such occasions, the national level and global level (e.g., colonial time inheritance) trump familial-level time inheritance.

There is also the occasion where national-level unequal time inheritance (e.g., city-tier inequalities as manifested though unequal rights granted by *hukou*) can play equally destructive roles as the global-level time inequality. This has been manifested in how discriminations exercised by China's first-tier cities on its internal migrants from lower-tiered cities are deemed as equivalent to those exercised by global-cities like New York and London.

As such, part 3 contributes significantly to substantiating and clarifying how time inheritance works across familial, national, and global levels in intricate and nuanced ways.

# Conclusion

## Moving Beyond Bourdieu:
## A Road Map for Global Time Inheritance Research

### Homage to Bourdieu

This book's time inheritance framework owes clear debt to Bourdieu's salient scholarship, especially his foundational conceptualizations of time, capital, and habitus. In fact, this book pays homage to Bourdieu and Passeron's (1979) seminal work *The Inheritors*, on which this book's title plays. In this concluding chapter, I argue that while rooted in Bourdieu's theoretical work, this book's time inheritance framework innovates in four main ways. Let's begin by revisiting his conceptualizations.

In his classic work *Forms of Capital*, Bourdieu (1986) theorizes *economic capital* as resources that manifest as money or are convertible into property rights, *social capital* as resources that are made up of social connections, and *cultural capital* as resources that can be in an *embodied* state as dispositions of the mind and body, in an *institutionalized* state as educational qualifications, and in an *objectified* state as valued cultural goods. These forms of capital are closely linked to the field in which they are evaluated. Regarding the dispositions that are shaped by familial upbringing and education, Bourdieu (2002) employs *habitus* to capture them.

Building on Bourdieu's foundational theorization about capital, especially his emphasis that capital is accumulated (labor) time, this book's time inheritance framework centers on the role of time across all three foundational types of capital.

Regarding time, in Bourdieu's "Social Being, Time and the Sense of Existence" (2000), he places great emphasis on how time is not external

145

to social agents but is made by social agents in *practice*. This conceptual emphasis aligns with Serafin's (2016) construct of "time in action," which foregrounds the *subjective* nature of this type of time as it is produced and experienced intimately by social agents, according to the extent to which their subjective expectations correspond to the objective probabilities of the field in which they are situated. Bourdieu (2000) advocates a departure from treating time as a pre-given construct that is external to the social agent. This is what Serafin (2016) defines as "time of action," which is understood as "objective" time, that reckons the time of events and structures social life.

In chapter 1, I illustrated how nation-states and global capitalist and neoliberal forces alike perform their "temporal classifications," which arbitrarily construct hierarchies of power, thus according differentiated time wealth to different groups of social actors (e.g., rural versus urban *hukou* status, native speakers of English versus nonnative English speakers). Crucially, these hierarchies resultant from temporal classifications by states and global (Western/colonial) forces can manifest in a diverse array of capital as conceptualized by Bourdieu (1986).

Take the rural–urban divide in China, for example. As discussed in chapter 1, the inheritance of *hukou* (either rural or urban) status entails unequal access to a wide range of resources. For instance, rural *hukou* holders are generally found to be offered education that is of an inferior quality than that available to urban *hukou* holders. For their children to access better quality education, rural parents often must travel a long distance and give up their livelihoods in the countryside to accompany their children to study in the county seats or in bigger cities (Wei, 2022; J. Wu, 2016; Xiang, 2007). In this process, these rural families must pay extra money (economic capital) and seek help from connections (social capital) who may know more about educational opportunities in county seats and cities (cultural capital). In this context, the urban *hukou* itself can be deemed a form of *institutionalized cultural capital*, which readily guarantees urban families rights and access to quality education. Without the urban *hukou*, rural families are compelled to invest substantially more (economic, social, and cultural) capital to achieve similar access to quality education.

Within this analysis, time is a constant force and common denominator across the various types of capital identified. It boils down to Bourdieu's (1986, p. 241) foundational theorization that "capital is accumulated labor" and that it takes time to accumulate any type of capital. As such, the inheritance of an urban *hukou* in China entails inheritance of a wealth of unearned (labor) time. In contrast, the inheritance of a rural *hukou* implies the inheritance of deprivation of time, of substantial extra time necessary to acquire and convert various forms of capital in order to achieve similar access to quality education. A focus on time analysis, therefore, is rooted in Bourdieu's conceptualization of capital but moves beyond it by accentuating the constant force and common denominator of time. This is the first important characteristic of the time inheritance framework in this book.

Second, regarding conceptualization of time, this time inheritance framework incorporates and works with Bourdieu's predominant focus on the "subjective" and "qualitative" nature of time as it is made and produced in practice. Importantly, this time inheritance framework moves beyond that by also incorporating the more "objective" and "quantitative" nature of time—that is, the "time of action" (Serafin, 2016) understanding of time—through examining how nation-states and global forces carry out various temporal classifications, as previously discussed here. Crucially, this time inheritance framework furnishes opportunities to investigate how such more "objective" temporal classifications shape the subjective reckoning of time within the social agents while also demonstrating how individual agency and time reckoning can achieve unexpected distinction across different levels of analysis (i.e., familial, national, and international). Throughout this book, I have demonstrated empirically how the various temporal classifications such as rural–urban divides and class differences have shaped the subjective time reckoning of "gained time" or "wasted time," of "time poverty" or "time wealth." I have also shown how a focus on the present for the "time poor" can inadvertently lead to a coveted "future orientation." As such, moving beyond Bourdieu's focus on subjective, internal aspects of time conceptualization injects an extra layer of explanatory power and analytic vigor to this time inheritance framework.

Third, in Bourdieu's conceptualizations, he assigns different conceptual scopes to (forms of) capital than to habitus. Different from forms of capital (as discussed above), *habitus* is a concept that captures the host of dispositions embodied by the social agent, as shaped by the external field; such dispositions can, according to Bourdieu (2002), generate an indefinite number of practices that are broadly adjusted to the objective probabilities of the field. In the time inheritance framework, the time-shaped nature of these dispositions is foregrounded. If you recall (see figure 1.1), the time inheritance framework encompasses "accumulated labor time and freed-up leisure time," which are directly related to forms of capital, but it also includes "time that feeds into their dispositions and mentality," which corresponds to Bourdieu's concept of habitus. In this sense, the time inheritance framework unites both Bourdieusian capital and habitus. This makes it possible to tease out, in depth, how the inheritance of time wealth shapes a mentality of "time entitlement" and a mode of living called "banked time," while the lack of it leads to a "debt-paying" mentality and a mode of living called "borrowed time," or "time on loan."

Taking the above three characteristics into consideration in regard to how the time inheritance framework is built on and moves beyond Bourdieu's conceptualizations of time, capital, and habitus, I would like to emphasize how Bourdieu's foundational theorizations allow this time inheritance framework to achieve, arguably, elegance in articulating the complex nature of the inheritance of time. Let me articulate this by quoting what I wrote in chapter 1:

> Bourdieu's temporalization and capital/time accumulation theses furnish significant insights regarding the inheritance of time. That is, inheritance of time is both quantitative and qualitative. The family's passing on of economic and social capital, which themselves required time to acquire by previous generations, can be considered the quantitative bequest of time. On the other hand, the family's handing down of cultural capital, which manifests, for example, in everyday conversations, can be considered "effortless" and "natural" passing on of time wealth. . . . More importantly, the family's substantial amount of time wealth (as in the forms of economic, social, and cultural capital) can cultivate a secure relation with time (Adam, 1990)—a sense of assuredness about the future, a trusted and safe understanding that there is something to fall back on, an understanding that the inheritors are deserving of the resources bestowed on them. As such, the security, assuredness, and sense of entitlement jointly constitute the qualitative aspect of time inheritance—or, in Bourdieusian terms, the facets of the inheritors' habitus that manifest time security, entitlement, and assuredness.

Lastly, a further critique of Bourdieu's aforementioned theorizations is that these concepts are most often rooted in and applied to "static and unified" fields (C. L. Xu, 2018a, p. 256) delineated by "geographically-implied national borderlines" (C. L. Xu, 2018b, p. 1129). When it comes to examining issues around inequalities of inherited time, therefore, Bourdieu's original conceptualizations do not appear to have sufficient explanatory power to capture the multilevel (i.e., familial, national, and international) alignment or collision of temporal differences. On this front, time inheritance's built-in theorization across three levels offers exciting conceptual and analytical power to tackle complex empirical phenomena; an important example that this book has not covered yet pertains to gendered time inheritance.

## Gendered Time Inheritance

Take the case of China as an example. In chapter 1, I argued that the CCP-led state's temporal classifications manifest in constructed hierarchies include rural versus urban, Han majority versus ethnic minorities, and across city tiers. I hasten to point out here that another notable hierarchy resulting from such state temporal classifications is the male–female divide.

In mainland China, in particular, male superiority has been deeply embedded in a patriarchal tradition guided by Confucianism. Compared with male domination, female subordination confines women to the roles of mother and wife and continues to perpetuate itself in today's society (Shen, 2015, pp. 37–42; Q. Wang, 2021), where traditional public/private (male/female) division of gender roles still persists (Martin, 2022; National Bureau of Statistics of China & All-China Women's Federation, 2011).

Admittedly, since the Chinese Communist revolution in 1949, women's liberation has been forcefully incorporated into the socialist agenda. Women were visibly encouraged to shoulder "half the sky," receive education, and work outside the family (C. Lin, 2001). However, such reforms were carried out under the assumption that women were supposed to catch up with men in workplaces, but women's caring responsibilities in the home sphere were unaltered. As a result, women entered society carrying double burdens on their backs (X. Li & John, 2005, pp. 1595–1596). After the mid-1990s, with redundancies becoming a national issue, women in China were pressed to return home. Indeed, in the reform-era job market, "occupational gender segregation and increased discrimination against women" have been widely documented (Kajanus, 2015b, p. 95; Q. Wang, 2021).

Due to these long-held biases against women and devaluation of females in rural regions, where familial and educational resources are limited, parents are found to display notable son preference (Murphy, 2020). This led to especially acute elimination of female fetuses and babies when the one-child policy was in full swing (Gerlach, 2020). In certain rural areas where the one-child policy was not strictly enforced or enforced with certain allowances, it was typical to find families with one or more elder sisters and a younger or youngest brother (Kipnis, 2011). In this book, Xun is a youngest brother to two elder sisters, while Su, Meng, Cang, and Xin are among the female participants who have younger siblings, with the youngest siblings always being male.

Considering the systemic discrimination against women and the lack of value assigned to women in the familial sphere, workplace, and marriage market in China (Hong Fincher, 2023; To, 2013; Woodhams et al., 2014; Zeng, 2014), it could be argued that women, especially those from deprived familial backgrounds, where resources are scarce, have inherited temporal debts across familial and national levels. This can be seen through the fact that some female babies may not even be given the opportunity to live (killed during pregnancy because of son preference and the limits of the one-child policy; Gerlach, 2020); they are effectively deprived of their biological time.

Importantly, women are typically considered less worthy of the resources of the family.[1] In this book, we hear the stories of Ku's elder sister, who had to quit her education at the primary level in order to work and support Ku's education from high school to postgraduate studies, and of Zhen's younger sister, who worked as a migrant worker in Shenzhen to support Zhen's higher education. The female rural-origin participants such as Su and Meng who did receive investment in their education often felt so indebted to their families and so undeserving of such investment that they were compelled to pay back their debts. It could be argued that these female participants may consider the education that their families invested in them as "time loans" rather than entitlement.

Curiously, education mobility, especially at the higher education stage, can enable these disadvantaged female time inheritors to be inserted into different temporal spheres, where the time rules are different and where they can gain unexpected distinction. Anni Kajanus's (2015a) research demonstrates how a female rural-origin student, Hannah (pseudonym), cultivated her new educational desires during her higher education mobility from the rural to the urban. Shanshan Lan's (2021) research shows how five female students from rural regions of China realized their overseas education ambitions through enrolling in language schools in South Korea after they had initial rural-to-urban higher education mobility. Fran Martin's (2018, 2022) research on urban middle-class female Chinese students who moved to study in Australia finds that they entered a "zone of suspension" where they were free from the impositions of rules back in China and could reconfigure their preferred life and work choices. In all these cases, the female participants, no matter their familial circumstances, faced similar devaluation of their worthiness and merits in education and work. They all needed "extra" time and the crucial opportunities of higher education mobility to access and gain time in which they could achieve greater degrees of freedom, education, and career recognition. These existing empirical findings, when examined through the lens of gendered time inheritance, can potentially yield fruitful insights into the underlying workings of inherited gendered inequalities manifested through time.

While this book has not had the space to fully expand on this gendered aspect of inherited time inequalities, I invite researchers in the fields of educational inequality, migration studies, China studies, and beyond to investigate in depth how gendered inherited-time disparity shapes the life trajectories of women and men across sectors and societies. The latest research by Harris et al. (2024) that uses UK panel data to examine women's progression time cost in UK higher education reveals that it typically takes women 15 years longer to achieve the rank of full professor than men. How are women "punished" so much by the job market? Further in-depth time inheritance research informed by the latest findings, such as those of Harris et al., can yield significant insights into the "black box" of how women become disadvantaged time inheritors in relation to men. Furthermore, it may be worthwhile to explore how state-engineered gender hierarchies intersect and interact with global-level gendered inequalities or parities and how these shape policies, which in turn affect the livelihoods and outlooks of both men and women.

## Intersectional Time Inheritance: A Research Road Map

The theorization of the time inheritance framework entails that it is inherently conducive to intersectional analyses of social inequalities (Crenshaw, 1995). As this book has amply demonstrated, time inheritance at certain levels (e.g., familial and national), when intersected with other levels' (e.g., global) conditions, can have unexpected results, either further exacerbating inequalities (e.g., see chapter 5) or enabling the "underdogs" to gain distinction (e.g., see chapter 9). When it comes to how time inheritance manifests at different levels, this book has drawn on hierarchies like class (working class, middle class, and upper middle class), the rural–urban divide, language (native English speakers or not), and ethnicity (Han majority versus ethnic minorities). These hierarchies are just some of the many possible ones that can inform an analysis focusing on inherited time inequalities. Gender is another important one that should warrant substantial research attention and exploration, as I have pointed out in the previous section. Caste and race are some other hierarchies that could benefit from analytical strengths lent by the time inheritance framework.

Take the caste system in India and slave trades in the UK as examples. In 2023, Priyamvada Gopal from Cambridge University tweeted the following in response to a former conservative member of Parliament, Antoinette Sandbach, who threatened to sue Cambridge University over slavery research conducted by a Cambridge historian who pointed out that Sandbach's ancestors were slave owners and that she and her family had benefited from the slave trades (Mohdin, 2023): "None of us have a right to 'privacy' from the histories we carry, including the histories of our subjugating ancestors. My own dominant caste ancestors have a lot of oppression & violence to account for. And I inherited positional and cultural advantages from them." While Gopal publicly acknowledged her own inheritance of privileges from her "dominant caste ancestors," Sandbach sought to hide her families' generations of benefits from the slave trades. In both cases, however, there is significant evidence to show how their inherited "positional and cultural advantages" had shaped their advantageous life trajectories, not least through Sandbach's notable political career or Gopal's transnational academic accolades decorated from India to Cambridge, UK.

The distinguished and dominant social positions that both Sandbach (e.g., class) and Gopal (e.g., caste) occupy are part of a pecking order of social positions (dominated versus dominant) that are in fact a "temporal order" too (Bourdieu & Passeron, 1979, p. 96). The evolutionist and teleological logic, mentioned in chapter 1, that helps keep the dominated in place by promising a false hope that so long as you wait long enough or do as you are told, you will arrive at the coveted position, conceals the fact that this will never happen unless through struggle. Informed by this false logic, some people end up waiting their whole lifetime or for generations, only to still be trapped in the same subjugated position. This is aptly captured in Bourdieu and Passeron's (1979, pp. 95–96) discussion of class differences:

> By an apparent paradox, the maintenance of order, i.e., of the whole set of gaps, differences, "differentials," ranks, precedences, priorities, exclusions, distinctions, ordinal properties, and thus of

the relations of order which give a social formation its structure, is provided by an unceasing change in substantial (i.e., non-relational) properties. This implies that the social order established at any given moment is also necessarily a *temporal order*, an "order of successions" as Leibniz put it, each group having as its past the group immediately below and for its future the group immediately above (one sees the attraction of evolutionist models). The competing groups are separated by differences which are essentially located in the order of *time*. (my emphases)

The inheritance of "positional and cultural advantages" by dominant caste members and former slave owners thus is essentially an inheritance of time wealth.

Such inherited time inequalities can be applied to examine unequal racial lived experiences in contemporary societies, too. In sociologist Rahsaan Mahadeo's (2019, p. 195) research on how America's racialized youth experience whiteness and time inequality, he writes, "With time being money, the intergenerational transmission of wealth was also understood as an intergenerational transmission of (available or free) time. Coming from mostly poor and working-class backgrounds, the lineage of most youth at Run-a-Way [a multiservice center for youth] meant that they were also temporally bankrupt. Temporal bankruptcy must be understood in relation to temporal privilege, which is ultimately linked to racial privilege." The "intergenerational transmission of wealth" here is understood by Mahadeo as "an intergenerational transmission of (available or free) time" based on the idea that "time is money." This empirical application points to two important aspects of the three forms of time inheritance (i.e., accumulated labor time and freed-up leisure time), as expounded in the "Time Privilege Continuum" in this book (see figure 1.1).

Specifically, this book proposes that advantaged time inheritors live on "banked time" through inheriting (1) accumulated *labor time* from their ancestors, which manifests in different forms of capital; (2) *freed-up leisure time*, which allows them to pursue preferred life causes and consume and appreciate life; and (3) *time that feeds into their disposition and mentality*, through which they develop this secure, safe, confident, entitled, and relaxed approach to life and its vagaries. In contrast, the disadvantaged time inheritors live on "borrowed time," which shapes their debt-paying mentality. Mahadeo's (2019) analysis of the racialized youth's "temporal bankruptcy" (p. 195) vividly demonstrates how time inheritance and its associated concepts as a framework can be usefully applied in the realm of research on racial inequalities, serving as a unifying conceptual resource for future empirical research.

Indeed, as I articulated in the summary of part 2, "inherited time inequalities thus are arguably one of the most fundamental social mechanisms to human inequalities across societies." It will take concerted efforts for future research to comprehensively and expansively track how various hierarchies of inequalities intersect to complicate time inheritance manifestations and shape the life trajectories of individuals across familial, national, and global levels. To this end, I have devised a "road map" in table C.1.

As is shown in table C.1, in this book, I have analyzed the intersectional manifestations of unequal time inheritance by focusing on class (familial level), *hukou* (i.e., rural versus urban household registration; national level), and language (i.e., native English speaker or not; international level) as well as institutional status (both national and international levels). For future research, the types and combinations of intersectional analyses that can be done, as informed by table C.1, can be vast and varied. For example, in the context of China, it may be worth investigating how unequal time inheritance is shaped by an intersection of class (e.g., middle-class versus working-class families), language, and ethnicity (e.g., Mandarin-speaking Han majority versus dialect-speaking ethnic minorities; for empirical examples, see C. L. Xu and M. Yang, 2019; M. Yang and C. L. Xu, 2020). Globally, it may be intriguing to investigate how inherited time wealth differs as class (e.g., working-class families' children) intersects with race (e.g., White or racialized minorities), language (e.g., native English speakers), and institutional status (e.g., globally dominant HEIs)—see Adam Poole's (2023) and Esther Kim's (2015) empirical accounts about how working-class White academics fare in a global academic market. Relatedly, it may be worth exploring how middle-class racialized academics who are native speakers of English and have globally dominant PhD degrees navigate racism across national borders (Bhopal, 2022; Bhopal et al., 2016), from a time inheritance angle.

The examples of "possible hierarchies" outlined in table C.1 are not exhaustive. They are meant as catalysts to inspire researchers (including myself) to continue to think with and through the time inheritance framework, especially in informing the formation of their research agendas. It could be argued that these examples may lend themselves more readily to thinking about conducting research on higher education and its labor market outcomes. Nevertheless, the applications of this time inheritance framework can be extended to numerous other areas, such as in unequal access to health care

Table C.1. Empirical Applications of Time Inheritance: Road Map

| Level | Possible Hierarchies |
|---|---|
| **Familial** | Class (upper middle class, middle class, working class/grassroots/low income) <br> OR <br> Gender (female, male) |
| **National** (state-sanctioned characteristics) | Hukou (urban, rural; i.e., household registration) <br> OR <br> Ethnicity (Han majority, ethnic minorities) <br> OR <br> Race (White, racial minorities) <br> OR <br> Migration status (rural-to-urban migrants, lower-tier-city to first-tier-city migrants, internally displaced citizens) <br> OR <br> Institutional status (nationally dominant HEIs, nationally dominated HEIs) <br> OR <br> Language (Mandarin/Putonghua, dialects) <br> OR <br> Gender (female, male) |
| **International** (globally established dominant characteristics) | Language (native English speakers, nonnative speakers of English) <br> OR <br> Citizenship (developed countries' citizens, developing countries' citizens) <br> OR <br> Migration status (international immigrants, refugees, asylum seekers, national citizens) <br> OR <br> Institutional status (globally dominant HEIs, globally dominated HEIs) <br> OR <br> Gender (female, male) |

(Jebril, 2021) and housing (Crawford & McKee, 2018; Palm & Carrasco, 2019; Zhang [张], H. 慧. J. 婧, 2016) and in gender inequalities (Harris et al., 2024; B. Li & Shen, 2022), to name just a few.

In the long run, a field of research called global time inheritance studies can uncover the nuances and hidden workings of inherited time inequalities but also discover and propose ways of challenging and breaking down such barriers in order to achieve a more socially just society at familial, national, and global levels.

# Policy Implications

Building on the empirical findings of this book, which focuses on inter-generational transfer of privilege or deprivation as manifested through time in China's higher education mobility, I outline below two aspects of policy implications.

## IMPLICATION 1

Affirmative actions and practices have informed policies in different parts of the world to mitigate historical injustices done to marginalized groups such as the working class, women, and racial and ethnic minorities (Boliver et al., 2021; Fischer & Massey, 2007; Sautman, 1998; T. Wang, 2007; Yamada, 2015). This book proposes that in such affirmative action policies it is pivotal to also incorporate an attention to inherited time inequalities so as to more thoroughly right some of the wrongs done to these disadvantaged time inheritors.

For instance, the time inequalities generated by state-engineered hierarchies, such as China's *hukou* (household registration) divide between the rural and the urban, are far and wide. Such time inequalities manifest not only in the large gap in inherited labor time (or labor-time debt) and the substantially different "freed-up leisure time" versus extra labor time demanded but also in the differentiated time-shaped dispositions, which result in a sense of entitlement and of being at ease in contrast to a debt-paying mentality among the differentiated time inheritors. One aspect of policy implication could thus be the removal or reduction of such state-manufactured hierarchies. Indeed, the Chinese state has instituted successive reforms to the *hukou* system; however, their effectiveness in reducing inequalities between the urban and the rural can be complicated by conflicts between migrants and "locals" who perceive unfairness (P. Lin et al., 2024).

Based on the findings of this book, I suggest that there are ways to tackle the time inequalities brought about by the *hukou* division. For example, currently, it is commonplace for Chinese research-funding bodies and higher education institutions to impose age limits on applicants (e.g., 35 years old and 40 years old are the common age thresholds; Horta & Li, 2024). Considering the disadvantageous time inheritance of rural-origin individuals, policy changes could be instituted to allow rural-origin individuals (i.e., those who had a rural *hukou* before entering university) a higher age threshold. Similarly, considering that individuals from rural and low-income urban families may not have the information and networks to inform them to make time-wise and time-sensitive decisions at critical higher education and career junctures, time allowance can be made for them in terms of their workload and in evaluation of job applications and promotion applications (C. L. Xu, 2020; C. L. Xu & Y. Ma, 2023).

At the global level, international HEIs can make temporal allowance for students who are from the Global South and whose native tongue is not English. For example, such allowance can be made through extending assignment deadlines and exam time, so as to mitigate their inherited temporal debts. Peer-reviewed journals can make temporal allowances to give authors whose first language is not English extra time to revise their manuscripts or actively reduce the "wait time" of article handling and peer reviewing (Amano et al., 2023) for authors from backgrounds that are prone to disadvantageous time inheritance. Due attention can also be paid to an ethics of care (Madge et al., 2009) for ensuring that mobile students are supported to mitigate their political time debts (e.g., see chapter 11)—this can be done by alerting student-facing practitioners to the political aspects of time inequalities and creating an environment where mental health or peer support (H. Chen et al., 2020), for example, can be sourced.

Both in education (schools and universities) and in the workplace, time-inheritance-sensitive awareness raising and training can be incorporated as part of the curricula or workplace mandatory training programs. These can build on existing work on equality, diversity, and inclusion practices (Bhopal, 2018, 2020) and decolonization efforts (Doharty et al., 2021) with a specific focus on the time privilege and deprivations among individuals of diverse backgrounds.

IMPLICATION 2

Considering that education mobility played such a pivotal role in enabling disadvantaged time heirs at certain levels (e.g., familial or national) to remove themselves and temporarily (or semipermanently) place themselves in another temporal sphere or level where they stood a higher chance of gaining some "fast-tracked" time inheritance, it is pivotal for education institutions (especially those at the higher education stage) to be encouraging and enabling their new recruits in a time-inheritance-sensitive way. For example, as noted in chapter 9, some elite Chinese universities have begun to remove English-language tests from their compulsory education components, and schools are planning to eliminate English language as one of the three core subjects (i.e., Chinese, math, and English; Gan, 2023). Considering that English is akin to a temporal wealth accelerator for rural-origin and urban working-class students to achieve upward mobility, depriving them of the opportunity to learn and excel in English is effectively denying these disadvantaged time inheritors the possibility to accelerate their global-level time inheritance. Educators, policymakers, and institutions alike, when equipped with such empirical findings on time inheritance, can therefore do more to prevent such practices.

For HEIs in the Global North, in their efforts to recruit students from a greater diversity of backgrounds (Jiang, 2021; J. Lee & Waters, 2024; T. Liu et al., 2023), it is important to recognize and compensate for the disadvantaged time inheritance of students from the Global South, such as by providing extra academic advice and labor market guidance, in order to mitigate the inherited time debts of these students by showing them different temporal possibilities (C. L. Xu, 2021b). A practical example would be to connect these students from the Global South (especially those from rural-origin and working-class backgrounds) with alumni networks and facilitate meaningful and instrumental sharing of academic and labor market information and training.

Admittedly, the above are easier said than done, considering the fact that on a global scale, HEIs in the Global North continue to treat students from the Global South as significant financial sources (e.g., the derogatory term "cash cows" is often used to refer to these students studying in Western HEIs) and thus are unlikely to welcome too many students from the Global South who are also from rural-origin and working-class backgrounds (Mulvey, 2020; C. L. Xu, 2020, 2021a). However, there are indeed existing flagship scholarship programs such as the Chevening, Commonwealth, and Fulbright Scholarships and numerous institutional-level scholarships that can, in the future, incorporate a time-inheritance-sensitive approach when setting selection criteria for their future scholarship recipients.

On a structural level, however, education mobility should not be the reserve of a small percentage of elite students (either academically or financially) but rather should be made much more accessible to those from the most disadvantageous time inheritance backgrounds. This will require institutional and governmental efforts at national and institutional levels, which are beyond the scope of this book but should be explored in depth in future research.

## Key Contributions

To summarize, the preceding chapters demonstrate how the concept of "time inheritance" opens a previously unavailable avenue for understanding inequalities across social agents of "vertically" differentiated origins in our society. *The Time Inheritors* makes three signal contributions to contemporary scholarship in sociology of time, sociology of education, and China studies. First, departing from existing literature's predominant focus on the middle-class youth or socially advantaged transnational migrants, *The Time Inheritors* juxtaposes individuals of diverse social origins (from the rural and deprived to the urban working class and urban upper middle class) to demonstrate the vertical social differences and inequalities embodied by their differentiated education-migratory moves, such as from rural to urban, between mainland China and Hong Kong, and transnational moves. Its rich empirical contrasts vividly showcase the usefulness of the concept of time inheritance and its associated concepts of borrowed time, banked time, freed-up time, and labor-time wealth/debt in unpacking such vertical and contrasting social differences and inequalities.

Second, rather than treating time and temporality as somewhat mechanic sequences, tempo, and synchronicity or as quantitative accumulation in a life course in existing literature, *The Time Inheritors* advances a conceptual framework where intergenerational temporal inequalities manifest through different forms and play out at familial, national, and global levels. As such, *The Time Inheritors* extends our conceptualization of time and analysis of social inequalities in both breadth (not just in the individual-versus-institution struggle but encompassed by multilevel temporal inequalities) and depth (unequal access to time as embedded in our dispositions and informing our decision making).

Third, empirically speaking, this book furnishes a deep dive into how the scene of education mobility in China is highly varied and deeply unequal. The social agents of diverse social and political backgrounds have inherited substantially different temporal privileges, not only from their families' own accumulation but also from state-level sanctions, as typified through *hukou* (rural versus urban and first-tier cities versus lower-tier cities). When such familial- and national-level time inequalities encounter the global-level ones, however, individual agency can play important roles for the determined and diligent "underdogs" to achieve upward social mobility but can also endanger the "unqualified inheritors" to the verge of "downclassing." Beyond the case of education mobility in China, I argue that the concept of time inheritance can enable researchers to discover a bold new vista for thinking about forms of inequality through the lens of time. This thus potentially furnishes a field of global time inheritance studies that transcends the disciplines of sociology of education, migration, and China studies.

# Appendix

## Participant Profiles

# Data Set 1

|  | Pseudonym | Gender | Subject of study | Place of origin |
|---|---|---|---|---|
| 1 | Lingshan | F | Social science | Shandong |
| 2 | Kang | M | Business | Guangdong |
| 3 | Xiang | F | Business | Guangxi |
| 4 | Yu | M | Actuarial science | Hebei |
| 5 | Yingying | F | Finance | Shanghai |
| 6 | Nianci | F | Humanities | Beijing |
| 7 | Ruhua | F | Statistics | Shandong |
| 8 | Mingyan | M | Engineering | Jilin |
| 9 | Zijuan | F | Computer science | Guangdong |
| 10 | Yuhan | M | Business | Hubei |
| 11 | Xifeng | F | Business | Guangdong |
| 12 | Miaoyu | F | Education | Jilin |
| 13 | Keqin | F | Law | Guangdong |
| 14 | Qingwen | F | Actuarial science | Shanghai |
| 15 | Zhu | F | Engineering | Jiangxi |
| 16 | Longnv | F | Actuarial science | Shanghai |
| 17 | Fei | M | Psychology | Shanghai |

| | Pseudonym | Gender | Subject of study | Place of origin |
|---|---|---|---|---|
| 18 | Xiangyun | F | Social science | Heilongjiang |
| 19 | Xiren | F | Finance | Shenzhen, Guangdong |
| 20 | Guoxiang | F | Humanities | Inner Mongolia |
| 21 | Liwan | F | Actuarial science | Zhejiang |
| 22 | Wen | F | Actuarial science | Shenzhen |
| 23 | Zilong | M | Actuarial science | Jiangsu |
| 24 | Xue | F | Actuarial science | Heilongjiang |
| 25 | Guojing | M | Civil engineering | Guangdong |
| 26 | Ruping | F | Statistics | Shandong |
| 27 | Tong | F | Finance | Zhejiang |
| 28 | Bei | F | Law | Shanxi |
| 29 | Liang | M | Civil engineering | Jilin |
| 30 | Tai | M | Law | Shanghai |
| 31 | Miusi | F | Sociology | Shaanxi |

All participants were born in the 1990s.

| | Pseudonym | Father's profession | Mother's profession | Family monthly income in 2013 (in RMB) |
|---|---|---|---|---|
| 1 | Lingshan | Business owner | Accountant | 10,001 – 30,000 |
| 2 | Kang | Business manager | Business owner | 10,001 – 30,000 |
| 3 | Xiang | Doctor | Nurse | 5,001 – 10,000 |
| 4 | Yu | Professor | Professor | 10,001 – 30,000 |
| 5 | Yingying | Doctor | Teacher | 10,001 – 30,000 |
| 6 | Nianci | Researcher | Doctor | 30,001 or above |
| 7 | Ruhua | Business owner | Homemaker | 10,001 – 30,000 |
| 8 | Mingyan | Doctor | Doctor | 10,001 – 30,000 |
| 9 | Zijuan | Company manager | Kindergarten teacher | 10,001 – 30,000 |
| 10 | Yuhan | Doctor | Teacher | 10,001 – 30,000 |
| 11 | Xifeng | Worker | Worker | 5,001 – 10,000 |
| 12 | Miaoyu | Business owner | Accountant | 5,001 – 10,000 |
| 13 | Keqin | Registered accountant | Accountant | 10,001 – 30,000 |
| 14 | Qingwen | Civil servant | Civil servant | 10,001 – 30,000 |
| 15 | Zhu | Engineer | Homemaker | 10,001 – 30,000 |
| 16 | Longnv | Employee in a company | Freelancer | 5,001 – 10,000 |
| 17 | Fei | Secondary school teacher | Retiree of realty company | 5,001 – 10,000 |
| 18 | Xiangyun | Business owner | Civil servant | 10,001 – 30,000 |
| 19 | Xiren | Business owner | Homemaker | 5,001 – 10,000 |

| | Pseudonym | Father's profession | Mother's profession | Family monthly income in 2013 (in RMB) |
|---|---|---|---|---|
| 20 | Guoxiang | Business owner | Civil servant | 5,001 – 10,000 |
| 21 | Liwan | Civil servant | Primary school teacher | 5,001 – 10,000 |
| 22 | Wen | Doctor | Business owner | 30,001 or above |
| 23 | Zilong | Civil servant | Teacher | 10,001 – 30,000 |
| 24 | Xue | Teacher | Medical doctor | 30,001 or above |
| 25 | Guojing | Civil servant | Civil engineer | 10,001 – 30,000 |
| 26 | Ruping | Accountant | Statistician | 10,001 – 30,000 |
| 27 | Tong | Human resources consultant | Economist | 30,001 or above |
| 28 | Bei | Lawyer | Lawyer | 10,001 – 30,000 |
| 29 | Liang | Accountant | Civil engineer | 10,001 – 30,000 |
| 30 | Tai | Lawyer | Civil servant | 10,001 – 30,000 |
| 31 | Miusi | Civil servant | Civil servant | 10,001 – 30,000 |

Focus Group Participants Who Were From Hong Kong: Table 1 of 2

|  | Pseudonym | Gender | Subject of study | Father's profession | Mother's profession |
|---|---|---|---|---|---|
| 1 | Fiona | F | Business | Retired | Property officer |
| 2 | Stephanie | F | Engineering | Chef | Homemaker |
| 3 | Christy | F | Education | Worker | Homemaker |
| 4 | John | M | Science | Clerk | Clerk |
| 5 | Helena | F | Accounting | Insurance agent | Insurance agent |
| 6 | Chris | M | Finance | Bank officer | Police officer |
| 7 | Greg | M | Finance | Taxi driver | Security guard |
| 8 | Linda | F | Medicine | Medical doctor | Medical doctor |
| 9 | Kingsan | F | Science | Temporary job | Unemployed |
| 10 | Ingrid | F | Law | Security guard | Homemaker |
| 11 | Emilia | F | Nursing | Mechanical worker | Homemaker |
| 12 | Donald | M | Science | Businessman | Homemaker |

All participants were born in the 1990s.

| | Pseudonym | Father's education | Mother's education | Monthly household income in 2013/14 (in HKD) |
|---|---|---|---|---|
| 1 | Fiona | Secondary school | Secondary school | 15,001 ~ 40,000 |
| 2 | Stephanie | Primary school | Primary school | 15,001 ~ 40,000 |
| 3 | Christy | Primary school | Secondary school | 15,001 ~ 40,000 |
| 4 | John | Secondary school | Secondary school | 15,001 ~ 40,000 |
| 5 | Helena | Secondary school | University | 15,001 ~ 40,000 |
| 6 | Chris | Secondary school | Secondary school | 15,001 ~ 40,000 |
| 7 | Greg | Primary school | Primary school | 5,001 ~ 15,000 |
| 8 | Linda | University | University | Above 100,001 |
| 9 | Kingsan | Secondary school | Primary school | 5,001 ~ 15,000 |
| 10 | Ingrid | Primary school | Primary school | 5,001 ~ 15,000 |
| 11 | Emilia | Secondary school | Secondary school | 5,001 ~ 15,000 |
| 12 | Donald | Master's degree | Secondary school | 40,001 ~ 100,000 |

Data Set 2

Hong Kong Students in Mainland China: Table 1 of 2

| | Pseudonym | Gender | Subject of study | Family household income per month in 2016 (in HKD) |
|---|---|---|---|---|
| 1 | Norman | M | Law | 25,000 |
| 2 | Catherine | F | Law | Self-reported as from a low-income family |
| 3 | Frances | F | Law | Self-characterized as from a grassroots family |
| 4 | Christine | F | Law | 8,000 – 10,000 |
| 5 | Lawrence | M | Education | 20,000 |
| 6 | Vincent | M | Education | Self-characterized as "absolutely grassroots" |
| 7 | Apple | F | Education | 30,000 |
| 8 | Vivienne | F | Philosophy | 10,000 – 20,000 |
| 9 | Stephanie | F | Education | Above 15,000 |
| 10 | Jenny | F | Psychology | Up to 20,000 |
| 11 | Rihanna | F | History | 10,000 – 15,000 |
| 12 | Clive | M | Traditional Chinese medicine | 20,000 |
| 13 | Shane | M | Material chemistry | Self-characterized as below middle class but above grassroots |
| 14 | Honesty | F | Law | Self-characterized as from a grassroots family |
| 15 | Stuart | M | International relations | Self-characterized as barely middle class |

|    | Pseudonym | Gender | Subject of study | Family household income per month in 2016 (in HKD) |
|----|-----------|--------|------------------|---------------------------------------------------|
| 16 | Prudence | F | Investment management | 80,000 – 125,000 |
| 17 | Emily | F | Media studies | Self-characterized as middle class |
| 18 | Matra | F | Journalism and communication | 35,000 – 40,000 |
| 19 | Nancy | F | Finance | Above 33,000 (self-characterized as middle class) |
| 20 | Simon | M | History | Above 30,000 |
| 21 | Laura | F | Journalism | 33,000 – 66,000 |
| 22 | Sandra | F | International economics and trade | Self-characterized as middle class |
| 23 | Charles | M | A European language (preferred to not disclose the exact language) | Self-characterized as middle class |

All participants were born in the 1990s.

|  | Pseudonym | Father's occupation | Mother's occupation | Father's education level | Mother's education level |
|---|---|---|---|---|---|
| 1 | Norman | Retired engineer | Homemaker | Secondary school | Junior secondary school |
| 2 | Catherine | Retired engineer | Homemaker | Secondary school | Secondary school |
| 3 | Frances | Restaurant owner | Restaurant helper | Secondary school | Secondary school |
| 4 | Christine | Self-employed | Part-timer | Bachelor's degree through distance learning | Secondary school |
| 5 | Lawrence | Restaurant chef | Cleaner | Primary school | Junior secondary school |
| 6 | Vincent | Salesperson | Salesperson | Primary school | Junior secondary school |
| 7 | Apple | Did not disclose | Did not disclose | Vocational school | Primary school |
| 8 | Vivienne | Passed away | Security guard | Primary school | Primary school |
| 9 | Stephanie | Owner of a barbershop | Owner of a barbershop | Secondary school | Primary school |
| 10 | Jenny | Unemployed | Restaurant waitress | Junior secondary school | Junior secondary school |
| 11 | Rihanna | Retired | Petrol station worker | Secondary school | Primary school |
| 12 | Clive | Retired | Handy jobs | Primary school | Primary school |
| 13 | Shane | Electronic engineer | Accountant clerk | Secondary school | Junior secondary school |
| 14 | Honesty | Workshop owner | Homemaker | Secondary school | Secondary school |
| 15 | Stuart | Retired (former self-employed builder) | Retired (former secretary) | Secondary school | Secondary school |
| 16 | Prudence | Restaurant manager | International school teacher | Bachelor's degree | Bachelor's degree |
| 17 | Emily | Property management | Banking | Bachelor's degree | Bachelor's degree |

|  | Pseudonym | Father's occupation | Mother's occupation | Father's education level | Mother's education level |
|---|---|---|---|---|---|
| 18 | Matra | Manager in a company | Owner of a beauty salon | Junior secondary school | Secondary school |
| 19 | Nancy | Businessman | Homemaker | Vocational college | Bachelor's degree |
| 20 | Simon | Businessman | Homemaker | Vocational school | Vocational college |
| 21 | Laura | Marketing manager | Homemaker | Secondary school | Secondary school |
| 22 | Sandra | Banking | Banking | Subdegree | Subdegree |
| 23 | Charles | Businessman | Civil servant | Secondary school | Vocational college |

Data Set 3

Rural-Origin Participants: Table 1 of 3

| | Pseudonym | Gender | Born in ... | Place of origin | Position in 2018 | Academic discipline |
|---|---|---|---|---|---|---|
| 1 | Jiao | M | 1970s | Zhejiang | Associate professor in the West | Social science |
| 2 | Tan | M | 1990s | Jiangxi | Lecturer in the West | Social science |
| 3 | Ping | M | 1980s | Shandong | Assistant professor in a top university in a tier-one city | Engineering |
| 4 | Qin | F | 1970s | Hubei | Associate professor | Social science |
| 5 | Pu | M | 1970s | Hubei | Lecturer | Physics |
| 6 | Dan | F | 1980s | Guangdong | Lecturer | Humanities |
| 7 | Tian | F | 1980s | Shandong | Lecturer | Social science |
| 8 | Kai | F | 1980s | Sichuan | PhD candidate in Greater China area | Social science |
| 9 | Lian | M | 1980s | Guangdong | Lecturer | Social science |
| 10 | Shuan | M | 1970s | Shandong | Associate professor | Social science |
| 11 | Mang | M | 1980s | Shandong | Assistant professor | Social science |
| 12 | Xin | F | 1960s | Shanxi | Professor | Social science |
| 13 | Ming | M | 1980s | Shandong | Lecturer in a tier-one city | Social science |
| 14 | Su | F | 1970s | Hubei | Associate professor | Social science |
| 15 | Cang | F | 1980s | Jiangxi | Lecturer | Social science |

| | Pseudonym | Gender | Born in . . . | Place of origin | Position in 2018 | Academic discipline |
|---|---|---|---|---|---|---|
| 16 | Xiaozi | F | 1970s | Henan | Associate researcher | Social science |
| 17 | Xun | M | 1980s | Hunan | University English lecturer | Social science |
| 18 | Chen | M | 1980s | Shandong | Associate professor | Social science |
| 19 | Fen | M | 1960s | Shandong | Professor | Social science |
| 20 | Ku | M | 1980s | Hubei | Assistant professor | Social science |
| 21 | Zhi | F | 1970s | Shandong | Associate professor | Social science |
| 22 | Zhen | M | 1980s | Jiangxi | Lecturer | Social science |
| 23 | Meng | F | 1980s | Hebei | HEI administrator | Administration |
| 24 | Chunpu | F | 1970s | Zhejiang | Associate professor in a tier-one city, China | Social science |
| 25 | Bian | M | 1960s | Anhui | Professor in Greater China area | Humanities |
| 26 | Jingpi | M | 1960s | Fujian | Chief physician; PhD supervisor | Medicine |

| | Pseudonym | Father's occupation / education level | Mother's occupation / education level |
|---|---|---|---|
| 1 | Jiao | Peasant / junior primary school | Peasant / illiterate |
| 2 | Tan | Worker at a company / vocational college | Shop owner / senior high school |
| 3 | Ping | Peasant and laborer / senior high school | Peasant / illiterate |
| 4 | Qin | Manager / senior high school | Junior primary school |
| 5 | Pu | Peasant / junior high school | Peasant / some homeschooling |
| 6 | Dan | Chinese medicine doctor / junior high school | Peasant / no formal education but could recognize some characters |
| 7 | Tian | Peasant and former army member / junior high school | Peasant / senior high school |
| 8 | Kai | Peasant / junior high school | Peasant / senior high school |
| 9 | Lian | Peasant / junior high school | Peasant / junior high school |
| 10 | Shuan | Peasant / primary school | Peasant / primary school |
| 11 | Mang | Primary teacher and accountant / vocational college | Peasant / a few years of primary school |
| 12 | Xin | Peasant / junior primary school | Peasant / illiterate |
| 13 | Ming | Peasant and laborer / junior high school | Peasant and laborer / junior high school |
| 14 | Su | Peasant and village chief / primary school | Peasant and laborer / junior primary school |
| 15 | Cang | Peasant / senior high school | Peasant / junior high school |
| 16 | Xiaozi | Worker at state-owned enterprise / primary school | Peasant / primary school |
| 17 | Xun | Peasant / primary school | Peasant / illiterate |
| 18 | Chen | Peasant / senior high school | Peasant / junior high school |

| | Pseudonym | Father's occupation / education level | Mother's occupation / education level |
|---|---|---|---|
| 19 | Fen | Peasant / junior primary school | Peasant / illiterate |
| 20 | Ku | Peasant / junior high school | Passed away |
| 21 | Zhi | Peasant / junior high school | Peasant / illiterate |
| 22 | Zhen | Peasant / primary school | Peasant / primary school |
| 23 | Meng | Peasant and small business owner / senior high school | Primary school teacher and peasant / college |
| 24 | Chunpu | Peasant / primary school | Peasant / junior primary school |
| 25 | Bian | Peasant / illiterate | Peasant / illiterate |
| 26 | Jingpi | Peasant / only one month's schooling | Peasant / illiterate |

| | Pseudonym | Obtained doctorate from . . . | Obtained master's degree from . . . | University tier |
|---|---|---|---|---|
| 1 | Jiao | Greater China area | Europe | Second/lower tier |
| 2 | Tan | Europe | Europe | Second/lower tier |
| 3 | Ping | China | China | Second/lower tier |
| 4 | Qin | Greater China area | China | Second/lower tier |
| 5 | Pu | China | China | Second/lower tier |
| 6 | Dan | China | China | Second/lower tier |
| 7 | Tian | Greater China area | China | Second/lower tier |
| 8 | Kai | Greater China area | China | First tier |
| 9 | Lian | Greater China area | China | First tier |
| 10 | Shuan | China | China | Second/lower tier |
| 11 | Mang | China | China | Second/lower tier |
| 12 | Xin | China | China | First tier |
| 13 | Ming | Europe | China | Second/lower tier |
| 14 | Su | Europe | China | Second/lower tier |
| 15 | Cang | Greater China area | China | First tier |
| 16 | Xiaozi | China | China | Second/lower tier |
| 17 | Xun | China | China | Second/lower tier |
| 18 | Chen | Australasia | China | Second/lower tier |

| | Pseudonym | Obtained doctorate from . . . | Obtained master's degree from . . . | University tier |
|----|-----------|-------------------------------|-------------------------------------|-----------------|
| 19 | Fen | China | China | Second/lower tier |
| 20 | Ku | Greater China area | China | Second/lower tier |
| 21 | Zhi | China | China | Second/lower tier |
| 22 | Zhen | Greater China area | China | Second/lower tier |
| 23 | Meng | China | China | Second/lower tier |
| 24 | Chunpu | China | China | First tier |
| 25 | Bian | North America | China | Second/lower tier |
| 26 | Jingpi | China | China | Second/lower tier |

Data Set 4

URBAN STUDENTS WHO STUDIED IN THE UK: TABLE 1 OF 2

| | Pseudonym | Gender | City of origin | Cities of residence for education and career | City of residence in 2022 |
|---|---|---|---|---|---|
| 1 | Xiao | F | Kunming, Yunnan | Beijing – Paris – Oxford – Washington, DC | Washington, DC |
| 2 | Mengxi | F | Chongqing | Chongqing – Swansea – Chongqing | Chongqing |
| 3 | Bing | F | Chengdu, Sichuan | Chengdu – Oxford – Bath – Chengdu | Chengdu |
| 4 | Jing | F | Mianyang, Sichuan | Xiamen – Southampton – Xiamen – Chengdu – Sydney | Sydney |
| 5 | Man | F | Beijing | Beijing – London | London |
| 6 | Chang | F | Chengdu, Sichuan | Chengdu – Durham, UK – London – city in Switzerland | Switzerland |
| 7 | Yi | F | Beijing | Tianjin – Sydney + UCLA exchange – Oxford master's | Beijing |
| 8 | Ting | F | Fuzhou, Fujian | Beijing – Bath | Fuzhou |
| 9 | Nong | F | Nanning, Guangxi | London – Keele – London | Beijing |
| 10 | Wang | F | Chongqing | Chongqing – Swansea – Chongqing | Chongqing |
| 11 | Chuan | F | Jingdezhen, Jiangxi | Singapore – Manchester – London | London? |
| 12 | Ji | M | Jinzhou, Liaoning | Beijing – Manchester – London | London |
| 13 | Dao | M | Spain, Shanghai | Shanghai – Manchester – London | London |
| 14 | Dong | M | Taiyuan, Shanxi | Loughborough – Coventry | Coventry |

| | Pseudonym | Gender | City of origin | Cities of residence for education and career | City of residence in 2022 |
|---|---|---|---|---|---|
| 15 | Pan | F | Qingdao, Shandong | Suzhou – Loughborough – Glasgow – Shenzhen | Shenzhen |
| 16 | Tong | F | Shanxi-Shanghai | Shanghai – Manchester | Unknown |
| 17 | Qie | M | Shenzhen | Shenzhen – Preston, UK – Cambridge – London | London |
| 18 | Shi | M | Shenzhen | Shenzhen – London – Oxford | Hong Kong |
| 19 | Huan | F | Beijing | Beijing – Sheffield – Manchester | Manchester |
| 20 | Xian | F | Tianjin | Tianjin – Sydney – Cambridge – A village in Hunan – Beijing – Oxford | Oxford |
| 21 | Li | M | Guangzhou | Guangzhou – Oxford – London | London |

All participants were born in the 1990s.

| | Pseudonym | Father's profession | Mother's profession |
|---|---|---|---|
| 1 | Xiao | Business owner | Civil servant |
| 2 | Mengxi | Civil servant | Homemaker |
| 3 | Bing | Business owner | Business owner |
| 4 | Jing | Business owner | Business owner |
| 5 | Man | Business owner | Business owner |
| 6 | Chang | Business owner | Business owner |
| 7 | Yi | Business owner | Business owner (PhD degree holder) |
| 8 | Ting | State-owned enterprise manager | Banker |
| 9 | Nong | Business owner | Business owner |
| 10 | Wang | University professor | University professor |
| 11 | Chuan | Civil servant | Civil servant |
| 12 | Ji | State-owned enterprise manager | Accountant |
| 13 | Dao | Business owner | Business owner |
| 14 | Dong | Journalist | Nurse |
| 15 | Pan | Wage earner | Wage earner |
| 16 | Tong | Finance manager | Finance manager |
| 18 | Qie | Medical doctor | Medical doctor |
| 20 | Shi | Finance manager | Finance manager |

|  | Pseudonym | Father's profession | Mother's profession |
|---|---|---|---|
| 21 | Huan | Military official | Military official |
| 22 | Xian | Civil servant | Civil servant |
| 23 | Li | Finance manager | Finance manager |

# Notes

## Introduction

1. TOEFL is the short form for the Test of English as a Foreign Language, a standardized test to measure the English-language ability of nonnative speakers wishing to enroll in English-speaking universities. TOEFL scores are commonly used by US-based higher education institutions as admission conditions. GRE is the short form for the Graduate Record Examinations, standardized tests that are an admissions requirement for many graduate schools in the United States, Canada, and a few other countries. The GRE is owned and administered by Educational Testing Service.

2. This refers to mainland China, as paralleled to the Greater China areas such as Hong Kong and Macau, which had different historical, political, and economic development trajectories (Breitung, 2009; M. K. Chan, 2003).

3. These include professionals and managers, routine nonmanual workers, small-business owners, supervising and skilled manual workers, semiskilled and unskilled workers, and farmers.

4. These include state administrators; managers, private-enterprise owners; professionals; routine nonmanual workers; self-employed workers; service workers; manufacturing workers; farmers; and the jobless, unemployed, and semiemployed.

5. These ten social strata include peasants, rural cadres, collective workers, collective cadres, state workers and state cadres (these six mapped the pre-reform-era class division), plus managers and experts, unskilled laborers (the proletariat), capitalists, and petty bourgeoisie (under capitalism).

## Chapter 1

1. According to X. Wu (2019, p. 366), "some limited channels are available for those of rural origin to obtain urban status, such as receiving vocational/higher education or joining the party or military service (Zhang 2015). Access to these

resources, however, is constrained by family background, including *hukou* origin (Wu & Treiman 2004)."

2. As I will show in the rest of this chapter and this book, such temporal classifications are arguably the result of legislations and policymaking (e.g., the suite of policies that prioritize urban areas and distribute greater resources to higher tier cities) as well as social and political reifications that encompass stigmatization and relegation of marginalized populations such as those of rural origin, ethnic minority, and female gender (Cai, 2011; Howlett, 2021; Kipnis, 2011; Q. Wang, 2021; J. Wu, 2016).

# Chapter 2

1. Refer to the "Class in China" section in the introduction for a detailed discussion of how class is understood, defined, and operated in this book.

2. With the exception of Tan and Jiao in the rural-origin group and Norman in the working-class group (see the list of participant profiles in the appendix).

3. The literal translation of *enren* (恩人) is the person who bestows favors on me, and *guiren* (贵人) is the person who is precious in bringing good fortune and/or luck to me.

4. With the exception of Ruhua, Man, Guojing, Guoxiang, and Lingshan (see the list of participant profiles in the appendix).

# Chapter 3

1. *Guanxi* 关系 is a Chinese idiom that refers to social networks and relations characterized by an interpersonal nature, which is distinguished from those defined by legal institutions. Research has shown that *guanxi* is often manifested through such relations as family, kinship, colleagues, and neighbors and plays significant roles in contemporary China. See Xie and Postiglione (2016, p. 1016) for a more detailed discussion.

2. The HKDSE is Hong Kong's university entrance examination and is roughly the equivalent of Gaokao (i.e., the National College Entrance Examination) in mainland China and A-levels in the UK.

3. The Chinese government has categorized the country's HEIs into four tiers based on their selectivity. This tier system is closely linked with government funding allocations, with the most selective first-tier universities receiving the disproportionate share of government-allocated resources (R. Yang & M. Xie, 2015). Generally, 'the most selective public 4-year universities and programs comprise the first tier, less selective public 4-year universities and programs comprise the second

tier, still less selective 4-year private universities comprise the third tier and 3-year vocational institutions comprise the fourth tier. Each year provincial governments usually set official tier eligibility cutoff scores based on the overall results on an annual college entrance exam so that only higher scoring students are eligible to attend higher tier institutions" (Loyalka et al., 2012, p. 287).

4. There are different and contested ways to categorize UK universities—for instance, by institutional age (e.g., Ancient and post-92), group membership (e.g., Russell Group), or area (e.g., Scottish Ancient). Here, I adopt the most commonly known labels (Blyth & Cleminson, 2016).

5. This refers to the temporal wealth (i.e., inherited time privilege) of the Western HEIs in which they could afford to enroll. Refer to the corresponding "Global Temporal Classification" section in chapter 1 for more discussion.

# Chapter 4

1. In more recent years, China has started to encourage the setting up of branch campuses of HEIs and low-tier HEIs in certain county seats, but these branch campuses and HEIs are mostly privately funded or collaborated with the university sector and are considered to be of the least prestige in China's higher education sector (Xu [徐] & Wang [王], 2021; Xu [徐] & Hu [胡], 2017).

2. This resonates with existing research, such as H. Li (2013) and Y. Liu (2018, 2019), in which rural-origin and working-class students in China are found to congregate in lower-tier universities, despite their high marks, due to their lack of requisite social and cultural resources as well as the quota system, which favors candidates from urban areas.

3. Project 211 was a higher education development and funding allocation scheme engineered by the Chinese central government for strengthening approximately 100 universities and key disciplines for the 21st century. The project was initiated in November 1995. See L. Li (2004) for more details.

4. Man is one of the three exceptions who had a sibling among all urban participants; the other two are Lingshan and Ruhua. All the rest are from single-child families.

5. That is, Years 12 and 13 in secondary school in the UK's education system.

6. For example, Man was enrolled in a 2+2 articulation program wherein she spent two years studying at a university in China and then moved to London to finish the remaining two years of her bachelor's degree; Jing enrolled in a 3+1 program wherein she spent one year studying at the University of Southampton in the UK; and Qie enrolled in a 2+2 program wherein he first studied in Shenzhen and then finished his bachelor's at a university in northwestern England.

7. Man's and Li's families bought them properties in London.

## Chapter 5

1. The CSSCI is an interdisciplinary citation program in China. Established in 2000, this citation database covers about 500 Chinese academic journals of the humanities and social sciences. Until the early 2020s, many leading Chinese universities used CSSCI as a basis for the evaluation of academic achievements and promotion (see C. L. Xu, 2020; X. Xu, 2019).

## Chapter 6

1. Such excessive diligence is "excessive" because it is often at the expense of their family time, such as the case of Jingpi, or overall development, such as the case of Lawrence.

## Chapter 7

1. Normally, university graduates in Hong Kong are required to obtain a PGDE in order to qualify as a teacher. The PGDE can be completed within one year of full-time studies or two years of part-time studies.

2. See Chiang (2022) about how much advantage students in Beijing possess in getting offers from universities based in Beijing, including some of the country's most elite universities such as Peking, Tsinghua, and Renmin Universities.

3. Yi's mother has a PhD in landscaping design, while her father has a first degree in landscaping design and later switched to the real estate and construction industry. Yi's father retired in his late 40s and now enjoys his retirement life. Yi described her family's life in Beijing as "comfortable."

4. In order to complete her four-year degree course.

## Chapter 8

1. According to the CEIC (2021), based on data reported by the Guangzhou Bureau of Statistics in 2021, the average wage in Guangzhou is RMB 144,288 (USD 20,479) per year, which averages RMB 12,024 (USD 1,707) per month. Norman's salary of RMB 4,500 (USD 639) per month was less than half of the median salary in Guangzhou in 2021.

2. The Guangdong–Hong Kong–Macao Greater Bay Area is also referred to as the Greater Bay Area (GBA). It is a megalopolis that consists of nine cities (Guangzhou, Shenzhen, Dongguan, Zhuhai, Zhongshan, Huizhou, Jiangmen, Foshan, and Zhaoqing) and two special administrative regions (Hong Kong and Macau) in

South China. It is envisioned as an integrated economic area aimed at taking a leading role globally by 2035 (Kuhn, 2021).

3. In July 2021, the Chinese government unexpectedly promulgated what is known colloquially as the Double Reduction Policy, which effectively banned shadow education (private after-school tutorials) for academic subjects in schools in mainland China (H. Qian et al., 2024).

4. Christine confided about environments where the superordinates verbally abused subordinates such as herself due to issues of temper management.

# Chapter 9

1. *Biaoxian* 表现 is literally translated as "performance," while *guanxi* 关系 is "social relations" (see Xie & Postiglione, 2016, p. 1016). Political *biaoxian* therefore refers to political performance and political capital, while personal *guanxi* refers to social relations and social capital in this context.

2. The "Greater China area" here refers to the historically disparate regions including Hong Kong, Macau, and Taiwan (Breitung, 2009; P.-C. Lan & Y.-F. Wu, 2016; C. L. Xu, 2015).

# Chapter 10

1. Guoxiang studied at Peking University for one year before moving to study in Hong Kong. This was her preparatory year, an arrangement between her university in Hong Kong and Peking University.

# Chapter 11

1. This is in contrast with the disadvantaged status of the rural-origin and working-class youth from mainland China, who are largely excluded from such elite, top-tier HEIs in mainland China, as demonstrated throughout this book and in the literature (Cai, 2011; Jin and Ball, 2021).

2. Admittedly, this also opened up a new source of higher education destination for students from mainland China. As demonstrated in this book, however, these higher education resources in Hong Kong are only accessible to the middle-class and upper-middle-class fee-paying students from mainland China due to the relatively higher costs of studying in Hong Kong, which are unaffordable for the rural-origin and working-class students unless they manage to receive full-cost scholarships.

3. A controversial event in 1989, also known as the Tiananmen Square protests, was a student-led series of popular demonstrations that took place in

Beijing but was suppressed by a crackdown on student demonstrators on June 4 the same year (He, 2014).

4. This was Catherine's age in 2017 when the first interview was conducted. She had graduated and was working as an administrative staff member at a university then.

5. Guangdong borders Hong Kong; the people of Guangdong and Hong Kong share Cantonese as a common language. It was easier for a Hong Kong student like Frances to pass as a student from Guangdong.

6. The Umbrella Movement took place in 2014 in Hong Kong. During this movement, protesters occupied Hong Kong's central districts with a view to demanding a democratic election of the region's chief executive in 2017. Faced with the police's tear gas attacks, the protesters defended themselves by using umbrellas, thus giving the movement its popular name (J. Chan, 2014, p. 571).

7. An important procedure for any CCP applicant to be considered is that they should be recommended by an existing member or probationary member.

## Conclusion

1. This may not be the case for single-child middle-class families in urban areas, as revealed in existing research by Kajanus (2015a, 2015b), Tu (2018), and Martin (2022), among others.

# References

Adam, B. (1990). *Time and social theory*. Polity Press.

Ahlers, A. L., & Christmann-Budian, S. (2023). The politics of university rankings in China. *Higher Education, 86*, 751–770. https://doi.org/10.1007/s10734-023-01014-y

Altbach, P. G. (2004). Globalisation and the university: Myths and realities in an unequal world. *Tertiary Education and Management, 10*(1), 3–25. https://doi.org/10.1023/B:TEAM.0000012239.55136.4b

Amano, T., Ramírez-Castañeda, V., Berdejo-Espinola, V., Borokini, I., Chowdhury, S., Golivets, M., González-Trujillo, J. D., Montaño-Centellas, F., Paudel, K., White, R. L., & Veríssimo, D. (2023). The manifold costs of being a non-native English speaker in science. *PLOS Biology, 21*(7), Article e3002184. https://doi.org/10.1371/journal.pbio.3002184

Bailey, C., & Madden, A. (2017). Time reclaimed: Temporality and the experience of meaningful work. *Work, Employment & Society, 31*(1), 3–18. https://doi.org/10.1177/0950017015604100

Baldwin, C. (2015, February 6). China newspaper warns against "McCarthyism" at Hong Kong University. *Reuters*. http://www.reuters.com/article/2015/02/06/hongkong-students-idUSL4N0VG4XA20150206

Batel, S. (2020). Re-presenting the rural in the UK press: An exploration of the construction, contestation and negotiation of media discourses on the rural within post-carbon energy transitions. *Energy Policy, 138*, 111286. https://doi.org/10.1016/j.enpol.2020.111286

Bennett, A., & Burke, P. J. (2018). Re/conceptualising time and temporality: An exploration of time in higher education. *Discourse: Studies in the Cultural Politics of Education, 39*(6), 913–925.

Bernstein, B. (1962a). Linguistic codes, hesitation phenomena and intelligence. *Language and speech, 5*(1), 31–48.

Bernstein, B. (1962b). Social class, linguistic codes and grammatical elements. *Language and speech, 5*(4), 221–240.

189

Bernstein, B. (2003). On the classification and framing of educational knowledge. In D. Scott (Ed.), *Curriculum studies: Major themes in education* (pp. 245–270). Routledge.

Bhambra, G. K. (2014). Postcolonial and decolonial dialogues. *Postcolonial Studies, 17*(2), 115–121. https://doi.org/10.1080/13688790.2014.966414

Bhopal, K. (2014). Race, rurality and representation: Black and minority ethnic mothers' experiences of their children's education in rural primary schools in England, UK. *Gender and Education, 26*(5), 490–504.

Bhopal, K. (2018). *White privilege: The myth of a post-racial society.* Policy Press.

Bhopal, K. (2019). Success against the odds: The effect of mentoring on the careers of senior black and minority ethnic academics in the UK. *British Journal of Educational Studies, 68*(1), 79–95. https://doi.org/10.1080/00071005.2019.1581127

Bhopal, K. (2020). Confronting White privilege: The importance of intersectionality in the sociology of education. *British Journal of Sociology of Education, 41*(6), 807–816.

Bhopal, K. (2022). Academics of colour in elite universities in the UK and the USA: The "unspoken system of exclusion." *Studies in Higher Education, 47*(11), 2127–2137. https://doi.org/10.1080/03075079.2021.2020746

Bhopal, K., Brown, H., & Jackson, J. (2016). BME academic flight from UK to overseas higher education: Aspects of marginalisation and exclusion. *British Educational Research Journal, 42*(2), 240–257.

Bilby, J., Reid, M., Brennan, L., & Chen, J. (2020). Tiers and fears: An investigation of the impact of city tiers and uncertainty avoidance on Chinese consumer response to creative advertising. *Australasian Marketing Journal, 28*(4), 332–348. https://doi.org/10.1016/j.ausmj.2020.07.005

Blyth, P., & Cleminson, A. (2016, September). *Teaching Excellence Framework: Analysis of highly skilled employment outcomes.* Department for Education. https://assets.publishing.service.gov.uk/government/uploads/system/uploads/attachment_data/file/557107/Teaching-Excellence-Framework-highly-skilled-employment..pdf

Boliver, V., & Capsada-Munsech, Q. (2024). Intergenerational inequality in education. In E. Kilpi-Jakonen, J. Blanden, J. Erola, & L. Macmillan (Eds.), *Research handbook on intergenerational inequality* (pp. 13–26). Edward Elgar Publishing.

Boliver, V., Gorard, S., & Siddiqui, N. (2021). Using contextual data to widen access to higher education. *Perspectives: Policy and Practice in Higher Education, 25*(1), 7–13.

Born, A. M. (2024). The price of the ticket revised: Family members' experiences of upward social mobility. *The Sociological Review, 72*(2), 394–411.

Bourdieu, P. (1984). *Distinction: A social critique of the judgment of taste* (R. Nice, Trans.). Harvard University Press. (Originally published in 1979 by Les Éditions de Minuit, Paris, as *La distinction: Critique sociale du jugement*)

Bourdieu, P. (1986). The forms of capital. In J. G. Richardson (Ed.), *Handbook of theory and research for the sociology of education* (pp. 241–258). Greenwood Press.

Bourdieu, P. (1988). *Homo academicus.* Stanford University Press.

Bourdieu, P. (2000). Social being, time and the sense of existence. In P. Bourdieu, *Pascalian Meditations* (R. Nice, Trans.; pp. 206–245). Polity Press.

Bourdieu, P. (2002). Habitus. In J. Hillier & E. Rooksby (Eds.), *Habitus: A sense of place* (pp. 27–34). Ashgate Publishing.

Bourdieu, P. (2020). *General sociology: Lectures at the Collège de France (1982–1983): Vol. 2. Habitus and field* (P. Collier, Trans.). Polity Press.

Bourdieu, P., & Passeron, J.-C. (1979). *The inheritors: French students and their relation to culture.* University of Chicago Press.

Breitung, W. (2009). Macau residents as border people: A changing border regime from a sociocultural perspective. *Journal of Current Chinese Affairs, 38*(1), 101–127. http://journals.sub.uni-hamburg.de/giga/jcca/article/view/15/15

Brooks, R., & Waters, J. (2018). Signalling the "multi-local" university? The place of the city in the growth of London-based satellite campuses, and the implications for social stratification. *Social Sciences, 7*(10), 195. https://doi.org/10.3390/socsci7100195

Buzan, B., & Lawson, G. (2020). China through the lens of modernity. *The Chinese Journal of International Politics, 13*(2), 187–217.

Cai, S. (2011). China's household registration (*hukou*) system and its socioeconomic impacts. *The McNair Scholars Journal of the University of Washington, 10,* 13–22.

Callahan, W. A. (2009). The cartography of national humiliation and the emergence of China's geobody. *Public Culture, 21*(1), 141–173.

Cao, X. E. (2021). Navigating my way as a first-generation student. *Matter, 4*(2), 332–335.

CEIC. (2021). *Average wage: On duty: Guangdong: Guangzhou* [Data set]. Retrieved November 9, 2022, from https://www.ceicdata.com/en/china/average-wage-on-duty-prefecture-level-city/average-wage-on-duty-guangdong-guangzhou

Chan, A. K. W., Cheung, L. T. O., Chong, E. K., Lee, M. Y. K., & Wong, M. Y. H. (2022). Hong Kong's new wave of migration: Socio-political factors of individuals' intention to emigrate. *Comparative Migration Studies, 10,* Article 49. https://doi.org/10.1186/s40878-022-00323-y

Chan, J. (2014). Hong Kong's Umbrella Movement. *The Round Table, 103*(6), 571–580. https://doi.org/10.1080/00358533.2014.985465

Chan, M. K. (2003). Different roads to home: The retrocession of Hong Kong and Macau to Chinese sovereignty. *Journal of Contemporary China, 12*(36), 493–518.

Chan, Y. W., & Koh, S. Y. (Eds.). (2017). *New Chinese migrations: Mobility, home, and inspirations.* Routledge.

Chang, C. C., & Yang, A. H. (2020). Weaponized interdependence: China's economic statecraft and social penetration against Taiwan. *Orbis, 64*(2), 312–333. https://doi.org/10.1016/j.orbis.2020.02.002

Chau, W. F. (2023). *Reflections on their motivations to move: A case study of wealthy Chinese migration to western democratic countries in the past two decades* [Doctoral dissertation, University of Glasgow].

Chen, C., & Fan, C. C. (2016). China's hukou puzzle: Why don't rural migrants want urban hukou? *China Review, 16*(3), 9–39.

Chen, H., Akpanudo, U., & Hasler, E. (2020). How do Chinese international students view seeking mental health services? *Journal of International Students, 10*(2), 286–305. https://doi.org/10.32674/jis.v10i2.765

Chen, J. (2022). Hysteresis effects and emotional suffering: Chinese rural students' first encounters with the urban university. *Sociological Research Online, 27*(1), 101–117. https://doi.org/10.1177/1360780420949884

Chen, Y. (2008). *Muslim Uyghur students in a Chinese boarding school: Social recapitalization as a response to ethnic integration*. Lexington Books.

Cheng [程], Meng 猛. (2018a). 读书的料 ”及其文化生产—当代农家子弟成长叙事研究 [“College material” and their cultural production: A narrative study of contemporary rural kids' growth]. China Social Sciences Press.

Cheng [程], Meng 猛. (2018b). 农村出身: 一种复杂的情感结构 [Rural background: A kind of complex emotional structure]. 青年研究 [Youth Studies], *2018*(6), 64–73.

Cheng [程], Meng 猛., & Kang [康], Y. 永久. (2018). 从农家走进精英大学的年轻人: “懂事”及其命运 [Youth from rural families to elite universities: “Understanding” and their fates]. 中国青年研究 [China Youth Study], *2018*(5), 68–75.

Cheng, Meng, & Kang, Y. (2019). Rural youths admitted to elite universities: “Empathy” and destiny. *Chinese Education & Society, 52*(5–6), 363–377.

Cheng, Michelle W., Xie, Y., & Lo, S. K. (2023). Making the college transition in China—rural first-generation college students and their parents. *Social Education Research, 4*(1), 131–143.

Chiang, Y.-L. (2018). When things don't go as planned: Contingencies, cultural capital, and parental involvement for elite university admission in China. *Comparative Education Review, 62*(4), 503–521.

Chiang, Y.-L. (2022). *Study gods: How the new Chinese elite prepare for global competition*. Princeton University Press.

Choi, P. K. (2010). “Weep for Chinese university”: A case study of English hegemony and academic capitalism in higher education in Hong Kong. *Journal of Education Policy, 25*(2), 233–252. https://doi.org/10.1080/02680930903443886

Choi, S. Y. P. (2023). Doing and undoing gender: Women on the frontline of Hong Kong's anti-extradition bill movement. *Social Movement Studies, 22*(5–6), 786–801. https://doi.org/10.1080/14742837.2022.2086114

Chu, Y. (2023). Foster child of the family: An autoethnography of an international minority teacher educator in a US university. In M. Gutman, W. Jayusi, M. Beck, & Z. Bekerman (Eds.), *To be a minority teacher in a foreign culture: Empirical evidence from an international perspective* (pp. 269–283). Springer.

Chua, H.-w., Wong, A. K. W., & Shek, D. T. L. (2010). Social development in Hong Kong: Development issues identified by Social Development Index (SDI). *Social Indicators Research, 95*(3), 535–551. https://doi.org/10.1007/s11205-009-9525-7

Clegg, S. (2010). Time future—the dominant discourse of higher education. *Time & Society, 19*(3), 345–364.

Collins, F. L., & Shubin, S. (2015). Migrant times beyond the life course: the temporalities of foreign English teachers in South Korea. *Geoforum, 62,* 96–104.

Crawford, J., & McKee, K. (2018). Hysteresis: Understanding the housing aspirations gap. *Sociology, 52*(1), 182–197. https://doi.org/10.1177/0038038516661263

Crenshaw, K. (1995). Mapping the margins. *Critical race theory: The key writings that formed the movement, 3*(15), 357–383.

Crystal, D. (2003). *English as a global language* (2nd ed.). Cambridge University Press. https://doi.org/10.1017/CBO9780511486999

Deleuze, G., & Guattari, F. (1983). *Capitalism and Schizophrenia: Vol. 1. Anti-Oedipus* (R. Hurley, M. Seem, & H. R. Lane, Trans.). University of Minnesota Press.

Deng, Y. (2022, August 13). The Chinese mainland's education policy attracts Hong Kong students. *iChongqing.* https://www.ichongqing.info/2022/08/13/the-chinese-mainlands-education-policy-attracts-hong-kong-students/

Department for Levelling Up, Housing and Communities. (2021, April 8). *Hong Kong British Nationals (Overseas) Welcome Programme—information for local authorities.* https://www.gov.uk/guidance/hong-kong-uk-welcome-programme-guidance-for-local-authorities

Doharty, N., Madriaga, M., & Joseph-Salisbury, R. (2021). The university went to "decolonise" and all they brought back was lousy diversity double-speak! Critical race counter-stories from faculty of colour in "decolonial" times. *Educational Philosophy and Theory, 53*(3), 233–244. https://doi.org/10.1080/00131857.2020.1769601

Du, F., Wang, W., & Dong, X. (2023). *Chinese people's time use and their quality of life: Research report of Chinese time use survey* (Y. Guan, Trans.). China Social Sciences Press / Springer.

Duncheon, J. C., & Tierney, W. G. (2013). Changing conceptions of time: Implications for educational research and practice. *Review of Educational Research, 83*(2), 236–272.

Esping-Andersen, G. (2005). Social inheritance and equal opportunity policies. In S. Delorenzi, J. Reed, and P. Robinson (Eds.), *Maintaining momentum: Promoting social mobility and life chances from early years to adulthood* (pp. 14–30). IPPR.

Fischer, M. J., & Massey, D. S. (2007). The effects of affirmative action in higher education. *Social Science Research, 36*(2), 531–549. https://doi.org/10.1016/j.ssresearch.2006.04.004

Fong, B. C. (2014). The partnership between the Chinese government and Hong Kong's capitalist class: Implications for HKSAR governance, 1997–2012. *The China Quarterly, 217*, 195–220.

Fong, V. L. (2011). *Paradise redefined: Transnational Chinese students and the quest for flexible citizenship in the developed world*. Stanford University Press.

Forbes, J., & Lingard, B. (2013). Elite school capitals and girls' schooling: Understanding the (re)production of privilege through a habitus of 'assuredness.' In C. Maxwell & P. Aggleton (Eds.), *Privilege, agency and affect: Understanding the production and effects of action* (pp. 50–68). Palgrave Macmillan.

Forbes, J., & Lingard, B. (2014). Assured optimism in a Scottish girls' school: Habitus and the (re)production of global privilege. *British Journal of Sociology of Education, 36*(1), 116–136. https://doi.org/10.1080/01425692.2014.967839

Ford, K. A. (2011). Race, gender, and bodily (mis)recognitions: Women of color faculty experiences with White students in the college classroom. *The Journal of Higher Education, 82*(4), 444–478.

Friedman, E. (2022). *The urbanization of people: The politics of development, labor markets, and schooling in the Chinese city*. Columbia University Press.

Friedman, S., & Laurison, D. (2019). *The class ceiling: Why it pays to be privileged*. Policy Press.

Gan, N. (2023, 21 September). Top Chinese university scraps English tests in move cheered by nationalists. *CNN*. https://edition.cnn.com/2023/09/21/china/china-university-english-test-intl-hnk/index.html

Gao, F. (2024). Avoiding the "rat race": Hong Kong students' sense of belonging to a Chinese university in the Greater Bay Area. *International Journal of Educational Development, 108*, 103059. https://doi.org/10.1016/j.ijedudev.2024.103059

Gao, L. (2023). *Cultural capital and urban-rural educational inequality in high school enrollment in China: A mixed-methods study* [Doctoral dissertation, University of Hong Kong].

Gao, X. (2014). "Floating elites": Interpreting mainland Chinese undergraduates' graduation plans in Hong Kong. *Asia Pacific Education Review, 15*(2), 223–235.

Garcia, Z., & Bianco, C. (2023). The impact of Chinese history on perceptions of the Law of the Sea in the South China Sea. *Territory, Politics, Governance*, 1–21. https://doi.org/10.1080/21622671.2023.2218427

Gasparini, G. (1995). On waiting. *Time & Society, 4*(1), 29–45.

Gerlach, A. (2020). The abortion of female foetuses and the killing of newborn girls in China—the power of unconscious phantasies. *Psychoanalysis and Psychotherapy in China, 3*(2), 221–229.

Gibran, Kahlil. (2021). *The prophet*. Alfred A. Knopf; Project Gutenberg. https://www.gutenberg.org/files/58585/58585-h/58585-h.htm (Original work published 1923)

Glass, C. R., & Cruz, N. I. (2023). Moving towards multipolarity: Shifts in the core-periphery structure of international student mobility and world rankings (2000–2019). *Higher Education, 85*(2), 415–435.

Goodman, D. S. G. (Ed.). (2008). *The new rich in China: Future rulers, present lives*. Routledge.

Goodman, D. S. G. (2014). *Class in contemporary China*. Polity.

Goody, J. (1962). *Death, property and the ancestors: A study of the mortuary customs of the Lodagaa of West Africa*. Stanford University Press.

Grose, T. (2010). The Xinjiang class: Education, integration, and the Uyghurs. *Journal of Muslim Minority Affairs, 30*(1), 97–109.

Grose, T. (2015). (Re)embracing Islam in *neidi*: The "Xinjiang class" and the dynamics of Uyghur ethno-national identity. *Journal of Contemporary China, 24*(91), 101–118.

Gross, D. (1985). Temporality and the modern state. *Theory and Society, 14*(1), 53–82. https://doi.org/10.1007/BF00160928

Gu, M., & Tong, H. K. (2012). Space, scale and languages: Identity construction of cross-boundary students in a multilingual university in Hong Kong. *Language and Education, 26*(6), 505–515. http://www.tandfonline.com/doi/abs/10.1080/09500782.2012.734686

Gu, Q., & Schweisfurth, M. (2015a). Transnational connections, competences and identities: Experiences of Chinese international students after their return "home." *British Educational Research Journal, 41*(6), 947–970. https://doi.org/10.1002/berj.3175

Gu, Q., & Schweisfurth, M. (2015b). Transnational flows of students: In whose interest? For whose benefit? In S. McGrath & Q. Gu (Eds.), *Routledge handbook of international education and development* (pp. 359–372). Routledge.

Gu, X. (2022). Sacrifice and indebtedness: The intergenerational contract in Chinese rural migrant families. *Journal of Family Issues, 43*(2), 509–533.

Guiheux, G., & Wang, S. (2018). A case of double socialisation in the social sciences: The experience of Chinese researchers trained in France (J. Hall, Trans.). *China Perspectives, 2018*(4), 21–30.

Guinto, J. (2023, July 6). Four arrested in Hong Kong after bounty set up for activists abroad. *BBC News*. https://www.bbc.co.uk/news/world-asia-66117142

Guo, J., & Chen, J. (2023). Can China's higher education expansion reduce the educational inequality between urban and rural areas? *The Journal of Higher Education, 94*(5), 638–663. https://doi.org/10.1080/00221546.2023.2168408

Guo, X. G., & Gu, M. M. (2016). Identity construction through English language learning in intra-national migration: A study on Uyghur students in China. *Journal of Ethnic and Migration Studies, 42*(14), 2430–2447. http://dx.doi.org/10.1080/1369183X.2016.1205942

Guryan, J., Hurst, E., & Kearney, M. (2008). Parental education and parental time with children. *Journal of Economic Perspectives, 22*(3), 23–46.

Hail, H. C. (2015). Patriotism abroad: Overseas Chinese students' encounters with criticisms of China. *Journal of Studies in International Education, 19*(4), 311–326.

Hamnett, C., Hua, S., & Liang, B. (2019). The reproduction of regional inequality through university access: The Gaokao in China. *Area Development and Policy*, *4*(3), 252–270.

Hansen, A. S. (2015). The temporal experience of Chinese students abroad and the present human condition. *Journal of Current Chinese Affairs*, *44*(3), 49–77.

Harrell, S. (1985). Why Do the Chinese Work So Hard? Reflections on an Entrepreneurial Ethic. *Modern China*, *11*(2), 203–226. http://www.jstor.org/stable/188906

Harris, R., Mate-Sanchez-Val, M., & Ruiz Marín, M. (2024). Gender disparities in promotions and exiting in UK Russell Group universities. *Applied Economics*, 1–17. https://doi.org/10.1080/00036846.2024.2361384

He, R. X. (2014). *Tiananmen exiles: Voices of the struggle for democracy in China*. Palgrave Macmillan.

Ho, E. L.-E. (2011). Migration trajectories of "highly skilled" middling transnationals: Singaporean transmigrants in London. *Population, Space and Place*, *17*(1), 116–129. https://doi.org/10.1002/psp.569

Hong Fincher, L. (2023). *Leftover women: The resurgence of gender inequality in China* (10th Anniversary Ed.). Bloomsbury Academic.

Horta, H., & Li, H. (2024, January 15). Ageism and age anxiety experienced by Chinese doctoral students in enacting a "successful" career script in academia. *Higher Education*. https://doi.org/10.1007/s10734-023-01176-9

Hou, M., Cruz, N., Glass, C. R., & Lee, S. (2021). Transnational postgraduates: Navigating academic trajectories in the globalized university. *International Studies in Sociology of Education*, *30*(3), 306–324. https://doi.org/10.1080/09620214.2020.1853590

Howlett, Z. (2021). *Meritocracy and its discontents: Anxiety and the national college entrance exam in China*. Cornell University Press.

Interactive Employment Service. (2020). *Greater Bay Area Youth Employment Scheme*. Labour Department, Government of Hong Kong Special Administrative Region. Retrieved November 9, 2020, from https://www2.jobs.gov.hk/0/en/information/gbayes/

Jebril, M. (2021, November). *The political economy of health in the Gaza Strip (Occupied Palestinian Territory)*. Centre for Business Research, University of Cambridge.

Jiang, S. (2021). Diversity without integration? Racialization and spaces of exclusion in international higher education. *British Journal of Sociology of Education*, *42*(1), 32–47. https://doi.org/10.1080/01425692.2020.1847635

Jin, J. (2024). The relevance and dissonances of "class" in China: An imaginative dialogue with Bourdieu and Bourdieusian studies. In G. M. Mu and K. Dooley (Eds.), *Recontextualising and recontesting Bourdieu in Chinese education: Habitus, mobility, and language* (pp. 64–80). Routledge.

Jin, J., & Ball, S. J. (2021). Precarious success and the conspiracy of reflexivity: Questioning the "habitus transformation" of working-class students at elite universities. *Critical Studies in Education, 62*(5), 608–623. https://doi.org/10.1080/17508487.2019.1593869

Jokila, S. (2015). The internationalization of higher education with Chinese characteristics: Appadurai's ideas explored. *Asia Pacific Journal of Education, 35*(1), 125–139. https://doi.org/10.1080/02188791.2014.940029

Kajanus, A. (2015a). *Chinese student migration, gender and family.* Palgrave Macmillan.

Kajanus, A. (2015b). Overthrowing the first mountain: Chinese student migrants and the geography of power. *Journal of Current Chinese Affairs, 44*(3), 79–102.

Kim, E. C. (2015). International professors in China: Prestige maintenance and making sense of teaching abroad. *Current Sociology, 63*(4), 604–620.

Kim, T., & Ng, W. (2019). Ticking the "other" box: Positional identities of East Asian academics in UK universities, internationalisation and diversification. *Policy Reviews in Higher Education, 3*(1), 94–119. https://doi.org/10.1080/23322969.2018.1564886

King, R., & Sondhi, G. (2018). International student migration: A comparison of UK and Indian students' motivations for studying abroad. *Globalisation, Societies and Education, 16*(2), 176–191.

Kipnis, A. (2011). *Governing educational desire: Culture, politics, and schooling in China.* University of Chicago Press.

Kong, S. T., Jackson, S., & Ho, P. S. Y. (2023). Seeking love and justice amid Hong Kong's contentious politics. *Feminist Encounters, 7*(2), 19–32.

Kuang, R. F. (2022). *Babel: An arcane history.* Harper Voyager.

Kuhn, B. (2021). China's Greater Bay Area. *Wirtschaftsdienst, 101*(4), 311–315. https://doi.org/10.1007/s10273-021-2901-x

Kurata, T. (2015). Support for and opposition to democratization in Hong Kong. *Asia-Pacific Review, 22*(1), 16–34.

Lai, R. Y. S. (2024). Home as a site of resistance/repression? The intersection of family, politics and the Hong Kong 2019 protest movement. *The Sociological Review, 72*(2), 412–431. https://doi.org/10.1177/00380261231175226

Lam, K. W. K., Zhong, H., & Gu, G. Y. (2023). Classic assimilation, self-selection and parent status: An analysis of the central–local political trust among highly educated Mainland migrants in Hong Kong. *Asian and Pacific Migration Journal, 32*(1), 83–104. https://doi.org/10.1177/01171968231167922

Lamont, M., & Lareau, A. (1988). Cultural capital: Allusions, gaps and glissandos in recent theoretical developments. *Sociological Theory, 6*(2), 153–168.

Lan, P.-C., & Wu, Y.-F. (2016). Exceptional membership and liminal space of identity: Student migration from Taiwan to China. *International Sociology, 31*(6), 742–763.

Lan, S. (2021). Finding a *chulu* (way out): Rural-origin Chinese students studying abroad in South Korea. *Pacific Affairs, 94*(4), 661–681.

Lareau, A. (2003). *Unequal childhood: The importance of social class in family life.* University of California Press.

Lee, E. M. (2017). "Where people like me don't belong": Faculty members from low-socioeconomic status backgrounds. *Sociology of Education, 90*(3), 197–212. https://doi.org/10.1177/0038040717710495

Lee, J., & Waters, J. (2024). "Wow. What's going on?" Emotional geographies of international student mobility to the UK in a time of crisis. *Emotion, Space and Society, 51,* Article 101015. https://doi.org/10.1016/j.emospa.2024.101015

Lehmann, W. (2023). Mobility and stability: Post-graduate employment experiences of working-class students. *Journal of Education and Work, 36*(1), 79–93. https://doi.org/10.1080/13639080.2022.2128188

Leibold, J., & Dorjee, T. (2023). Learning to be Chinese: Colonial-style boarding schools on the Tibetan plateau. *Comparative Education, 60*(1), 118–137. https://doi.org/10.1080/03050068.2023.2250969

Lem, P. (2022, October 10). Concern as Hong Kong admits record student intake from mainland China. *Times Higher Education.* https://www.timeshighereducation.com/news/concern-hong-kong-admits-record-student-intake-mainland-china

Leung, M. W. H., & Waters, J. (2013). Transnational higher education for capacity development? An analysis of British degree programmes in Hong Kong. *Globalisation, Societies and Education, 11*(4), 479–497. https://doi.org/10.1080/14767724.2013.834180

Leung, M. W. H., & Waters, J. L. (2017). Educators sans frontières? Borders and power geometries in transnational education. *Journal of Ethnic and Migration Studies, 43*(8), 1276–1291.

Levinson King, R. (2023, 25 November). Harvard under fire for helping elite skip the queue. *BBC News.* https://www.bbc.co.uk/news/world-us-canada-67523348.amp

Li, B., & Shen, Y. (2022). Publication or pregnancy? Employment contracts and childbearing of women academics in China. *Studies in Higher Education, 47*(4), 875–887. https://doi.org/10.1080/03075079.2020.1817888

Li, H. (2013). Rural students' experiences in a Chinese elite university: Capital, habitus and practices. *British Journal of Sociology of Education, 34*(5–6), 829–847. https://doi.org/10.1080/01425692.2013.821940

Li, H. (2020). Changing status, entrenched inequality: How English language becomes a Chinese form of cultural capital. *Educational Philosophy and Theory, 52*(12), 1302–1313. https://doi.org/10.1080/00131857.2020.1738922

Li, H., Loyalka, P., Rozelle, S., Wu, B., & Xie, J. (2015). Unequal access to college in China: How far have poor, rural students been left behind? *The China Quarterly, 221,* 185–207. https://doi.org/10.1017/S0305741015000314

Li, L. (2004). China's higher education reform 1998–2003: A summary. *Asia Pacific Education Review, 5,* 14–22.

Li, X., & John, M. E. (2005). Women and feminism in China and India: A conversation with Li Xiaojiang. *Economic and Political Weekly, 40*(16), 1594–1597. http://www.jstor.org/stable/4416497

Liao [廖], Q. 青. (2016). 精英大学中农村学生的学习经历—对再生产理论的省思 [Learning experiences of rural students in elite universities: Reflections on the theory of production]. 高等教育研究 [Journal of Higher Education], 37(11), 77–84.

Liao, Q., & Wong, Y.-L. (2019). An emotional journey: Pursuing a bachelor's degree for rural students in four elite universities in Shanghai, PRC. *Cambridge Journal of Education*, 49(6), 711–725. https://doi.org/10.1080/03057 64X.2019.1592114

Lin, C. (2001). Whither feminism: A note on China. *Signs*, 26(4), 1281–1286.

Lin, P., Pan, Y., Wang, Y., & Hu, L. (2024). Reshaping unfairness perceptions: Evidence from China's Hukou reform. *China Economic Review*, 83, 1–19. https://doi.org/10.1016/j.chieco.2023.102081

Lin, T., & Wu, X. (2009). The transformation of the Chinese class structure, 1978–2005. In K.-b. Chan (Ed.), *Social stratification in Chinese societies* (pp. 81–112). Brill.

Lingard, B., & Thompson, G. (2017). Doing time in the sociology of education. *British Journal of Sociology of Education*, 38(1), 1–12.

Lipura, S. J., & Collins, F. L. (2020). Towards an integrative understanding of contemporary educational mobilities: A critical agenda for international student mobilities research. *Globalisation, Societies and Education*, 18(3), 343–359. https://doi.org/10.1080/14767724.2020.1711710

Liu, J. (2012, September 1). Hong Kong debates "national education" classes. *BBC News*. http://www.bbc.com/news/world-asia-china-19407425

Liu, S. (2020). *Neoliberalism, globalization, and "elite" education in China: Becoming international*. Routledge.

Liu, T., Sato, Y., & Breaden, J. (2023). Factors influencing international students' trajectories: a comparative study of Chinese students in Japan and Australia. *International Journal of Comparative Education and Development*, 25(1), 23–39. https://doi.org/10.1108/IJCED-08-2022-0060

Liu, W. (2017). Intergenerational emotion and solidarity in transitional China: Comparisons of two kinds of "ken lao" families in Shanghai. *The Journal of Chinese Sociology*, 4(1), Article 10. https://doi.org/10.1186/s40711-017-0058-1

Liu, Y. (2013). Meritocracy and the Gaokao: A survey study of higher education selection and socio-economic participation in East China. *British Journal of Sociology of Education*, 34(5–6), 868–887. https://doi.org/10.1080/0142569 2.2013.816237

Liu, Y. (2018). When choices become chances: Extending Boudon's positional theory to understand university choices in contemporary China. *Comparative Education Review*, 62(1), 125–146. https://doi.org/10.1086/695405

Liu, Y. (2019). Choices, risks and rational conformity: Extending Boudon's positional theory to understand higher education choices in contemporary China. *Higher Education*, 77, 525–540. https://doi.org/10.1007/s10734-018-0285-7

Liu, Y., Huang, Y., & Shen, W. (2022). Building halos: How do Chinese elites seek distinction through (mis)recognising studying abroad? *International Journal of Educational Development*, *91*, 102589. https://doi.org/10.1016/j.ijedudev.2022.102589

Lomer, S. (2018). UK policy discourses and international student mobility: The deterrence and subjectification of international students. *Globalisation, Societies and Education*, *16*(3), 308–324. https://doi.org/10.1080/14767724.2017.1414584

Loyalka, P., Song, Y., & Wei, J. (2012). The effects of attending selective college tiers in China. *Social Science Research*, *41*(2), 287–305. https://doi.org/10.1016/j.ssresearch.2011.11.015

Lu [陆], X. 学. Y. 艺. (2002) 当代中国社会阶层研究报告 [Report on social class study in contemporary China]. Social Sciences Academic Press.

Lui, L., Sun, K. C.-Y., & Hsiao, Y. (2022). How families affect aspirational migration amidst political insecurity: The case of Hong Kong. *Population, Space and Place*, *28*(4), Article e2528. https://doi.org/10.1002/psp.2528

Lui, T.-L. (2003). Rearguard politics: Hong Kong's middle class. *The Developing Economies*, *41*(2), 161–183. https://doi.org/10.1111/j.1746-1049.2003.tb00936.x

Lui, T.-L. (2009). Hong Kong's changing opportunity structures: Political concerns and sociological observations. In K.-b. Chan (Ed.), *Social stratification in Chinese societies* (pp. 141–163). Brill. https://doi.org/10.1163/ej.9789004181922.i-270.42

Luo [罗], P. 平. (2021). 中国为世界提供现代化道路新选择 [China provides the world a new choice of modernization path]. 历史评论 [Historical Review], *5*, 16–21.

Ma, A., & Holford, J. (2023, July 25). Mainland Chinese students in Hong Kong: Coping with the socio-political challenges of 2017 to 2020. *Journal of Studies in International Education*. https://doi.org/10.1177/10283153231187142

Ma, E. K.-W. (2012). *Desiring Hong Kong, consuming south China: Transborder cultural politics, 1970–2010*. Hong Kong University Press.

Ma, Y. (2020). *Ambitious and anxious: How Chinese college students succeed and struggle in American higher education*. Columbia University Press.

Macfarlane, B. (2014, October 16). Hong Kong's students ask: If not now, when? *Times Higher Education*.

Macfarlane, B. (2017). "If not now, then when? If not us, who?" Understanding the student protest movement in Hong Kong. In R. Brooks (Ed.), *Student politics and protest: International perspectives* (pp. 143–156). Routledge.

Madge, C., Raghuram, P., & Noxolo, P. (2009). Engaged pedagogy and responsibility: A postcolonial analysis of international students. *Geoforum*, *40*(1), 34–45. https://doi.org/10.1016/j.geoforum.2008.01.008

Madge, C., Raghuram, P., & Noxolo, P. (2015). Conceptualizing international education: From international student to international study. *Progress in Human Geography*, *39*(6), 681–701.

Mahadeo, R. (2019). Why is the time always right for white and wrong for us? How racialized youth make sense of whiteness and temporal inequality. *Sociology of Race and Ethnicity*, 5(2), 186–199. https://doi.org/10.1177/2332649218770 469

Marginson, S. (2008). Global field and global imagining: Bourdieu and worldwide higher education. *British Journal of Sociology of Education*, 29(3), 303–315. https://doi.org/10.1080/01425690801966386

Marginson, S. (2014). Academic freedom: A global comparative approach. *Frontiers of Education in China*, 9(1), 24–41.

Martin, F. (2018). Overseas study as zone of suspension: Chinese students re-negotiating youth, gender, and intimacy. *Journal of Intercultural Studies*, 39(6), 688–703. https://doi.org/10.1080/07256868.2018.1533538

Martin, F. (2022). *Dreams of flight: The lives of Chinese women students in the West.* Duke University Press.

Maxwell, C., & Aggleton, P. (2013). Becoming accomplished: Concerted cultivation among privately educated young women. *Pedagogy, Culture & Society*, 21(1), 75–93.

Maxwell, C., & Aggleton, P. (2014). The reproduction of privilege: Young women, the family and private education. *International Studies in Sociology of Education*, 24(2), 189–209.

Maxwell, C., & Yemini, M. (2019). Modalities of cosmopolitanism and mobility: Parental education strategies of global, immigrant and local middle-class Israelis. *Discourse: Studies in the Cultural Politics of Education*, 40(5), 616–32. https://doi.org/10.1080/01596306.2019.1570613

McNamee, S. J., & Miller, R. K., Jr. (1989). Estate inheritance: A sociological lacuna. *Sociological Inquiry*, 59(1), 7–29. https://doi.org/10.1111/j.1475-682X.1989.tb01077.x

Meinhof, M. (2017). Colonial temporality and Chinese national modernization discourses. *InterDisciplines: Journal of History and Sociology*, 8(1), 51–80.

Miao, L., & Wang, H. (2024, 16 March). China still leading source of foreign students. *China Daily*. https://www.chinadaily.com.cn/a/202403/16/WS65f4e78ba31082fc043bcf71.html

Ministry of Education of the People's Republic of China. (2011, March 2). *2010 年我国出国留学人数和留学回国人数双增长* [In 2010 there was a double increase in the number of students who studied abroad and the number of returnees in China]. http://www.moe.gov.cn/jyb_xwfb/gzdt_gzdt/s5987/201103/t20110302_128436.html

Mohdin, A. (2023, August 31). Ex-Tory MP threatens to sue Cambridge University over slavery research. *The Guardian*. https://www.theguardian.com/world/2023/aug/31/ex-tory-mp-threatens-sue-cambridge-university-slavery-research-antoinette-sandbach

Mok, K. H. (2016). Massification of higher education, graduate employment and social mobility in the Greater China region. *British Journal of Sociology of Education, 37*(1), 51–71. https://doi.org/10.1080/01425692.2015.1111751

Mok, K. H., Wen, Z., & Dale, R. (2016). Employability and mobility in the valorisation of higher education qualifications: The experiences and reflections of Chinese students and graduates. *Journal of Higher Education Policy and Management, 38*(3), 264–281.

Mulvey, B. (2020). Conceptualizing the discourse of student mobility between "periphery" and "semi-periphery": The case of Africa and China. *Higher Education.* https://doi.org/10.1007/s10734-020-00549-8

Mumford, A. (2007). Inheritance in socio-political context: The case for reviving the sociological discourse of inheritance tax law. *Journal of Law and Society, 34*(4), 567–593. https://doi.org/10.1111/j.1467-6478.2007.00405.x

Murphy, R. (2020). *The children of China's great migration.* Cambridge University Press.

Murphy, R. (2022). What does "left behind" mean to children living in migratory regions in rural China? *Geoforum, 129*, 181–190. https://doi.org/10.1016/j.geoforum.2022.01.012

National Bureau of Statistics of China & All-China Women's Federation. (2011, 21 October). Xinwenban jieshao disanqi zhongguo funv shehui diwei diaocha deng qingkuang [Information Office introduces data of the third survey of Chinese women's social status]. http://www.gov.cn/wszb/zhibo479/wzsl.htm

Nungsari, M., Chin, J. W., Ngu, K., Abdullah, M. F. S., & Flanders, S. (2024). Dreams vs reality: Urban and rural female youth aspirations. *Journal of Career Assessment, 32*(1), 79–100. https://doi.org/10.1177/10690727231177911

O'Sullivan, M., & Tsang, M. Y.-h. (2015). Educational inequalities in higher education in Hong Kong. *Inter-Asia Cultural Studies, 16*(3), 454–469. https://doi.org/10.1080/14649373.2015.1069007

Ohnesorge, H. W., & Owen, J. M. (2023). Mnemonic soft power: The role of memory in China's quest for global power. *Journal of Current Chinese Affairs, 52*(2), 287–310. https://doi.org/10.1177/18681026231193035

Osburg, J. (2013). *Anxious wealth: Money and morality among China's new rich.* Stanford University Press.

Palm, M., & Carrasco, S. (2019, December 5). *Affordability and availability in Melbourne's self-organizing student housing markets* [Paper presentation]. State of Australian Cities Conference and PhD Symposium, Perth, Australia.

Piketty, T. (2014). *Capital in the twenty-first century* (A. Goldhammer, Trans.). Belknap Press.

Piketty, T., & Yang, L. (2022). Income and wealth inequality in Hong Kong, 1981–2020: The rise of pluto-communism? *The World Bank Economic Review, 36*(4), 803–834.

Poole, A. (2023). From recalcitrance to rapprochement: Tinkering with a working-class academic bricolage of "critical empathy." *Discourse: Studies in the*

*Cultural Politics of Education*, *44*(4), 522–534. https://doi.org/10.1080/015 96306.2021.2021860

Prazeres, L. (2019). Unpacking distinction within mobility: Social prestige and international students. *Population, Space and Place*, *25*(5), Article e2190. https://doi.org/10.1002/psp.2190

Qian, H., Walker, A., & Chen, S. (2024). The "Double-Reduction" education policy in China: Three prevailing narratives. *Journal of Education Policy*, *39*(4), 602–621. https://doi.org/10.1080/02680939.2023.2222381

Qian, L. (2022). *Jizhu Xiangchou: Rural nostalgia and revitalization in Xi-era China* [Doctoral dissertation, University of Oxford]. https://ora.ox.ac.uk/objects/ uuid:3ffaa59b-40e3-4a33-b86e-295ab0084294/files/rp2676w14d

QS. (2014). *QS World University Rankings 2014/15*. Retrieved September 17, 2014, from http://www.topuniversities.com/university-rankings

Ren, R., & Qi, Y. (2024). Conflicting geographical imaginaries in globalised labour markets: The local valorisation of international education among employers and returned international students. *Transactions of the Institute of British Geographers*, Article e12681. https://doi.org/10.1111/tran.12681

Robertson, S. (2022). *Temporality in mobile lives: Contemporary Asia-Australia migration and everyday time*. Bristol University Press.

Said, E. W. (2003). *Orientalism*. Penguin Books. (Original work published 1978)

Sautman, B. (1998). Preferential policies for ethnic minorities in China: The case of Xinjiang. *Nationalism and Ethnic Politics*, *4*(1–2), 86–118.

Savage, M. (2014). Piketty's challenge for sociology. *The British Journal of Sociology*, *65*(4), 591–606. https://doi.org/10.1111/1468-4446.12106

Serafin, M. (2016). *The temporal structures of the economy: The working day of taxi drivers in Warsaw*. International Max Planck Research School on the Social and Political Constitution of the Economy.

Shahjahan, R. A., & Edwards, K. T. (2022). Whiteness as futurity and globalization of higher education. *Higher Education*, *83*(4), 747–764. https://doi. org/10.1007/s10734-021-00702-x

Shahrokni, S. (2018). The collective roots and rewards of upward educational mobility. *The British Journal of Sociology*, *69*(4), 1175–1193.

Shen, Y. (2015). *Transforming life in China: Gendered experiences of restaurant workers in Shanghai* [Doctoral dissertation, London School of Economics and Political Science].

Shive, G. (2010). Exporting higher education services: An engine of growth for Hong Kong. *Hong Kong Journal Archives*. Retrieved in 2014 from http:// www.hkjournal.org/PDF/2010_spring/4.pdf

Snyder, B. H. (2016). *The disrupted workplace: Time and the moral order of flexible capitalism*. Oxford University Press.

Song, H., & Zhang, Y. (2022). Unpacking the emotional experiences of English majors preparing for postgraduate entrance exam in China. *English Language Teaching*, *15*(4), 117–128.

Starmass. (n.d.). *China tiered cities*. Starmass International. Retrieved May 3, 2023, from http://www.starmass.com/china-tiered-cities/

Sun, K. C.-Y. (2021). *Time and migration: How long-term Taiwanese migrants negotiate later life*. Cornell University Press.

Szydlik, M. (2004). Inheritance and inequality: Theoretical reasoning and empirical evidence. *European Sociological Review, 20*(1), 31–45. https://doi.org/10.1093/esr/20.1.31

Thomas-Alexander, T. (2023, August 15). University provides safe haven for scholars fleeing Hong Kong: University of Surrey sets up Hong Kong studies hub as political pressures drive Hong Kong academics to the UK. *Times Higher Education*. https://www.timeshighereducation.com/news/university-provides-safe-haven-scholars-fleeing-hong-kong

Thompson, E. (1967). Time, work-discipline, and industrial capitalism. *Past & Present, 38*, 56–97.

Times Higher Education. (2014). *World university rankings 2014–15*. Retrieved January 8, 2015, from http://www.timeshighereducation.co.uk/world-university-rankings/2014-15/world-ranking

To, S. (2013). Understanding *sheng nu* ("leftover women"): The phenomenon of late marriage among Chinese professional women. *Symbolic Interaction, 36*(1), 1–20.

Tse, T. K. C. (2007). Remaking Chinese identity: Hegemonic struggles over national education in post-colonial Hong Kong. *International Studies in Sociology of Education, 17*(3), 231–248. https://doi.org/10.1080/09620210701543908

Tu, M. (2018). *Education, migration and family relations between China and the UK: The transnational one-child generation*. Emerald Group Publishing.

Tu, M., & Nehring, D. (2019). Remain, return, or re-migrate? The (im)mobility trajectory of mainland Chinese students after completing their education in the UK. *International Migration, 58*(3), 43–57. https://doi.org/10.1111/imig.12589

Tung, C. H. (1998). *Policy address: From adversity to opportunity*. H. K. G. Printing.

Vickers, E. (2015). A civilising mission with Chinese characteristics? Education, colonialism and Chinese state formation in comparative perspective. In E. Vickers & K. Kumar (Eds.), *Constructing modern Asian citizenship* (pp. 50–79). Routledge.

Vickers, E. (2024). The motherland's suffocating embrace: Schooling and public discourse on Hong Kong identity under the National Security Law. *Comparative Education, 60*(1), 138–158. https://doi.org/10.1080/03050068.2023.2212351

Vickers, E., & Kumar, K. (Eds.). (2015). *Constructing modern Asian citizenship*. Routledge.

Wakeling, P., & Savage, M. (2015). Entry to elite positions and the stratification of higher education in Britain. *The Sociological Review, 63*(2), 290–320.

Wang [王], C. 春光., Zhao [赵], Y. 玉峰., & Wang [王], Y. 玉琪. (2018). 当代中国农民社会分层的新动向 [New trends of social stratification in rural China]. 社会学研究杂志 [Sociological Studies], *2018*(1), 63–88.

Wang, B. (2019). A temporal gaze towards academic migration: Everyday times, life-times and temporal strategies amongst early career Chinese academic returnees. *Time & Society, 29*(1), 166–186. https://doi.org/10.1177/0961463x19873806

Wang, B., & Collins, F. (2020). Temporally distributed aspirations: New Chinese migrants to New Zealand and the figuring of migration futures. *Sociology, 54*(3), 573–590. https://doi.org/10.1177/0038038519895750

Wang, Jing. (2023). Chinese parental academic socialization prior to college entrance examination: Insights from urban and rural areas. *Journal of Family Studies, 29*(1), 389–406. https://doi.org/10.1080/13229400.2021.1934516

Wang, Jue. (2023). Young children's negotiation of language policies and multilingual curriculum at an ethnic minority elementary school in rural China. *Global Studies of Childhood, 13*(2), 149–164. https://doi.org/10.1177/20436106231177879

Wang, Q. (2021). *Unexpected nvboshi: The making of new womanhood in contemporary China* [Doctoral dissertation, University of York]. White Rose eTheses Online. https://etheses.whiterose.ac.uk/30396/

Wang, S., & Shane, D. (2019, 16 April). Jack Ma endorses China's controversial 12 hours a day, 6 days a week work culture. *CNN Business.* https://edition.cnn.com/2019/04/15/business/jack-ma-996-china/index.html

Wang, T. (2007). Preferential policies for ethnic minority students in China's college/university admission. *Asian Ethnicity, 8*(2), 149–163.

Wang, X., Liu, C., Zhang, L., Shi, Y., & Rozelle, S. (2013). College is a rich, Han, urban, male club: Research notes from a census survey of four tier one colleges in China. *The China Quarterly, 214*, 456–470. https://doi.org/10.1017/S030574 1013000647

Wang, X., & Shen, Y. (2014). The effect of China's agricultural tax abolition on rural families' incomes and production. *China Economic Review, 29*, 185–199. https://doi.org/10.1016/j.chieco.2014.04.010

Wang, Z. (2023). *Transnational student return migration and megacities in China: Practices of Cityzenship.* Palgrave Macmillan.

Waterfield, B., Beagan, B. L., & Mohamed, T. (2019). "You always remain slightly an outsider": Workplace experiences of academics from working-class or impoverished backgrounds. *Canadian Review of Sociology / Revue canadienne de sociologie, 56*(3), 368–388. https://doi.org/10.1111/cars.12257

Waters, J. (2006a). Emergent geographies of international education and social exclusion. *Antipode, 38*(5), 1046–1068.

Waters, J. L. (2006b). Geographies of cultural capital: Education, international migration and family strategies between Hong Kong and Canada. *Transactions of the Institute of British Geographers, 31*(2), n.s., 179–192. https://doi.org/10.1111/j.1475-5661.2006.00202.x

Waters, J. L. (2007). "Roundabout routes and sanctuary schools": The role of situated educational practices and habitus in the creation of transnational professionals. *Global Networks, 7*(4), 477–497. https://doi.org/10.1111/j.1471-0374.2007.00180.x

Waters, J. L. (2018). International education is political! Exploring the politics of international student mobilities. *Journal of International Students*, *8*(3), 1459–1478.

Waters, J., & Brooks, R. (2011). "Vive la différence?": The "international" experiences of UK students overseas. *Population, Space and Place*, *17*(5), 567–578. https://doi.org/10.1002/psp.613

Waters, J., & Brooks, R. (2021). *Student migrants and contemporary educational mobilities*. Palgrave Macmillan.

Waters, J., & Leung, M. (2013). A colourful university life? Transnational higher education and the spatial dimensions of institutional social capital in Hong Kong. *Population, Space and Place*, *19*(2), 155–167. https://doi.org/10.1002/psp.1748

Waters, J., & Leung, M. (2014). "These are not the best students": Continuing education, transnationalisation and Hong Kong's young adult "educational non-elite." *Children's Geographies*, *12*(1), 56–69. https://doi.org/10.1080/14733285.2013.850851

Wei, X. (2022, 9 April). A studied sacrifice: Why China's moms bet all on education. *Sixth Tone*. https://www.sixthtone.com/news/1010049

Weiss, J. C. (2019). How hawkish is the Chinese public? Another look at "rising nationalism" and Chinese foreign policy. *Journal of Contemporary China*, *28*(119), 679–695. https://doi.org/10.1080/10670564.2019.1580427

Wong, T.-H. (2023). Different postcolonial conditions, different education histories: The cases of Taiwan, Singapore and Hong Kong. *History of Education*, *52*(2–3), 246–269.

Wong, Y.-L. (2022). "Entitlement" and "legitimacy" as emotional capital: Living out class through a critical educational failure by community-college students in Hong Kong. *Studies in Higher Education*, *47*(3), 616–629. https://doi.org/10.1080/03075079.2020.1776244

Woo, E., & Wang, L. (2024). Crisscrossing scapes in the global flow of elite mainland Chinese students. *Higher Education*, *87*, 551–566. https://doi.org/10.1007/s10734-023-01023-x

Woodhams, C., Xian, H., & Lupton, B. (2014). Women managers' careers in China: Theorizing the influence of gender and collectivism. *Human Resource Management*, *54*(6), 913–931.

Wu, J. (2016). *Fabricating an educational miracle: Compulsory schooling meets ethnic rural development in southwest China*. State University of New York Press.

Wu, X. (2019). Inequality and social stratification in postsocialist China. *Annual Review of Sociology*, *45*, 363–382. https://doi.org/10.1146/annurev-soc-073018-022516

Xia, Y., Wu, A., Li, D., Wu, L., & Han, J. (2024). Exploring the value of children in the context of China's modernization transition. *Journal of Family Issues*, *45*(9), 2182–2205. https://doi.org/10.1177/0192513x231197407

Xiang, B. (2007). How far are the left-behind left behind? A preliminary study in rural China. *Population, Space and Place, 13*(3), 179–191. https://doi.org/10.1002/psp.437

Xiang, B. (2016). Beyond methodological nationalism and epistemological behaviouralism: Drawing illustrations from migrations within and from China. *Population, Space and Place, 22*, 669–680. https://doi.org/10.1002/psp.1929

Xiang, B., & Shen, W. (2009). International student migration and social stratification in China. *International Journal of Educational Development, 29*(5), 513–522. https://doi.org/10.1016/j.ijedudev.2009.04.006

Xiao, L., & North, D. (2017). The graduation performance of technology business incubators in China's three tier cities: The role of incubator funding, technical support, and entrepreneurial mentoring. *The Journal of Technology Transfer, 42*(3), 615–634. https://doi.org/10.1007/s10961-016-9493-4

Xie [谢], A. 爱. L. 磊. (2016). 精英高校中的农村籍学生——社会流动与生存心态的转变 [Rural students in China's elite university: Social mobility and habitus transformation]. 教育研究 [Education Research], *16*(4), 74–81.

Xie, A., & Postiglione, G. A. (2016). *Guanxi* and school success: An ethnographic inquiry of parental involvement in rural China. *British Journal of Sociology of Education, 37*(7), 1014–1033. https://doi.org/10.1080/01425692.2014.1001061

Xie, A., & Reay, D. (2020). Successful rural students in China's elite universities: Habitus transformation and inevitable hidden injuries? *Higher Education, 80*(1), 21–36. https://doi.org/10.1007/s10734-019-00462-9

Xu [徐], J. 军. W. 伟., & Hu [胡], K. 坤. (2017). 县域办学: 经济发达地区高等教育地方化的新探索 [An analysis on the transformation and development of county-based independent colleges in Zhejiang Province]. 宁波大学学报: 教育科学版 [Journal of Ningbo University (Educational Science Edition)], *39*(1), 51–55.

Xu [徐], J. 军. W. 伟., & Wang [王], Y. 韵. C. 晨. (2021). 县域高校协同治理模式构建研究: 基于 CAS 理论 [CAS research on the construction of collaborative governance model in county-based colleges]. 宁波大学学报 (教育科学版) [Journal of Ningbo University (Educational Science Edition)], No. 2, 27–34.

Xu, C. L. (2015). When the Hong Kong Dream meets the anti-mainlandisation discourse: Mainland Chinese students in Hong Kong. *Journal of Current Chinese Affairs, 44*(3), 15–47. https://doi.org/10.1177/186810261504400302

Xu, C. L. (2018a). Political habitus in cross-border student migration: A longitudinal study of mainland Chinese students in Hong Kong and beyond. *International Studies in Sociology of Education, 27*(2–3), 255–270. https://doi.org/10.1080/09620214.2017.1415768

Xu, C. L. (2018b). Transborder habitus in a within-country mobility context: A Bourdieusian analysis of mainland Chinese students in Hong Kong. *The Sociological Review*, *66*(6), 1128–1144. https://doi.org/10.1177/0038026117732669

Xu, C. L. (2019). "Diaspora at home": Class and politics in the navigation of Hong Kong students in mainland China's universities. *International Studies in Sociology of Education*, *32*(2), 178–195. https://doi.org/10.1080/0962021 4.2019.1700821

Xu, C. L. (2020). Tackling rural-urban inequalities through educational mobilities: Rural-origin Chinese academics from impoverished backgrounds navigating higher education. *Policy Reviews in Higher Education*, *4*(2), 179–202. https:// doi.org/10.1080/23322969.2020.1783697

Xu, C. L. (2021a). Portraying the "Chinese international students": A review of English-language and Chinese-language literature on Chinese international students (2015–2020). *Asia Pacific Education Review*, *23*, 151–167. https:// doi.org /10.1007/s12564-021-09731-8

Xu, C. L. (2021b). Time, class and privilege in career imagination: Exploring study-to-work transition of Chinese international students in UK universities through a Bourdieusian lens. *Time & Society*, *30*(1), 5–29. https://doi.org/ 10.1177/0961463x20951333

Xu, C. L., & Ma, Y. (2023). Geography-mediated institutionalised cultural capital: Regional inequalities in graduate employment. *Journal of Education and Work*, *36*(1), 22–36. https://doi.org/10.1080/13639080.2022.2162018

Xu, C. L., & Montgomery, C. (2019). Educating China on the move: A typology of contemporary Chinese higher education mobilities. *Review of Education*, *7*(3), 598–627. https://doi.org/10.1002/rev3.3139

Xu, C. L., & Yang, M. (2019). Ethnicity, temporality and educational mobilities: Comparing the ethnic identity constructions of Mongolian and Tibetan students in China. *British Journal of Sociology of Education*, *40*(5), 631–646. https://doi.org/10.1080/01425692.2019.1576121

Xu, S., & Law, W.-W. (2015). Rural education and urbanization: Experiences and struggles in China since the late 1970s. *Global Education Review*, *2*(4).

Xu, W., & Poole, A. (2023). "Academics without publications are just like imperial concubines without sons": The "new times" of Chinese higher education. *Journal of Education Policy*, 1–18. https://doi.org/10.1080/02680939.2023.2288339

Xu, X. (2019). Performing under "the baton of administrative power"? Chinese academics' responses to incentives for international publications. *Research Evaluation*, *29*(1), 87–99. https://doi.org/10.1093/reseval/rvz028

Xu, Y. (2022). *Dongshi* as reflexive habitus to understand Chinese rural students' academic success. *Cambridge Journal of Education*, *52*(2), 255–270.

Yamada, N. C. (2015). From free to fee: Neoliberalising preferential policy measures for minority education in China. *Learning and Teaching*, *8*(3), 82–99.

Yan [阎], G. 光. C. 才. (2017). 学术职业选择、阶层趣味与个人机遇 [The choice of academic profession: Class taste or personal opportunities]. 华东师范大学学报

(教育科学版) [Journal of East China Normal University (Educational Sciences)], *6*, 1–10. https://xbjk.ecnu.edu.cn/EN/10.16382/j.cnki.1000-5560.2017.06.001

Yan, A. (2019, June 27). Why did one of China's elite universities need to offer big money to get the best students? *South China Morning Post.* https://www.scmp.com/news/china/society/article/3016360/why-did-one-chinas-elite-universities-need-offer-big-money-get

Yang, M. (2017). *Learning to be Tibetan: The construction of ethnic identity at Minzu University of China.* Lexington Books.

Yang, M., & Xu, C. L. (2020). Getting ahead while retaining ethnic salience: Educational mobilities, class, and empowerment of a Tibetan student in China. *Asia Pacific Journal of Education, 42*(2), 335–349. https://doi.org/10.1080/02188791.2020.1833835

Yang, R. (2018). Foil to the West? Interrogating perspectives for observing East Asian higher education. In J. Jung, H. Horta, & A. Yonezawa (Eds.), *Researching Higher Education in Asia: History, Development and Future* (pp. 37–50). Springer.

Yang, R., & Xie, M. (2015). Leaning toward the centers: International networking at China's five C9 League universities. *Frontiers of Education in China, 10*(1), 66–90. https://doi.org/10.1007/bf03397053

Yang, R., Xie, M., & Wen, W. (2018). Pilgrimage to the West: Modern transformations of Chinese intellectual formation in social sciences. *Higher Education, 77*, 815–829. https://doi.org/10.1007/s10734-018-0303-9

Yin, X. S., Hussain, J., & Kui, Z. (2022). The spatial distribution pattern and formation mechanism of the spatial agglomeration of Chinese higher education population: A cross-province comparison. *Applied Spatial Analysis and Policy, 15*, 315–338. https://doi.org/10.1007/s12061-021-09392-5

Yuan, Z., Qian, J., & Zhu, H. (2017). The Xinjiang inland class: Multi-ethnic encounters and the spaces of prescription and negotiation in an eastern coastal city. *The China Quarterly, 232*, 1094–1115.

Yuan, Z., & Zhu, H. (2020). Uyghur educational elites in China: Mobility and subjectivity uncertainty on a life-transforming journey. *Journal of Ethnic and Migration Studies, 47*(3), 536–556. https://doi.org/10.1080/1369183X.2020.1790343

Zeng, B. (2014). Women's political participation in China: Improved or not? *Journal of International Women's Studies, 15*(1), 136–150.

Zhang [张], H. 慧. J. 婧. (2016). 从"职住空间"到"社会空间"——在日中国新移民的生存适应策略探讨 [From "job-housing space" to "social space": The adaptation strategies of new Chinese immigrants in Japan]. 华侨华人历史研究 [Overseas Chinese History Studies], No. 3, 17–26.

Zhang [张], S. 思. Q. 齐. (2018). 社会网络中的"强连接"对留学生活的影响——基于英国伦敦政治经济学院中国留学生的实证研究 [Impacts of "strong ties" in social networks on overseas studies—an empirical investigation on Chinese international students in the London School of Economics and Political Science]. 江汉论坛 [Jianghan Tribune], No. 1, 138–144.

Zhang, Chen. (2023). *Recognition and misrecognition: Experiences of UK Chinese postgraduates after their return home* [Doctoral dissertation, University of Edinburgh].

Zhang, Chenchen. (2018). Governing neoliberal authoritarian citizenship: Theorizing *hukou* and the changing mobility regime in China. *Citizenship Studies, 22*(8), 855–881. https://doi.org/10.1080/13621025.2018.1531824

Zhang, J., Wang, R., & Lu, C. (2019). A quantitative analysis of *Hukou* reform in Chinese cities: 2000–2016. *Growth and Change, 50*(1), 201–221. https://doi.org/10.1111/grow.12284

Zhang, S., & Tang, X. (2021). Cultural capital as class strength and gendered educational choices of Chinese female students in the United Kingdom. *Frontiers in Psychology, 11*(3945). https://doi.org/10.3389/fpsyg.2020.584360

Zhang, S., & Xu, C. L. (2020). The making of transnational distinction: An embodied cultural capital perspective on Chinese women students' mobility. *British Journal of Sociology of Education, 41*(8), 1251–1267. https://doi.org/10.1080/01425692.2020.1804836

Zhao, K. (2023). Does higher education expansion close the rural-urban gap in college enrolment in China? New evidence from a cross-provincial assessment. *Compare: A Journal of Comparative and International Education, 53*(5), 802–819. https://doi.org/10.1080/03057925.2021.1965468

# Index

Page numbers followed by t or f refer to tables and figures.

www.ingramcontent.com/pod-product-compliance
Lightning Source LLC
Chambersburg PA
CBHW031126270326
41929CB00011B/1507